CAMBRIDGE LIBRARY COLLECTION

Books of enduring scholarly value

Medieval History

This series includes pioneering editions of medieval historical accounts by eye-witnesses and contemporaries, collections of source materials such as charters and letters, and works that applied new historiographical methods to the interpretation of the European middle ages. The nineteenth century saw an upsurge of interest in medieval manuscripts, texts and artefacts, and the enthusiastic efforts of scholars and antiquaries made a large body of material available in print for the first time. Although many of the analyses have been superseded, they provide fascinating evidence of the academic practices of their time, while a considerable number of texts have still not been re-edited and are still widely consulted.

Essays on Archaeological Subjects

Thomas Wright (1810–77), antiquarian, archaeologist and historian, wrote many works on all his areas of interest, including several reissued in the Cambridge Library Collection. He was the first excavator of the Roman city of Wroxeter, wrote on the history of Ludlow and of Cambridge, and was interested in ethnology, folklore, Old English, and etymology. This two-volume collection of his essays was published in 1861: he selected them 'to embrace in some manner the whole field of our own primeval history and that of the Middle Ages'. The subjects range from the excavation of tumuli in Yorkshire to the history of drama in the Middle Ages. Wright draws on sources ranging from medieval charters to modern linguistic studies, as well as the remains and artefacts uncovered by his own and others' excavations. Volume 1 considers prehistoric finds, aspects of Roman Britain, and the Anglo-Saxon and late medieval period.

T0382232

Cambridge University Press has long been a pioneer in the reissuing of out-of-print titles from its own backlist, producing digital reprints of books that are still sought after by scholars and students but could not be reprinted economically using traditional technology. The Cambridge Library Collection extends this activity to a wider range of books which are still of importance to researchers and professionals, either for the source material they contain, or as landmarks in the history of their academic discipline.

Drawing from the world-renowned collections in the Cambridge University Library and other partner libraries, and guided by the advice of experts in each subject area, Cambridge University Press is using state-of-the-art scanning machines in its own Printing House to capture the content of each book selected for inclusion. The files are processed to give a consistently clear, crisp image, and the books finished to the high quality standard for which the Press is recognised around the world. The latest print-on-demand technology ensures that the books will remain available indefinitely, and that orders for single or multiple copies can quickly be supplied.

The Cambridge Library Collection brings back to life books of enduring scholarly value (including out-of-copyright works originally issued by other publishers) across a wide range of disciplines in the humanities and social sciences and in science and technology.

Essays on
Archaeological Subjects

*And on Various Questions Connected with the History
of Art, Science, and Literature in the Middle Ages*

VOLUME 1

THOMAS WRIGHT

CAMBRIDGE
UNIVERSITY PRESS

CAMBRIDGE
UNIVERSITY PRESS

University Printing House, Cambridge, CB2 8BS, United Kingdom

Cambridge University Press is part of the University of Cambridge.
It furthers the University's mission by disseminating knowledge in the pursuit of
education, learning and research at the highest international levels of excellence.

www.cambridge.org
Information on this title: www.cambridge.org/9781108083478

© in this compilation Cambridge University Press 2018

This edition first published 1861
This digitally printed version 2018

ISBN 978-1-108-08347-8 Paperback

The original edition of this book contains a number of oversize plates
which it has not been possible to reproduce to scale in this edition.
They can be found online at www.cambridge.org/9781108083478

ESSAYS ON ARCHÆOLOGICAL
SUBJECTS.

ESSAYS ON ARCHÆOLOGICAL SUBJECTS,

AND ON VARIOUS QUESTIONS CONNECTED
WITH THE HISTORY OF ART, SCIENCE,
AND LITERATURE IN THE
MIDDLE AGES.

BY

THOMAS WRIGHT, Esq. M.A., F.S.A., M.R.S.L., Etc.

CORRESPONDING MEMBER OF THE IMPERIAL INSTITUTE OF
FRANCE (ACADEMIE DES INSCRIPTIONS ET
BELLES LETTRES.)

IN TWO VOLUMES.
VOL. I.

LONDON:
JOHN RUSSELL SMITH,
SOHO SQUARE.
1861.

TO

JOSEPH MAYER,

OF LIVERPOOL,

WHOSE NAME IS ENDEARED TO ALL WHO ARE INTERESTED IN

THE HISTORY AND ANTIQUITIES OF THEIR COUNTRY

BY HIS GENEROUS EXERTIONS TO COLLECT

AND PRESERVE THEIR RELICS,

AND AT WHOSE EXPRESS DESIRE SEVERAL OF THE

FOLLOWING ESSAYS WERE WRITTEN,

These Volumes

ARE DEDICATED, AS A MARK OF THE AUTHOR'S

SINCERE REGARD

PREFACE.

THE Essays which compose the following volumes are selected from a considerable number of papers written during some years past as communications to the periodical press, or to learned societies, such as the British Association of Science, the Society of Antiquaries, the British Archæological Association, and other similar bodies, or as lectures in which it was the design of the author to give sketches of the history or literature of the Middle Ages in a popular form. Some friends have thought that a few of them were worthy of preservation in a less temporary form, and in deference to their opinion I venture to give this selection to the public. The subjects of these Essays, although more or less connected with each other, are rather varied, and embrace in some manner the whole field of our own primeval history and of that of the Middle Ages. I have arranged them, as far as that could conveniently be done, chronologically, so that the first volume belongs chiefly to the Romano-British and Anglo-Saxon periods of our history, while the second volume is occupied with subjects of a more general character belonging to the later mediæval period.

As might naturally be expected, the form and style of these several Essays are influenced a little by the times when and the circumstances under which they were written, and, although they have all been revised, and many of them considerably modified, I have preferred retaining somewhat of their original characteristics, as it would have been necessary almost to re-write them all to produce anything like a perfect uniformity. This will explain a few slight repetitions, in cases where the same fact or the same notion is introduced in reference to its bearing on different questions.

Some opinions are published in these Essays, the result of my own observation or reflections, which are contrary to what have long been those of our antiquaries and historians. Some of these, I confess, are supported by my own firm conviction of their truth; but others I only offer as suggestions which appear to me to be supported by very cogent reasons, while many of them require further researches and discoveries before they can either be confirmed or refuted. I trust, therefore, that my readers will acquit me of any intention of offering these opinions dogmatically, or of wishing them to be taken for anything more than they may seem to be worth.

In conclusion, I have to return my thanks, in the first place, for the loan of the engravings which illustrate some of these Essays, to Mr. Mayer of Liverpool, at whose expense the lecture on Anglo-Saxon Antiquities was first printed in the " Transactions of the Historic Society of Lancashire ;" to the British Archæ-ological Association, in the Journal of which scientific body several of these Essays were first published ; to the Cambrian Archæological Association; to the Society of Antiquaries; and to Mr. J. H. Parker, of Oxford. I have also to thank Messrs. Longmans, for their ready consent to my reprinting, in this separate form, the Essay on Saints' Legends and Miracles from the " Edinburgh Review ;" and my thanks are due, for a similar reason, to Mr. Harrison Ainsworth, Mr. J. H. Parker, &c., in regard to articles similarly reprinted from the "New Monthly Magazine," "Bentley's Miscellany," the "Gentleman's Magazine," and other periodicals.

THOMAS WRIGHT.

Sydney Street, Brompton,
December, 1860.

CONTENTS.

PLATE.

ESSAYS ON ARCHÆOLOGICAL
SUBJECTS.

I.

ON THE REMAINS OF A PRIMITIVE PEOPLE IN
THE SOUTH-EAST CORNER OF
YORKSHIRE.

WITH SOME REMARKS ON THE EARLY ETHNOLOGY
OF BRITAIN.

N the southern part of the coast of Yorkshire there is a tract of country secluded
by its natural features from the other
parts of the county. From the coast
on the north the wild elevated tract of the Wolds
makes a sweep out in a south-westerly direction, until
it descends into the district now called Holderness;
over which, formerly, thick and extensive forests and
morasses stretched, towards the south-east, to the
mouth of the Humber. The Wolds must have been
in early times almost uninhabitable, the forest forming
with them a continuous line of barrier, resting at each
extremity upon the sea. In the small district included
within this barrier the geographer Ptolemy places a
tribe called the Παρίσοι, who dwelt περὶ τὸν εὐλίμενον

I.   B

κόλπον, "round the well-havened bay," which, I have
no doubt, we must identify with the present bay of
Bridlington. Ptolemy has been quoted as further
giving to this tribe a capital town, named Petuaria;
but to me the language of the ancient geographer
does not seem to countenance such a statement, and
I think that we must take Petuaria as a town coming
next after the territory of the Parisi, and probably
situated on the banks of the Humber. A not improbable suggestion has been made by our modern
ethnologists, that the name of the tribe, Parisi, is only
a corruption of that of Frisii, or rather that the two
words represent the same original name, and that
the primitive people who dwelt round the bay of
Bridlington were originally settlers from the opposite
coasts of Friesland. I mention this suggestion as
being rather a happy one, for it seems agreeable to
what we might expect in such a tribe so situated; but
at the same time I would urge how extremely cau-
tious we ought to be in accepting arguments founded
on, I fear, too often fanciful derivations of the old
names of places and peoples, ascribed to languages of
which we really know nothing, and which, sometimes,
have existed only in the imaginations of those to whom
we owe the derivations.

It is probable enough, from its physical character,
that the district thus described remained· in primitive
simplicity long after the other parts of the island had
made great advances in civilization. During a recent
visit I have ascertained facts which leave no doubt
that it was occupied by the Romans, though I can
discover no reason for believing that they had any
important station here. Indeed, I have at this moment in my possession Roman coins which I am assured

were dug up at Bridlington; and I have an authenticated statement, by Mr. Cape of that town, of the
discovery, a few years ago, of the remains of a Roman
villa in the parish of Rudstone—a place well known
to antiquaries by the upright stone in its churchyard,
which probably dates from as far back as the Roman
period, and which may, perhaps, mark the head
seat of the tribe. At a later period, Flamborough
became celebrated as the landing-place of Ida, the
leader of the Northumbrian Angles; and this particular district appears to have fallen to the lot of one
of the families, or septs, of the settlers, which bore
the name of Bridlingas, and who fixed their head-
quarters at the spot called from that circumstance
Bridlinga-tun, *i. e.* " the mansion of the Bridlingas," a
name which has been but slightly softened down in
the modern Bridlington. During the whole of the
earlier Saxon period this country appears to have
lost nothing of its secluded and almost inaccessible
character. The Wolds to the north-west remained as
wild as ever, while in the forest to the south of them,
which was known as the Derawald, (a name that may
be interpreted either "the wood of the Deiri," or "the
wood of wild animals,") the solitude was so great that
the little river of Hull, which passed through it, was
celebrated for its numerous beavers, an animal which
is known to avoid the haunts of men. One spot,
probably an open place in the forest, which was known
by the name of Befor-leag, or "the lea, or field, of
beavers," was chosen, as late as the latter end of the
seventh century, by archbishop John, on account of
its solitude, for the establishment of a religious house,
which was afterwards famous as the abbey of Beverley. Indications of the earliest Anglo-Saxon settlers

in this district are not wanting, for a Saxon cemetery
of the pagan period has been met with in the immediate neighbourhood of the Roman villa already mentioned.

The traces of Romans or Saxons are, however, very
trifling in comparison with the numerous examples of
another description of objects which are found scattered over the whole of this district.   These are implements of various kinds made of chipped flint; among
which the most common are arrow-heads, with others
of similar form but of larger size, which probably
served for small spears or javelins.   A large and very
interesting collection of these curious implements has
been made by Mr. Edward Tindall, of Bridlington;
and Mr. Thomas Cape, of the same town, possesses,
also, a considerable number, all found in that immediate neighbourhood by himself.   Among them are
observed fish-hooks, so delicately formed that we cannot but feel astonished at the labour it must have
required to chip them out of a piece of flint.   Nor is
the accuracy with which the barbed arrow-heads are
formed less surprising.   I am inclined to think that
some of the latter, from the sharpness of the barb, and
from the middle spike being notched, as though for
the purpose of being tied to a line, may have been
intended also to serve as fish-hooks.   Others appear
to have been designed to serve as tools, knives,
chisels, &c.   We have examples, also, of flints finely
and regularly notched on the edge, as though for
saws; and one or two instruments which appear to
have been intended for boring.   A fine stone axe was
found by Mr. Cape, at Lissett, between Bridlington
and Driffield.   Flat circular pieces of flint, about the
size of a half-crown, are also rather common, and

present all the appearance of having been intended to be thrown with a sling, or with a stick.

A comparison of these implements at once impresses us with the notion that they belonged to a people whose life was simple and uncultivated. They evidently supported themselves upon fish, which were caught with the hook, and upon birds and wild animals, which they shot with arrows, or struck down with rounded flints thrown from slings. Mr. Tindall informs me that the arrow-heads, and heads of spears or javelins, are found most abundantly in old moorland on the sides of rather steep hills; and that when such land is first broken up and tilled they are sometimes found scattered about in considerable numbers. It is evident that they belonged to a tribe confined within this district, because they appear not to be found in any abundance beyond it. Mr. Tindall further informs me, from his own experience, that the sling-stones are found chiefly in and around Flamborough; that in the neighourhood of Sewerby, about three miles from Flamborough, the rudest of the arrow-heads are found; and that, as far as his own observation goes, those of more perfect make are found furthest inland. This circumstance may be quite accidental, and is probably to be explained by the abundance or peculiar character of the game which frequented particular spots. We should naturally expect to find more of it on the edges of the Wolds, and on the borders of the forests, than near the shore; but the cliffs about and above Flamborough have from time immemorial been celebrated for the immense number of wild-fowl which resort to them, and for the slaughter of which the sling would, perhaps, be the most useful implement.

Another circumstance must be mentioned with regard to the localities in which these flint implements are found. It appears that in particular fields, in the immediate neighbourhood of Bridlington, they are met with in much greater quantities than in other places—in such quantities, indeed, that I am assured that a person who looks for them can hardly, at any time, walk across one of these particular fields without picking up one or two implements of chipped flint. I must, in connection with this part of the subject, call attention to other pieces of flint, which are evidently, in some cases, the chippings from the flints out of which the other implements have been made, or the rough beginnings of implements which were either spoilt in the making, or were never completed. These seem to prove that the implements I have been describing were made in the district where they were used. I understand that these fragments and imperfect implements are found chiefly in these same fields to which I have just alluded, and we seem, therefore, to be led irresistibly to the conclusion that these spots are the sites of establishments of people whose occupation it was to make the objects in question, and that these fragments, &c. are the refuse of their workshops (if we may apply such a term to them), mixed, perhaps, with the remains of their stock, when they may have been obliged to leave the place through hostile invasion, or for other reasons at which we cannot now even guess.

To whom, we may ask, do these curious implements belong? I think, when we consider the locality, their primitive character, and the other circumstances of the case, we can have no hesitation in ascribing them to the same people whom Ptolemy places in this very

spot under the name of Parisi; and I believe that
they belong to a period extending, from a limit which
we have no means of fixing, down, perhaps, to the
time of the Anglo-Saxon invasion, or even it may be
to a rather later period; though I should be inclined
to ascribe the great mass of them to a date not later
than the period of the Roman occupation. Thus
from these few flints, gathered in the fields, we are
enabled to add some important knowledge to the bare
testimony of the ancient geographer; and we may
now venture to state that the Parisi were a small
tribe inhabiting the district round the bay of Bridlington, separated by the natural features of the
country from the inland districts, living peaceably
and very rudely on the produce of fishing and the
chase, who were little, if at all, acquainted with the use
of metals, or of any of the improvements of civilization; and, probably, they were few in number. We
have, as yet, no facts to enable us to say whether they
were a fragment of an early Celtic population remaining in primitive ignorance, while their brethren in
the interior advanced towards refinement, or whether they were some rude fisher tribe whom boats and
the accidents of the sea had brought from Scandinavia, or from the opposite shores of the continent of
Europe, to settle on this distant coast. Further
observation may show whether remains, with very
similar characteristics, are found on the coasts of
northern Europe, and whether we find remains indicating a similar population, under similar circumstances, in other parts of the coast of our own island.
I would merely observe, that it is a fact which must
not be overlooked, that the tribe of the Parisi, though
small, must have possessed some peculiarity distinc-

tive from the tribes around, to entitle it to separate
mention in the geography of Ptolemy.

This particular subject, or rather this particular
case of an important subject, leads us naturally to
consider that subject in its more general form, and I
seize the opportunity for offering a few remarks on
the ante-Roman ethnology of Britain. It is a subject which has been singularly obscured by baseless
theories and speculations, arising out of the ignorance
and prejudice of writers who have treated upon it in
anything but a carefully scientific spirit. It is a subject on which the ethnologist has need of the co-ope-
ration of the archæologist; and yet, in this country
at least, archæology is a younger *science* than ethnology itself. Both are, I fear, too much exposed to
the two great dangers of a love for theoretic speculation on the one hand, and of a tendency to generalize
too hastily on the other.

In the geography of Ptolemy we see our island
distributed among numerous tribes, differing much
in name, and differing also in the extent of their ter-
ritories. Cæsar, the first who describes the island
from personal observation and inquiry on the spot,
tells us that the interior of the island was inhabited
by people who were said, by tradition, to be the in-
digenous race, but that the sea coasts were occupied
by Belgian settlers. We learn further, from his account, that there was in his time a wide difference
in the degree of civilization between these midland
aborigines and the inhabitants of the maritime settlements. Cæsar assures us that the Belgæ on the continent were mostly of German blood (*plerosque Belgas
esse ortos ab Germanis*), and that they had crossed the

Rhine to settle in districts from which they had ex-
pelled the Gauls. In another place he tells us that
the Belgæ of his time differed as much from the Gauls,
in language and manners, as the Gauls themselves
differed from the Aquitani, which we know was an
entire difference of race and language. Without wishing to enter, at present, on a much debated question,
I would remark that Cæsar's statements amount to a
declaration of facts which do not seem to me to be
overruled by the theory of modern ethnologists; and
I am inclined to believe that at least a considerable
portion of the population on the eastern and south-
eastern coast of Britain, at the earliest period with
which we are acquainted with it, was really of Teutonic
origin. The account given by Tacitus, at a somewhat
later period, I think countenances this view of the
subject, and he expressly points out physical characteristics in the Caledonians of the north which bespoke
their German descent. All these are facts which I
think are not shaken by speculative inductions. It
seems evident, indeed, that, at the earliest period at
which we can hope to gain any information on the
ethnology of our island, it was inhabited by a number
of different tribes, differing in manners and in civilization, and of different race—in fact, that Britain had
afforded a home for colonies, at different periods, from
the whole line of coasts stretching from the Baltic to
the Bay of Biscay, and that it was not occupied by
a uniform population which passed uniformly through
different grades of civilization.

In fact, uniformity of condition, among the population of an extensive district of varied country, can
only exist either in a state of absolute barbarism,
where there is no intellectual development at all, or

in the very highest degree of civilization, where inter-communication is general and extremely rapid. Yet it is on the implied assumption of some such uniformity that the antiquaries of Denmark have built their system of *periods.* " We are now," says Mr. Worsaae, from whose manual of Danish Antiquities I take the expression of this theory, " we are now enabled to pronounce with certainty, that our antiquities belonging to the times of paganism may be referred to three chief classes, referable to three distinct *periods.* The first class includes all antiquarian objects formed of *stone,* respecting which we must assume that they appertain to the *stone-period,* as it is called, that is, to a period when the use of metals was in a great measure unknown. The second class comprises the oldest metallic objects; these, however, were not as yet composed of iron, but of a peculiar mixture of metals, copper and a small portion of tin melted together, to which the name of bronze has been given; from which circumstance the period in which this substance was commonly used has been named the *bronze-period.* Finally, all objects appertaining to the period when iron was generally known and employed are included in the third class, and belong to the *iron-period.*"

Such is the system adopted by the antiquaries of the north, and which has been rather hastily accepted by some of our own writers on antiquarian subjects. It is ingenious, and has, no doubt, something attractive about it; but I believe it to be unnatural as well as un-historical, and I think it may easily be shown that it is even contradicted by facts. I ascribe this erroneous classification, first, to too great a tendency of the northern antiquaries to hasty generalization; and secondly, and, perhaps, more especially, to what

I will term a vicious system of arranging museums which has prevailed to some degree in all countries. The proper, and the only correct, arrangement of a museum of antiquities is, no doubt, the *ethnological* one. Relics of antiquity should be classed according to the peoples and tribes to whom they are known or believed to have belonged, and to the localities in which they are found, and then only have they any intelligible meaning. Thus, to take an example, flint articles found in the district of Bridlington have not necessarily any connection with articles of flint which might be found, for instance, in Herefordshire, or in Wiltshire, either with respect to the people who made them or originally possessed them, or to the period to which they belonged. If, therefore, we wish to understand these relics, and to derive advantage from them, we must look at those of each locality by themselves, and pay attention in each case to the circumstances connected with them individually. But people have been adopting a practice of placing flint implements with flint implements, bronze with bronze, and iron with iron, until, forgetting entirely the real elements which give them an individual meaning, they begin to look at them just as if they were so many fossils belonging to such and such geological strata, and thus form systems which are pretty and attractive to look at, but which, in truth, belong only to the imagination.

It will, perhaps, not be occupying the time of the Society quite fruitlessly if we enter a little more in detail into this now rather celebrated system of periods. And first, with regard to the stone-period,—I do not mean at all to deny that the prevalence of implements, like those I have been describing, made of stone,

must be considered as characteristic of a low degree
of social development; and, in fact, it seems to imply
the ignorance of metals, or the incapacity to work
them. This, however, is by no means a necessary
consequence. When communication between one
place and another, even at short distances, was slow
and difficult—which was the case not only among
the ancient inhabitants of this island, but compara-
tively even down to very recent times—people were
commonly obliged to use the materials they had ready
at hand, from the impossibility of obtaining a regular
supply of material of a more appropriate character.
It is probable that, if one of the tribe of the Parisi,
or several together, set off to a place no farther off
than York to seek a supply of materials, he or they
ran the imminent risk of never returning. Metal of
any kind, therefore, might be an article of which they
depended for a small and precarious supply on some
itinerant dealer, who, of course, could not be expected
to carry with him any large quantity. It is, therefore,
quite possible that the use of metal and the use of
stone for such implements may have existed contemporaneously. We have, indeed, sufficient evidence
that they did so exist. We find stone implements
along with bronze implements, in what are considered
as the earliest sepulchral tumuli in this island. Stone
implements have sometimes been found on Roman
sites. Douglas found one of the stone implements
usually called a celt, in a Saxon grave, in Greenwich
Park. I myself recently took from an Anglo-Saxon
grave in the Isle of Wight, lying among implements
of iron, pieces of chipped flint closely resembling
those met with in the neighbourhood of Bridlington.
I believe, indeed, that one of the chroniclers of the

Norman Conquest speaks of weapons of stone as used by some of the Anglo-Saxon troops at the battle of Hastings.   Again, there are two circumstances to which I would particularly call your attention.   Many of these implements in stone must have been made with metal tools.   This is particularly the case with some stone articles of a higher finish.   It appears to me that even the common flint implements can only have been chipped with metal, and I suspect, moreover, that that metal was iron.   Secondly, it seems to me equally evident that most of these implements in stone were really copies of similar implements in metal.   A stone axe found by Mr. Cape in the neighbourhood of Bridlington, is, I believe, a mere copy of a Roman axe.   I cannot imagine that any one would have thought of making a barb to a fishing hook of flint, unless he had previously seen a barbed hook of metal.   Nor does it seem any more natural that people who were reduced to making such articles by chipping them out of flint should have thought of making a barbed arrow-head, when one without barbs would have served his purpose equally well, unless he took his idea from a model made of some kind of metal, and furnished by a more civilized or a richer people.

Secondly, with regard to the so-called *bronze-period*, I confess that I see no reason why the use of bronze should naturally precede that of iron.   I need hardly remark that bronze is a mixed metal, and that it was first made, in countries where there was no iron, (as in Greece and Italy,) in the attempt to harden copper that it might be made available for weapons, or for other edged or pointed instruments. But I know not why, in a country like Britain, in some parts of which iron was found almost on the surface of the ground, and at times so extremely rich in ore as to be almost malleable, this metal should not be in use quite as early as either bronze or copper. I must remind you that Cæsar tells us that in his time, while iron was procured in the island, the brass (*æs*), by which, no doubt, he meant bronze, used by the Britons was imported from abroad.

There are certain peculiarities in the articles of bronze, usually ascribed to the *bronze-period*, which deserve our special attention. They consist, chiefly, of swords of a form which antiquaries seem agreed in describing by the epithet of leaf-shaped, and of bronze axes, chisels, and other similar weapons, to which has been given the rather incongruous name of "celts," concerning which I will only remark that the sooner it is laid aside the better. The leaf-shaped swords are found, I believe, in almost all parts of the Roman empire, as well as in the barbaric countries on its border, though more numerous in the latter, and under different circumstances. They are found not unfrequently within the Roman province of Britain; but always, I think, in places where they seem to have been thrown accidentally, and not under circumstances which would lead us to identify at once the people who left them there. On the contrary, when they are found in Ireland, (where they are rather plentiful,) in the parts of Scotland beyond the limits of the Roman province, in Scandinavia, and even as far eastwardly as Hungary, we are naturally led to assume that they belonged to the natives of those countries, and, in fact, they are sometimes found interred in their graves. It has, therefore, been assumed that these swords were the weapons peculiar to the primitive populations of those countries which the Romans had not conquered, and of the Celtic populations of these islands before the Romans visited them. The same remarks apply to the so-called bronze celts, except that the latter have been found in our island more undoubtedly with Roman remains. It must be remarked, as at least partly explaining the difference in the circumstances of the finding of these articles, that the Romans were not in the habit of burying *their arms with the dead,* which, on the contrary, was a general custom among the Celtic and Teutonic races.

Now it is a remarkable circumstance that, whenever we find the swords, or the " celts," along the whole line of the European limits of the empire, whether in Ireland in the far-west, in Scotland, in distant Scandinavia, in Germany, or still further east in the Sclavonic countries, they are the same—not *similar* in character, but *identical.* It is certain that these countries were not occupied by peoples of the same race, nor is it at all probable that there was at any time (except through the Romans) a direct intercourse between the people on the borders of Russia and those of Ireland; and it seems to me that we should be led almost irresistibly, by the fact just stated, to the conclusion, particularly since we find them within the Roman empire, that these objects did not really belong to the countries where they are found, but that they must have been manufactured for them in some central position common to them all—in fact, that they were made in the Roman empire, and sold to the barbarians, just as now, at Birmingham and in others of our great manufactories, articles are made for exportation to suit the tastes of the Indian of America or of the Negro of Africa. There are known facts which corroborate this view of the matter.

At an early period local-intercommunication was extremely difficult and extremely slow, for people in general had to travel on foot, and their travelling was surrounded with danger. We know that not many years ago, before stage-coaches were generally introduced, the whole population of a village or small town remained so closely attached to the spot, that any one of them who had visited a distant village or two was looked upon as a remarkable personage. Much more was this the case at the remote period of which we are speaking. Under such circumstances, the internal commercial relations of a country were very small. At a later period of the Middle Ages the inconvenience arising from this circumstance was in a small degree obviated by the establishment of fairs, to which merchants and manufacturers repaired at certain periods of the year, and at which people bought and laid up sufficient stores for the interval. But, before the establishment of these fairs, a great part of the trade and manufactures of a country was in the hands of wandering dealers or workmen, such as in more modern times are termed *pedlers*,—a name probably derived from the circumstance that many of these dealers went on foot. Men who sold certain articles, or who practised certain arts, wandered thus over an immense extent of territory; they received, to a certain degree, the same kind of protection as minstrels, and passed often from one country to another. Their arrival was looked forward to with anxiety by those who needed their services, and who had saved money for purchases, or collected materials for work. Thus, even in greater matters, people prepared their malt and other ingredients for the time when the itinerant brewer came round and made their ale; and, after gunpowder came into use, each town or great lord expected the visit at a certain period of the man skilful in making it, at whose arrival they had the materials ready. So people who had articles of any kind that needed mending, if they were not mendable in a very easy manner, laid them aside, and waited till the periodical visit of men professing to make the repairs they required.

There are curious facts, illustrating this practice, connected with the immediate subject on which I am treating. In various places in England, especially in the eastern and south-eastern districts, and under circumstances which leave no doubt in my mind of their belonging to the Roman period, are found, not unfrequently, the remains of the working stock of people who evidently went about, in the manner just described, to make implements of bronze, and numerous discoveries prove that these articles were the bronze celts and leaf-shaped swords. Thus, in 1845, a quantity of bronze celts, with punches, gouges, and other instruments of the same material, as well as several pieces of unused metal, one of which appeared to be the residuum left in the melting pot, were found at a village near Attleborough, in Norfolk. No less than seventy so-called celts, and ten spear-heads of bronze, were found together in a field near Stibbard, in the same county. A similar collection of bronze chisels, &c. with portions of a leaf-shaped sword, was found at Sittingbourne, in Kent. At Westow, in Yorkshire, a collection of sixty such implements, together with a piece of a broken sword, and a piece of bronze which appeared to be the re-

siduum from melting, was found in an earthen jar
or vase.   I have myself seen some of a collection of
whole and broken celts, gouges, &c. found, under similar circumstances, at the foot of the Wrekin, in Shropshire, not far from the Roman town of Uriconium.
I might easily extend the list of such discoveries
which have been made at different times in our island;
and similar discoveries have been made also in various
parts of Germany, in Switzerland, and in France.
Leland, writing in the time of Henry VIII, and
speaking of Cornwall, tells us, " There was found of
late yeres spere heddes, axis for warre, and swerdes
of coper, wrapped up in lynin scant perishid, nere
the mount in St. Hilaries paroch in the tynne workes."
Here we find the manufactures of these articles actually brought into relation with the mining districts
from which the metals were derived.

Now here, I think, the whole mystery of these
bronze implements is solved.   It is evident, from the
frequency of these discoveries, that the *makers* were
rather a numerous class throughout the Roman empire.   They travelled about with their melting pot,
and a certain quantity of material, to which was added
the broken bronze they found at the places where
they stopped to work, and which had, no doubt, been
carefully preserved until their arrival, perhaps to be
taken in part payment.   The actual molds in which
the celts were cast are found commonly enough.
These " celts," with the chisels and gouges, appear
to have been the articles made in greatest quantities within the civilized parts of the empire, because
they were articles for domestic purposes; but we see
that the same manufacturers did make the leaf-shaped
swords, and the spear-heads.   There were various

reasons why bronze should be used for such purposes.
In the first place, it is far more easily fusible than
iron, or any other hard metal; and it is evident that
an itinerant manufacture like this could not be carried on conveniently with a metal which was not
easily fusible.   I think we may trace, also, among
the Romans themselves, a sort of superstitious reverence for bronze as a metal; and it was probably considered by the barbarians themselves as handsome,
and more valuable than iron.   After this statement
of facts, no one will, I think, be surprised when I
state that on the Continent these leaf-shaped swords
have been found, under circumstances which leave
little doubt of their being Roman.   In France, one
of these swords was found at Heilly, in the department of the Somme, with other articles, among which
were four brass coins of Caracalla; and another was
found, in another locality, along with skeletons, and
coins, some of which were of the emperor Maxen-
tius, so that they could not have been deposited in
the place where they were met with before the fourth
century of the Christian era.

   With regard to the *iron-period* it is not necessary
to say much.   We all know that, from the first period
at which we trace the knowledge of iron, the use of
it has continued without interruption.   But we know,
also, that iron is the most perishable of all metals.
We have only to wet the blade of a knife, and in that
state expose it to the air, and decomposition begins
immediately.   Beyond a certain date no article in
iron is preserved, except under very favourable
circumstances.   Every one who has been present at
the opening of Anglo-Saxon graves, the average date
of which may be considered as the sixth century, and

in which abundance of iron implements, and especially weapons, such as swords and spears, were buried,
knows how often the former existence of such articles
is only traced by a darker tinge in the earth. We
must not, therefore, conclude that, at a period before
the Roman age, (when we know that that metal was
used,) iron was *not* in use, because we find no remains
of it.

These various considerations lead me to the conclusion, that the system of periods adopted by the
northern archæologists must be rejected as having
no foundation in facts. The use of stone, no doubt,
marked a low state of civilization, but it depended
partly on localities and their peculiar conditions, and
did not belong to any particular period, or to any
particular people; nor was it incompatible with the
use of metals at the same time. The same considerations seem to show that there was no *bronze-period*
in the sense those archæologists give to the term;
but that the articles in bronze on which they build
their theory were really of Roman manufacture, or,
at least, made in Roman provinces, and were obtained
by commerce. In saying this, I do not mean to deny
that in the sequel, and towards the latter period of
Roman rule, the barbarians themselves may have
learned and practised the manufacture; because this,
we know, was the common course in most manufactures; and, indeed, we can trace in many of these
articles, especially in the more elaborately ornamented
examples, an evident falling off from the tasteful
forms which the Romans had given to them. It is
to this period of degenerate art, indeed, that I attribute the mass of the more peculiar articles in bronze
found in Scandinavia. Lastly, I feel convinced that

the notion of there having been a period, in western
or northern Europe, during which bronze was in
common use for manufactures, and iron was *not* known,
is a mere gratuitous assumption.   The inconvenience
of such extensive generalizations will be apparent at
once to the ethnologist who feels the necessity of
studying peoples in detail, and taking them in their
tribes and small divisions, instead of beginning with
extensive and fanciful theories.

II.

ON SOME ANCIENT BARROWS OR TUMULI,
RECENTLY OPENED IN EAST
YORKSHIRE.

HE town of Bridlington stretches from east to west along sloping ground which rises towards the north. The higher ground above the town is called Hunton, and commands, towards the south, an extensive prospect of Bridlington Bay and Holderness. This high ground is divided into fields; in one of which, occupied by Mr. William Brambles, as tenant of the Corporation of Beverley, and in other fields adjoining, there is a continuous embankment, inclosing a long square, within which are remarked many pit-formed hollows in the ground; and boulders and other stones, which appear to have been brought from the beach, are turned up by the plough, especially near the embankment. According to the popular tradition of the locality, this place was at some remote period the site of a town or village: but such traditions are to be received with caution; and the number of large barrows scattered about would seem rather to point to the brow of the hill as a primeval cemetery. Its position is exactly such a one as the early inhabitants of our island were accustomed to choose for that purpose.

Five of these barrows have been recently opened by a Yorkshire friend, Mr. Edward Tindall, of Bridlington—a gentleman who has made himself remarkable for the zeal and success with which he investigates the remains of antiquity in that district; and I have thought it would not be without interest to the members of the Society to give them a brief account of the result of his investigations, according to the information I have received from Mr. Tindall himself. Mr. Tindall commenced his labours (assisted by his friend Mr. Collinson) at the beginning of the month of April, 1857, and opened a tumulus standing by itself, and the nearest of them all to the town. At the depth of about two feet from the top of the tumulus the remains of two skeletons were found, among burnt earth and a little charcoal. The bones were much decayed; but the jawbone of one of them, which was better preserved than the rest, was pronounced by a medical gentleman present (Dr. Allison) to be that of a youth under fourteen years of age. Mixed with the burnt earth and charcoal were several strippings of flints and a quantity of light-grey vegetable ashes. Mr. Tindall continued the excavation until he came down to the chalk, but found no other object of interest.

At a short distance from this tumulus are two others, near together, in a field belonging to Yarborough Lloyd, esq. One of these was opened on the 10th of April, and presented some peculiarities of construction. The chalk rock had first been uncovered and hollowed out into the form of a bowl about eighteen inches deep, and nine feet in diameter, for the reception of the deposit. After the latter had been placed in it, the bowl was filled in with fine

mould, and above this was raised the tumulus, formed
of large chalk stones, covered over, when finished, with
a coating of rubble, and earthed up at the top with fine
soil. This tumulus was about five feet high from the
surface of the chalk. No traces of human remains
were found in it; but there were a considerable
quantity of bones of carnivorous and ruminating
animals, fowls, &c., and three articles in bronze,
one of them a fibula of rather unusual form. This
object will be best understood by the accompanying
figures, (Figs. 1 and 2,) representing it as seen in two
positions:—

Fig. 1.

Fig. 2.

Figs. 1 and 2. A Roman Fibula.

The other two objects were also bronze fibulæ, in the
shape of a plain ring, and exactly resembling each
other, (Fig. 3.)

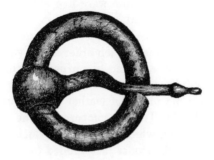

Fig. 3. Circular Roman Fibula.

These three articles are undoubtedly Roman, and I should think not of the earlier period of the occupation of our island.

The other of these two barrows, which was next opened, closely resembled the former in its construction, though the hollow in the chalk was not quite so deep; but nothing further was found in it than a few fragments of bones, with charcoal, burnt earth, a small quantity of dark-coloured fatty earth, and four flint implements.

At the beginning of May, Mr. Tindall opened a fourth tumulus, in another field at some distance from the others, and on the highest ground in the lordship, which was attended with discoveries of a somewhat remarkable character. It was nearly forty yards in circumference, and, as the shortest way of arriving at the probable place of deposit, the workmen were directed to sink a shaft from the top. In their passage down they found " a remarkable quantity of boulder or cobble stones, placed in the same manner as a grave is generally sodded up in a churchyard, and at each corner there were five stones placed in a horizontal line," and radiating as it were from the centre. At the ends of two of these lines of stones, which were opposite to each other and a yard deeper in the barrow, were found two urns of slightly baked earth, containing " a sort of brown paste or fat matter," with some pieces of leather and a quantity of hair, which Mr. Tindall compares to the hair of a cow. The urns, which were below, but not immediately under, the stones just alluded to, were placed in hollows in the chalk made for their reception. A flat piece of flag-stone was placed over one of the urns, and a similar piece of chalk over the other, and one of them stood nearly in its original upright position, while the other was crushed to pieces. There was here also a bowl-shaped hollow in the chalk, over which was a làyer of ashes, charcoal, and burnt wood. Among this was found a piece of leather, some bits of iron, which appeared to have been nails, and two pieces of flint chipped into the form of crescents. It is worthy of remark also that some of the leather was cut and jagged at the edges in a manner that would lead us to believe that it had belonged to some ornamental part of the dress.

The fifth tumulus was opened, on the 26th of May, by a trench cut through it from east to west, about five feet wide. About a foot beneath the surface occurred a layer of boulders, and under these, burnt bones and earth, and some much corroded nails. Mr. Tindall also found here a few cinders of *mineral coal*, about seven pieces of mineral coal unburnt, each about the size of a walnut, and one similar bit of kennel coal; and also, which was the most extraordinary of all, a piece of a tobacco pipe made of pipeclay. In the body of the tumulus were found the branches, remarkably well preserved, of what was believed to have been a blackthorn tree, and several decayed pieces of wood.

Tobacco pipes have been found before in very singular approximations with objects of remote antiquity, and they have even been supposed to belong to a period long antecedent to the introduction of tobacco into Europe, when some other plant is conjectured to have been used as a narcotic. My friend, Dr. Bruce, in his excellent work on the Roman Wall, has engraved two of these pipes, and mentioned others, found on Roman sites in the North of England. Another friend, well known for his careful as well as learned antiquarian investigations, the Abbé Cochet, found both shanks and bowls of similar pipes in the Roman cemetery at Dieppe, in Normandy, and they have also been met with in a Roman cemetery near Abbeville. They all seem to me to present by far too close a resemblance to the pipes in use about the time of James I. to belong to any much earlier period; and we must, I think, ascribe these anomalous positions in which they are sometimes found to mere accident. We know how common a practice it was in former days to dig into these ancient tumuli in search of imaginary treasures, and it seems to me not impossible that some subject of our first kings of the Stuart dynasty, engaged in a search of this kind, may have dropped his broken pipe in the Bridlington tumulus. With regard to the mineral coal and cinders, Mr. Tindall assures me that they were found at the bottom of the tumulus, among the original deposit;

and although the circumstance is a very extraordinary
one, it is not impossible or even very improbable. It
has been fully ascertained that the Romans in this
island used mineral coal. Extensive remains of their
coal-mining operations have been found in Northumberland, and I believe in North Wales, where the
seams cropped out at the surface; and the cinders of
mineral coal have been met with in more than one
instance in the fire-places of Roman villas.*   I will
mention, as rather a curious coincidence with what
was observed in these Yorkshire tumuli, that the Abbé
Cochet found, as the usual accompaniments of the
urn interments in the Roman cemeteries he opened
in Normandy, pieces of chipped flint, generally formed into the shape of wedges, which would of course
hardly differ in shape from what we are accustomed

to call flint axes.   Of
the two urns, of which
Mr. Tindall has sent me
drawings from which the
accompanying cuts were
made, one (Fig. 4.) I
consider to be Roman,
that is, belonging to the
Roman period; the other
(Fig. 5) belongs to those
ruder forms which are
common in the York-

Fig. 4. Supposed Roman Urn.   shire barrows, and which
are generally called, without any positive reason,
British.

* It may be further stated that mineral coal, both burnt and
unburnt, has been found in the excavations now in progress at
Wroxeter, near Shrewsbury, on the site of the Roman city of
Uriconium.

In this example, how-
ever, it appears to me
that we may distinctly
recognize debased copies
of the ornaments of the
Samian and other Roman
ware, such as (in this
case) the egg-and-
tongue and the platted
band ornaments,* and it
strengthens me rather in
a suspicion that this class

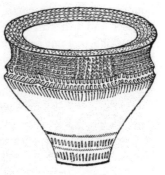

Fig. 5. Sepulchral Urn.

of Yorkshire tumuli will prove eventually to belong, not to the British, but to a very late Roman
period. In spite, too, of the coarseness of the manufacture, the outline, when drawn correctly, as in my
cut, is an evident imitation of Roman forms.

While speaking of urns found in this neighbourhood, I may mention two which came into the possession of Mr. Tindall that are especially deserving
of notice. One, represented in
the cut (Fig. 6), is barrel-shaped,
with peculiar ornamentation, and
was filled with black earth, in
which was found a large bead of jet.
An urn of similar shape and character, and equally ornamented,
is in the possession of Mr. Cape,
of Bridlington. The other urn
to which I allude, was extracted
in Mr. Tindall's presence, from a
barrow, in a field in his neigh-

Fig. 6. Sepulchral Urn.

* I may remark, that the resemblance is much more apparent
in the original urn than in the cut, which has been necessarily
made on a small scale.

bourhood, when the earth was cleared away by the farmer, and was still more remarkable in character. Its surface was not only embellished with ornaments, but with a pictorial representation of a warrior in a chariot drawn by two men, and preceded by two others carrying spears. Unfortunately, this curious urn was very dishonestly purloined from Mr. Tindall soon after it came into his possession, but he preserved a rough drawing of it, from which the accompanying cut (Fig. 7.) is reduced. I may add that the group here represented is repeated on the other side. It may be remarked that the swords in this group bear a close resemblance to one represented in a sculpture found at Birdoswald, (Amboglanna,) on the Roman Wall, which was intended to represent a soldier of the Dacian cohort established at that place.

Fig. 7.   Roman Urn.

It is to be hoped that Mr. Tindall will continue his exploration of the barrows in the neighbourhood of Bridlington, as I believe there are still several which remain unopened. I will merely call attention to one, at some distance to the north of that town, which has been partially excavated since the foregoing remarks were first laid before the society.

At the beginning of October last (1857), I paid a visit to lord Londesborough, who was then in his residence at Scarborough, and it had been arranged that we should take that opportunity of opening a very large barrow at some distance to the south of that town.

This barrow, which is a mound of earth above sixty
feet in height, and about 300 feet in circumference,
is popularly known by the name of Willey-hou (*hou*
being in that part of the country synonymous with
barrow).   It stands on the slope of one of the lower
chalk hills of the wolds, a few miles inward from the
coast, at a distance of somewhat less than a mile from
the village of Wold-Newton (which is rather to the
northward of it), and about a mile and a half from
that of North Burton (which lies nearly south). At the
foot of the bank, below Willey-hou, runs one of those
curious intermitting streams common to the chalk
districts, which is known by the name of *The Gypsies*.

On Monday, the 5th of October, a sufficient number of men were set to work in cutting a large trench
from one side of the tumulus to the centre; but the
time required for such an excavation had been much
underrated, and up to the Thursday the only result
was the clearing of a large portion of a level floor, at
some elevation from the base of the tumulus, which
was covered with a coating of wood ashes and other
burnt materials.   On the day just mentioned our attention was carried away to another discovery, that
of some interesting Anglo-Saxon interments near
Scarborough, which proved for the moment the more
attractive of the two.

This discovery had interrupted our plans with regard to the great tumulus of Willey-hou, and as it
would have required another week or more to explore
it properly, it was abandoned for the present. I have
no doubt whatever that it is a sepulchral interment
of the Roman period, but it may probably contain
nothing but an urn filled with bones.   This great
tumulus is, however, especially interesting from its

connection with the stories and legends of ancient times, which are as much characteristic of races as language itself, and travel with them or with their divisions in the same manner. The example I have to relate shows how durable such stories are in the minds of peoples. We sometimes find, in opening these tumuli, the traces of depredations committed upon them in former times in the belief, which prevailed generally, that vast treasures were concealed beneath them; but fortunately they were protected also by another article of the superstitious creed—the belief that these treasures were placed under the charge of fearful dragons, or of still more powerful fairies or demons, who were sure to take vengeance upon any one who attempted to rob them. The treasure-hunters, therefore, who went to work in earnest, sought the assistance of magical incantations, which were not always easily obtained. The tumulus of Willey-hou, which is one of the most celebrated in this part of England, was the subject of a legend of very remote date.

One of our most valuable historians of the twelfth century was born at Bridlington, in the first year of the reign of king Stephen (A.D. 1136), and afterwards becoming a canon of Newburgh, in the same county, is commonly known by the name of William of Newburgh. He seems to have been fond of the legends and popular antiquities of his native place, and he tells us that he had often remarked the tumulus to which the following legend belongs, which he has taken the trouble to hand down to us. There can be no doubt that it is the barrow of Willey-hou. He describes it as standing about half a mile from a village, of which he has omitted to tell us the name, but which was, no doubt, Wold-Newton; it was near "those celebrated waters, which are commonly called *Vipse*, and spring from the earth in a copious stream, not continually, but at intervals, after intervals of years." This stream was no doubt *The Gypsies* already mentioned.

One day a rustic of the village just mentioned, went to visit one of his friends in a neighbouring village, (no doubt North Burton,) the road to which lay near our tumulus, a road, therefore, which we may easily suppose people would not then willingly choose to pass at night. However, the love of beer, which was then even more powerful than at the present day, kept the rustic visitor until a late hour at night, and when at length he started on his way home he was at least all the happier for his entertainment. As he approached the tumulus his astonishment was great to hear merry sounds issuing from it, which betokened that it was occupied by a party who were feasting and singing. Wondering who could have come to that lonely spot to enjoy themselves at such an hour, he approached nearer to the mound, and then, for the first time, he saw a door open in its side. Our rustic friend, who was well mounted, rode boldly up to this door, looked through it, and beheld, inside, a spacious apartment, brilliantly illuminated, and a large company of men and women seated at a magnificent entertainment. As he stood there staring at the door, one of the cup-bearers, seeing him, approached and offered him the cup to drink. Now it must be remarked that, according to the doctrines of fairy lore, (for these were fairies,) when a mere mortal approached their assemblies accidentally, the fairy-folk always offered him some of the liquor they were

drinking, and, if he drank it, he immediately lost all
power of returning home, and was carried away into
fairy-land.   But the rustic of East Yorkshire was
too wise for that, for he poured the contents on the
ground, and, grasping firmly the cup, started off at
full gallop.   The fairy feasters rushed from the tumulus, and gave chase; but the horse of the fugitive was
a good and swift one, and almost by miracle he reached his village in safety, and secured his valuable prize.
He had, however, a chance in his favour which William
of Newburgh has forgotten to state.   It was an article
of popular belief, equally in the time of the fairies and
in that of the witches, that if you once placed a running
stream between yourself and your unearthly pursuers,
they had no longer any power over you.   At a very
little distance from Willey-hou the stream of the
Gypsies must have protected the fugitive in his flight
to Wold-Newton.   His prize turned out to be a vase
of unknown material, and equally strange in form and
colour, (*vasculum materiæ incognitæ, coloris insoliti, et
formæ inusitatæ.*)   This extraordinary cup was soon
talked of far and near, and at last it was given to
King Henry I.—for it was in his reign that this
event occurred.   Henry subsequently presented it
to his brother-in-law, king David of Scotland; and
many years afterwards the second king Henry, visiting the Scottish court, was shown this wonderful cup,
and begged it of William the Lion, who then occupied the Scottish throne.   " This story," says William of Newburgh, " may appear strange, and people
would not believe it if it had not been attested by the
most trustworthy witnesses."

And, in fact, there may have been some truth in
it; for it is not impossible that somebody digging into

the tumulus may have found an urn which, from its rarity, may have been thought not unworthy to be presented to the king, and that the legend may have been added to give more interest to it. It is a common legend, and has been repeated under various forms and circumstances.

This legend, as we see, existed early in the twelfth century, or more than seven hundred years ago. I learnt, during my visit to the spot, that it still exists, though in a debased form. The peasantry now tell us that, one winter's night, a farmer returning from market heard, much to his astonishment, sounds of mirth and revelry proceed from Willey-hou, whereupon he rode up to the hill to ascertain the cause of this extraordinary occurrence. As he approached, a little dapper man presented himself, with a cup of welcome. The farmer, supposing it to be silver, drank the contents, and setting spurs to his horse rode off with the treasure; but on his arrival at home, to his great disappointment, he found that it was nothing but base metal.

This is not the only legend which the peasantry of the neighbourhood have preserved relative to Willey-hou. They tell you gravely that years ago some avaricious personage dug into the tumulus in order to gain possession of the treasure it was supposed to contain. At length, after much labour, he came to an immense iron chest, the receptacle of the coveted riches, but the lid was no sooner uncovered than it lifted itself up a little, and out sprang an immense black cat, which seated itself upon the chest, and glowered with eyes of fire upon the insolent intruders. Not daunted by this, after making various ineffectual attempts to move the chest, the digger for treasure fixed to it a strong chain or rope, to which he attached so numerous a team of horses, according to some accounts, or bullocks, according to others, that they reached two and two from the tumulus to North Burton, a distance of full a mile and a half. When all these preparations were completed, the director of these operations gave the order for moving exultingly in the following words—of course addressing his animals:—

"Hep Joan! prow Mark!
Whether God will or no,
We'll have this ark."

He had hardly uttered the words when the rope and the traces broke in a hundred places, and the chest of treasure disappeared for ever.

There is a certain air of quaintness about the rhymes which seems to speak for the antiquity of this legend. The peasantry assure you further, that if any one run nine times round the tumulus without stopping, and then put his ear against it, he will distinctly hear the fairies dancing and singing in the interior. The old superstitious feeling relating to the spot seems, indeed, to exist almost as strong amongst the peasantry of the present day as it did ages ago; our proceedings excited general alarm among the lower classes, who expected to see some manifestation of vengeance on the part of the beings believed to hold the guard of the tumulus; and few would have ventured out in its neighbourhood after dark.

III.

ON SOME CURIOUS FORMS OF SEPULCHRAL
INTERMENT FOUND IN EAST
YORKSHIRE.

HE sepulchral interments of the earlier inhabitants of our island are often very indefinite, and are not easily identified by themselves with any particular race of people, but by means of careful observation and of patient comparison with other examples, they may be ultimately made to throw some light upon primæval history. It is in the hope of contributing to this object that I would call attention to a very curious class of sepulchral chests, or coffins, which appear to me quite novel, and which seem to be peculiar to East Yorkshire.

On the summit of the high cliffs near the village of Gristhorpe, about six miles from Scarborough, and fifteen to the northward of Bridlington, are, or were, three ancient tumuli. That in the centre, a tolerably large one, was opened on the 10th of July, 1834, and was found to contain what was at first taken for a mere rough log of wood; but on further examination it proved to be a wooden coffin, formed of the rough trunk of an old oak tree, the external bark of which was still in good preservation. It had been merely hewn roughly at the extremities, split, and then hollowed internally to receive the body. The accompanying cut will give the best notion of the appearance of

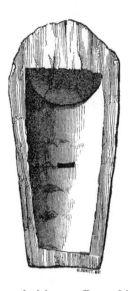

this primitive coffin, which was much damaged in its removal from the tumulus. The trunk of the tree had been split tolerably equally, for the coffin and its cover were of nearly the same dimensions. The only attempt at ornament was what was taken for a rude figure of a human face cut in the bark at one end of the lid, which appeared to have been held to the coffin only by the uneven fracture of the wood corresponding on each part. At the bottom of the coffin, near the centre, a hole, three inches long and one wide, had been cut through the wood, apparently for the purpose of carrying off the aqueous matter arising from the decomposition of the body. This

coffin was about seven feet long by three broad.
When first opened it was nearly full of water; but,
on this being cleared away, a perfect and well preserved skeleton presented itself, which was laid on
its right side with its head to the south. The body,
of which the skeleton measures six feet two inches,
having been much too long for the hollow of the
coffin, which was only five feet four inches long, the
legs had been necessarily doubled up.

Several small objects were found in the coffin with
the skeleton, most of which are represented in the
accompanying cut. They are, three pieces of chipped flint (Figs. 1, 2, and 6); a well-executed ornament,

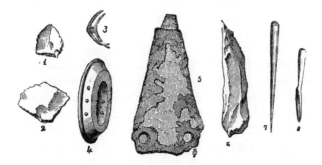

resembling a large stud or button, apparently of horn,
which had every appearance of having been formed
by the lathe (Fig. 4); a pin of the same material,
which lay on the breast, and had apparently been
used to secure a skin, in which the body had evidently been enveloped (Fig. 7); an article of wood,
also formed like a pin, but having what would be its
point rounded and flattened on one side to about half
its length (Fig. 8); fragments of an ornamental ring,

of similar material to the stud, and supposed, from its
large size, to have been used for fastening some part
of the dress (Fig. 3); the remains of a small basket
of wicker-work, the bottom of which had been formed
of bark, and a flat bronze dagger or knife (Fig. 5).
None of these articles give us any assistance in fixing
the age of this curious interment, except the dagger,
and that is not very certain. Chipped flints are found
very frequently in Roman interments, both in this
country and on the continent; and I have also found
them in Saxon graves: but the dagger belongs to a
type of which several examples have been found in
the Wiltshire barrows, as well as in similar interments
in other parts of England, which, from all the circumstances connected with them, we should be led
to ascribe to a remote date, perhaps to the earlier
period of the Roman occupation of the island. A
quantity of vegetable substance was also found in
the coffin, which was rather hastily conjectured to
be the remains of mistletoe. The coffin, after being
deposited in its grave, had been covered over with
large oak branches. The tumulus above this was
formed of a layer of clay, then a layer of loose stones,
another layer of clay, and a second layer of loose
stones, and the whole was finally covered with soil,
which had no doubt collected upon the tumulus
during the long period since it was raised.*

The wooden coffin from Gristhorpe, with its contents, were deposited in the Scarborough Museum,
where they have always excited considerable interest.

---

* An account of the opening of this tumulus, and of its contents, was published by Mr. W. C. Williamson, curator of the
Manchester Natural History Society. Second edition. Scarborough, 1836. 4to.

The skeleton, which has been unadvisedly called
that of a "British chief," has by some chemical influence become as black as ebony, from which circumstance some pleasant archæologist jokingly gave
to the British chief the title of the *Black Prince*.
It remained an unique example of barrow-inter-
ments, until I received from a friend in that part
of Yorkshire, Mr. Edward Tindall, of Bridlington,
information of the discovery of a similar interment near Great Driffield, in the August of last
year; and soon afterwards I learnt that another oak
coffin of this description had been found near Beverley in 1848.   Of the latter I have received, through
Mr. Tindall, some account from Dr. Brereton, of
Beverley.   It appears that in the year just mentioned
a labourer named Fitzgerald, while digging a drain
in the ground called Beverley Parks, near that town,
came upon what he supposed to be a portion of the
trunk of a tree, which had been turned quite black
from the chemical action of the iron and gallic acid in
the soil.   On further examination it proved to be
a coffin, which was formed very similarly to that at
Scarborough.   A slab, which had been cut, or split
from the rest, formed the lid; but it had been fastened

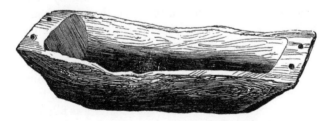

to the chest by means of four oaken thrindles, or pegs,

about the size of the spokes of a common ladder, and
the ends of the coffin had been bevelled off, so as to
leave less of the substance of the wood where the
holes for the pegs were drilled through. This coffin
was nearly eight feet and a half long externally, and
seven feet and a half internally ; and it was four feet
two inches wide. It is understood to have contained
some fragments of human bones, not calcined; but no
careful examination appears to have been made at the
time of the discovery. A quantity of bones of different kinds of animals were found in the soil about the
spot. The tumulus, in this case, had probably been
cleared away long ago, without disturbing the interment, in consequence of the position of the latter
below the surface of the ground. This, I understand,
was the case also with the coffin at Gristhorpe, which
had been placed in a hole some depth below the original surface of the ground.

From the description I have received it seems
rather doubtful whether the barrow in which the
third oak coffin was found, and which is situated by
one of the fine clear streams in the neighbourhood of
Great Driffield, near a place called Sunderlandwick,
be altogether artificial, or whether an original rise in
the ground had not been taken advantage of by those
who erected it. If the latter were the case, then a
hole has been dug here also for the reception of the
coffin; but if the whole mound, which was composed
of clay, were artificial, the coffin must have been laid
upon the surface of the ground. Two large and thick
branches of trees had here, as at Gristhorpe, been
placed over the coffin before the mound was filled in.
The coffin in this instance was, like the others, hollowed from the solid trunk of a tree, but it differed from

them in having no ends; and, although it came in two pieces when taken out of the earth, (or rather in three, for the lid broke in two,) it was supposed by those who found it that it had been originally one entire piece, a sort of large wooden tube, or pipe, formed

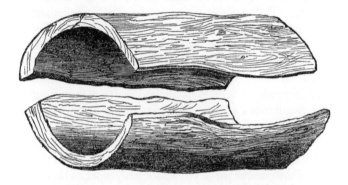

by hollowing through the heart of the timber. This coffin was about six feet in length and four in breadth, the disproportion in breadth being accounted for by the circumstance that it was intended to contain three bodies, two of which were laid with their heads turned one way, and the other turned in the contrary direction. The coffin, in consequence of the ends being unprotected, was filled with clay and sand, which had become mixed with the human remains, and the skulls and other bones were in so fragile a condition through decay that they fell to pieces when disturbed, and did not admit of any profitable examination.   I understand that no articles of any kind, which might assist in fixing the date of this interment, were found; but a quantity of ashes lay mixed with the surrounding soil, which are described as still retaining a burnt smell. The coffin in this instance lay due east and west.*

No circumstance connected with these two last interments is calculated to throw any light upon their dates, which, however, I think we may safely consider as not more recent than the close of the Roman period. But, as I was putting these notes together, information reached me of a still more singular discovery. During the last two years the local board of health at Selby has carried on extensive excavations for sewerage, &c. in that town, which have brought to light numerous ancient remains, including the foundations of a fortified gate, or bridge, of very massive character. In the month of June of the present year, while cutting through a piece of ground called the Church Hill, which is understood to be the site of the ancient parish church, destroyed when the old abbey church was made parochial, and in which considerable foundations of stone were found, the workmen met with not one, but fourteen wooden coffins, all made, like those I have been describing, out of the solid trunks of oak trees, which had been separated into two pieces in order to form a chest and lid, and had been scooped out to form a receptacle for the corpse. I have been favoured with an account of this discovery by Mr. George Lowther, of Selby. These coffins, he informs me, were found near the surface of the ground, some of them at a depth of not more than eighteen inches, lying parallel to each other, not exactly east and west, but rather E. N. E. by W. S. W., a variation of two points. To Mr.

---

* This coffin has, I believe, been given, by the proprietor of the estate on which it was found, to the Museum of the Yorkshire Philosophical Society at York.

Lowther, also, I am indebted for a drawing of one of
these coffins, found on the third of June, 1857, which
is copied in the annexed woodcut.   It was the only one

which appears to have been very carefully examined;
but, as far as I can gather, they all contained remains
of human skeletons, though accompanied by no articles which might assist us in assigning a date to them.
The skeleton contained in this coffin was pronounced
by a medical gentleman present at the examination to
be that of a full-grown female.   This coffin was six
feet ten inches long; one which lay near it measured
nearly eight feet.   It differs in one rather remarkable circumstance from those previously described, namely, that although similarly cut and hollowed
from a solid trunk of oak, the interior work is finished
in a less workmanlike manner.   In the Gristhorpe
and Beverley coffins the cavity for the reception of
the body must have been finished internally by the
chisel, as their ends stand at right angles, or nearly
so, to the bottom, which is flat in the whole length;
but in the Selby coffin the cavity has been formed by
an adze, or similar instrument, fitted for hollowing or
scooping a block of wood, but not for cutting it out
clean at right angles.   It is also deserving of remark
that the upper part, or lid, is hollowed out in a corresponding manner to the lower part.   The two parts

of the coffin were in this, as in the others found at
the same place, fastened together by oval wooden
pegs, driven down into the sides; resembling in this
respect the Beverley coffin.   When it was first discovered, and the soil cleared away from it, the wood
of the upper part was found decayed and broken
away, so as to expose to view the face of the skeleton,
as shown in our engraving.

Although we have nothing to define the age of the
Selby wooden coffins, we have the certainty that they
belonged to Christian interments, and that they were
laid in regular juxtaposition in a churchyard.   All
the circumstances connected with them would lead
us to ascribe them to a remote period, and I do not
think it improbable that they may be anterior to the
Norman Conquest.   I am not at this moment aware
of the discovery of coffins of the same description
in other parts of the island; and they seem to show,
which would indeed be a curious fact, that a peculiar
burial practice had continued to exist in this district
(Eastern Yorkshire) from a period dating as far back
as the commencement of the Roman occupation of the
island to probably a late Anglo-Saxon period, that is,
during a thousand years.   This should be a sufficient
warning against our assuming too hastily that a particular form of interment must be characteristic of a
particular date.   I must, however, add that I am
rather inclined to doubt whether the contents of the
Gristhorpe tumulus do not rather prove that the peculiar shaped dagger or knife found in it was in use at
a later period than is commonly supposed, than that
the dagger proves the extremely remote age of the
coffin.   From various circumstances which have come
to my knowledge, through the researches of Mr. Tin-

dall and others, I am inclined to think that most of
the barrows in the maritime district of Yorkshire to
the south of Scarborough belong to the later Roman
period; in which case we may much more easily understand how a particular form of coffin then in use may
have continued in use during the Anglo-Saxon period.
It must be added, as a fact of considerable importance
with regard to these interments in England, that, as
I learn from the English edition of Worsaae's " Primeval Antiquities of Denmark" (Parker, 1849), examples of exactly similar coffins have been found, in
one or two instances, in barrows in Denmark and
Germany, which date, probably, from about the fourth
century.

IV.

TRÉAGO, AND THE LARGE TUMULUS AT
ST. WEONARD'S.

N the old coach road from Hereford to Monmouth, rather more than ten miles from the former place, and about seven from the latter, stands the little village of St. Weonard's; a saint who is, I believe, unknown to the calendar, though we gather from Leland that he was a hermit, who had sought retirement in this spot, and that he was figured in the painted glass which then adorned the window of the church. In a document, preserved in the *Liber Landavensis*, relating to the territory of Ergyng, or Archenfield, in which St. Weonard's is situated, it is called Llansant-Gwainerth, St. Gwainerth's Church. The village is situated on the top of a hill, amid a rich and varied country, and the tower of the church is a bold object from whatever side we approach it. To the south-west, another hill of about the same elevation, at a distance of about a quarter of a mile, incloses a valley, which is partly occupied by the park and mansion of Treago, the seat of Peter Rickards Mynors, esq.

Treago, from the East, as it appeared before the alterations.

Treago, which stands on the lower part of the slope of the hill opposite that which is crowned by St. Weonard's, is a house of great antiquity, probably of the thirteenth century, and presents an example of the old fortified mansion, resembling no other with which I am acquainted in this country. It forms a square, with a small tower or tourelle at each corner. The south and north sides of the house are fifty-four feet between the tourelles, and the east and west fifty-three feet and a half. The southern tower was larger and loftier than the others, and its wall was extremely massive. It had a stone staircase, in a sort of narrow buttress tower. The upper part of this tower was taken down, a century ago, by Charles Morgan, esq., who married the widow of Robert Mynors, esq., and came to reside at Treago, and who built in its place a rather unsightly addition, in the shape of a

I.   D

large circular smoking room, which now serves as
a bed room. The upper part of this staircase was
formed of solid logs of wood, and part of it still
remains. The ground-floor of this corner of the
building appears to have been occupied by the offices
connected with the kitchen, the remains of which
are still very interesting. The site of the oven is
marked outwardly by a bulge in the wall, between
the staircase turret and the present entrance to the
house, which latter seems to have been originally a
door communicating from these domestic offices with
the outward court. The old hall formed the northern
side of the house, now turned into a kitchen, and
was open to the roof, which is of very early character,
and still perfect, though a bed room has been inserted
between it and the hall. Its timbers and arches bear
a close resemblance to those in Westminster Hall.
The old kitchen, with its two enormous fire-places,
is now divided into two rooms. It adjoined and
opened into the inner court, and communicated
through the court with the old hall. Each of the
corner tourelles had eyelet holes; and there were
on the outside of the house two rows of small windows, each about one foot wide, by a foot and a half
high, with strong cross-bars of iron. There was one
three-light window, high up in the south-eastern face
of the building; and the eastern tower, which perhaps contained the ladies' " chamber," had also three
windows of stone, one of three lights and two of two
lights, which were, like the others, strongly barred.
The western and northern tourelles had three rows
of eyelets, with projecting stones internally, as though
to support persons who might discharge arrows, or
other small missiles, at the asailants, in case of an

assault.   This side of the house, commanded by the
slope of the hill, was, of course, more exposed than
the others.

The entrance porch, in the middle of the north-
east side, is supposed to have been added about the
time of Henry VIII ; it is built against, and not
let into, the old wall of the house, and a door with a
new Tudor arch was made in the wall as an entrance
into the old hall, which communicated with the internal court.   The dimensions of this court were 25
feet 5 inches, by 25 feet 9 inches.   There were four
doors from this internal court into the house, all very
small and low, not more than two feet wide, with angular heads, resembling somewhat the angular-headed
doorways of the old Anglo-Saxon churches.   It is worthy of remark that this form of door is found at Goodrich Castle, and perhaps it may be traced on other
buildings in this part of the border.   It may be remarked, also, that there are three different masons'
marks, found severally repeated on all the facing stones
of the building, the surface of which has not been destroyed,—a key, a plane, and a square,—which would
seem to imply that there were three master-masons
employed in its erection.   It would be interesting to
ascertain whether these marks are found in other
buildings in this part of the country.   There were two
rows of windows, of larger dimensions than the external windows, and curiously carved in oak, looking into
the interior court from the rooms above and below.
This court contained a good and deep well, sunk
through the rock on which the house is built, which
still supplies a pump.   In the interior of the house there
are remains of secret rooms and hiding places, which,
in the unsettled times in which such fortified edifices

were built, were necessary for concealing property
of value and persons during short periods of unex-
pected and unavoidable occupation by an enemy.
The rooms were low and small, and naturally rather
dark.   The principal fire-places were very large,
about twelve feet wide, within a round arch, with a
strong pointed one above.   The external walls of the
house are very massive, that on the south-east side
being still seven feet thick; nevertheless it stood
within an inclosure, or external court, surrounded by
strong massive walls, which were taken down about
seventy years ago; and there are reasons for believing
that it was further protected on the east by a wet moat.

Such was Treago but a few years ago, when it had
undergone very little change from its original appearance. It had then been partly occupied for many years
as a farm-house, and was surrounded with the ordinary
buildings of a farm-yard. About ten years ago (this
was written in 1855) Mr. Mynors determined, on leaving his seat at Evancoyd, in Radnorshire, to reside
here; and the house of Treago, the place of his birth,
underwent the necessary repairs and alterations to
fit it for a modern residence, which, unfortunately for
its archæological character, were unavoidably great.
The interior court was necessarily sacrificed, and all
that remains is a small yard.   Externally, the alterations were less considerable, consisting chiefly in the
insertion of substantial windows with stone mullions,
and the general outline of the building has not been
changed.   The old entrance on the south-east side
of the house has been formed into a modern principal
entrance, and a handsome terrace has been raised on
this side, to form an appropriate approach to it.
Fortunately, the outward appearance of the house,

before these alterations were made, has been preserved in a drawing by Mrs. Mynors, from which I
am permitted to give the first of the accompanying
cuts.   The second cut (from a sketch by myself) represents the same portion of the house as it appears
at present.

Treago, from the East, in its present condition.

Treago has experienced a fortune of which few
houses in this country, of anything like similar antiquity, can boast, that of having remained continu-
ously in the possession of the same family since it
was built.   According to that document of worse
than doubtful authenticity, the Roll of Battle Abbey,
the head of the English family of Mynors was a
Norman, who came over with the Conqueror, and
fought at Hastings.   The name, however, expressed
in Latin by De Mineriis, is rather suspicious, when

we consider its proximity to the Forest of Dean, for *mineria, minerium,* and *minera,* were the mediæval Latin words for a mine. Treago appears to have been the original seat of the family of Mynors, though it, or branches of it, had possessions, at an early period, at Burghill in Herefordshire, and at Westbury in Gloucestershire; and also, at a more recent period, at Duffield in Derbyshire, this latter by grant from Henry VIII. The earliest deeds now at Treago refer to the lands at Burghill and Westbury. We find in one deed Henry de Miners granting certain lands in Burghill to Roger fitz Eilaf, the brother of Roger, dean of Stratton. In another deed, Henry de Stratton restores these lands to William de Myners. We learn, from a third deed of confirmation by Isabella de Longchamp, that William de Mynors was the grandson of Henry de Miners, Richard de Miners, son of the former, and father of the latter, having intervened. As Richard de Miners passed over to his son William, in the year 1226, the lands he had received in Burghill from his father, Henry de Miners, we have thus three generations of the family, which must have commenced as early as the middle of the twelfth century.* Whether these were

* The four of these ancient deeds which follow are interesting on several accounts. We see in them, at this early period, the growing jealousy in the lords of the soil of the grasping temper of the monastic orders :—

(1.) Sciant presentes et futuri, quod ego Henricus de Mineriis dedi et concessi Rogero filio Eilaf', fratri Roberti decani de Stratone, pro homagio suo et servitio, decem et octo acras terre in manerio meo de Burghulle, et quoddam mesuagi . . . . in eodem manerio, quod Willelmus de la Lamese aliquando tenuit, tenendum de me et he . . ᵥ . s meis, sibi et heredibus suis, libere et quiete et honorifice, reddendo inde mihi et heredibus meis ille et heredes sui, annuatim unum bisantum ad

Mynors of Treago is not quite clear, though I am
rather inclined to think they were so,—at a later

festum sancti Michaelis, pro omni servitio et exactione quod ad
me vel heredibus meis pertineat vel pertinere possit, salvo
tamen servitio regali. Et si forte contigerit quod predictus
Rogerus de legitima uxore sua sine herede obierit, statuet
quemcunque voluerit heredem, excepto in religionem. Has
vero prenominatas acras, cum mesuagio et pertinentiis suis, ego
predictus Henricus et heredes mei contra omnes homines et
feminas predicto Rogero vel cuicunque assignaverit waranti-
zabimus. Pro hac autem donatione et concessu et warantatione
dedit mihi predictus Rogerus quinque marcas argenti. Et
quia vol . . . . ratum . . . convulsum permaneat,
presenti scripto et sigilli mei attestatione confirmo. His
t . . . . Thom' de Maurdem, Reg' de Tulintune, Henr'
filio Rog. (?), Henr' filio Wim'. Rob' vicario, Will' de Heliun,
Ric' de Mineriis, et multis aliis.

(2.) Sciant presentes et futuri quod ego Henricus de Stretone relaxavi et quietum clamavi, pro me et heredibus meis
vel assignatis meis imperpetuum, Willelmo de Myners, et heredibus suis vel assignatis suis, totum jus meum et clamium quod
habui vel aliquo jure habere potui, in uno mesuagio et in decem
et octo acris terre cum omnibus suis utrique pertinentiis in
manerio de Borhulle, pro quindecem marcas quas mihi nume-
raverit pre manibus. Quod mesuagium et quas acras Henricus
de Myners dedit et incartavit Rogero filio Eliaph, fratri Roberti
decani de Stretone, habend' et tenend' sibi et heredibus suis
vel assignatis suis, libere, integre, bene, et in pace, quibuscunque et quandocunque dictum messuagium et dictas acras cum
suis pertinentiis dare, vendere, legare, vel assignare voluerit,
preterquam domui religionis, secundum tenorem carte quam
Henricus de Myners confecit predicto Rogero filio Eliaph. Et
quia volo quod hec mea relaxatio et quieta clamatio predicto
Willelmo et heredibus suis vel assignatis suis rata et stabilis
imperpetuum permaneat, huic scripto sigillum meum apposui.
Hiis testibus, domino Gilberto Talebot, Willelmo Torel, Nicholao de Wormel', Roberto de Brunehope, Nicholao de Hulle,
Henrico Wymund, Gilberto de Broy, et aliis.

(3.) Sciant presentes et futuri, quod ego Isabella de Longo-
campo inspexi et audivi cartam quam Ricardus de Myneriis
filius Henrici de Myneriis fecit Willelmo filio suo de duabus

period we know that the Burghill estates were in a branch of the family. Not long after the date of

virgatis terre cum omnibus pertinentiis suis in Burhhulle et in Westbur', in hiis verbis: Sciant presentes et futuri quod ego Ricardus de Myneriis, filius Henrici de Myner', dedi et concessi, et hac presenti carta mea confirmavi, Willelmo filio meo, pro servitio suo, duas virgatas terre, cum omnibus pertinentiis suis, quas Henricus de Myneriis, pater meus, dedit michi pro servitio meo, videlicet unam virgatam terre quam Arnaldus de la Mora et Willelmus de la Lamputte aliquando tenuerunt in manerio de Burhulle, et aliam virgatam terre quam Eynulf' Kyng et Ricardus Longus tenuerunt in manerio de Westburi, tenendas et habendas sibi et heredibus suis, vel suis assignatis, in feodo et hereditate, libere et quiete ab omni servitio, reddendo inde annuatim heredibus Henrici de Myneriis quedam paria calcarium deauratorum ad pascham, sicut ego facere consuevi, pro omni servitio, exactione, et demanda, que de terra exeunt vel exire possunt. In cujus rei testimonium presenti scripto sigillum meum apposui. Hiis testibus, Ric' de Westbur', Willelmo de Abbenhale, Rad' de Reddlee, Willelmo de Helion et Willelmo filio suo, Rad' Thorel, Waltero de Wormesle, Waltero Koldecoc, Henrico filio Wimund'. Actum fuit anno gratie m°. cc°. xx° vi°. Et ego Isabele concessi et confirmavi totas predictas duas virgatas terre, cum omnibus pertinentiis, habend' et tenend' eidem Willelmo de Myneriis et heredibus suis, vel suis assignatis, de heredibus predicti Henrici de Myneriis vel assignatorum suorum, sine omnibus calumpniis, clamiis, vexationibus, et impedimentis, mei et heredum meorum, imperpetuum. Quod ego Isabela, in propria viduitate mea et in libera potestate mea, recepi homagium dicti Willelmi de Myneriis, quod quid volo, ut hec mea concessio et confirmatio rata et stabilis permaneat, hoc presens scriptum sigilli mei impressione confirmavi. Hiis testibus, Ric' de Westbur', Willelmo de Abbenhale, Rad' de Redlee, Willelmo de Helion, et Willelmo filio suo, Rad' Thorel, Waltero de Wormesl', Waltero Koldecoc, Henr' filio Wymund', et multis aliis.

(4.) A touz yceux que cest lettre verrount ou orrount. Elisabethe de Pennebrugge, dame de Burghulle, salutz en Dieu. Sachez moy avoire doné et graunté à Johan de Bradewardyn la garde et les plites de totes les teres et tenementz que sount apelés warres tenementz, oue les apurtenaunces, les

the transaction between Richard de Mynors and his
son William de Mynors, though sufficient to have
allowed a son or a grandson of the latter to come into
the estates and influence of the family, John de
Miners, of Treago, was appointed by Edward II.
keeper of the castle of St. Briavel and of the Forest
of Dean. From this John the family of Mynors of
Treago is traced in direct descent from father to son,
to Robert Mynors, esq., who died in 1765, without
direct heir. The estates and representation of the
family then passed to Peter Rickards, esq., who was
the descendant of Robert Mynors, esq., of Treago
(b. 1616, d. 1672), by his daughter Theodosia, and
who assumed the name of Mynors. The present
representative of the family is his son. As might be
supposed of a family of wealth and influence, seated
so long in one place, that of Mynors became, in the
course of ages, allied with nearly all the great border
families, and its quarterings are unusually numerous.
Among these the most illustrious was that of Basker-
ville, of which the present possessor of Treago is now
the representative.

quels tenementz sount en ma meyn par resoun del nounage de
Thomas filz et heyr à Roger le Myners, à avoyre et tenyre les
avaunditz teres et tenementz oue les appurtenaunces à dite
Johan de Bradewardyn ou à ses atourneys taunqe l'avaundit
Thomas seit de pleyne age, rendaunt à moy et à mes heyrs, ou
à mes atourneys, les rentes et les services que sur les dites
teres et tenementz sount dues, duraunt le terme susdit. Et
jeo l'avaundit Elisabete et mes heyrs totes l'avaundites teres et
tenementz oue lour apurtenaunces à dit Johan et ses heyrs, ou
à ces atournés, duraunt le terme susdite encountre toutes gentz
garantyroms. En tesmoygnment de quele chose à cest pre-
sentez j'ay mys moun seal. Doné à Burghulle, le premere
jour de Fevere du rr. Edward tierce puys le conquest tren-
tisme seoptime.

The church of St. Weonard's is a rather late building, possessing no very remarkable architectural fea-
ture.   In a portion of it, called Mynors' Chapel,
there are inscriptions and other monuments to various
members of the family at Treago.   But at a short
distance from the church, and, indeed, almost adjoining the church-yard, stands one of those immense
artificial mounds, known here generally by the name
of " tumps," which are found in various places along
the border of Wales.   The circumstance, occurring
so often, of the proximity of these mounds to the

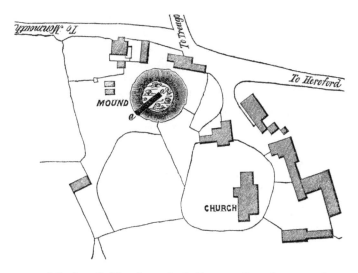

parish church,* leads to the inference that the mounds
themselves were originally regarded with supersti-

* Among the great tumuli thus adjacent to the churches
may be mentioned, in this immediate neighbourhood, one at
King's Capel, and another at Thruxton.   There was one formerly at Wormelow, and the place is still called Wormelow

tious reverence, and that the earlier preachers of the
Gospel in these parts resolved on taking advantage
of the worship already paid at the spot, by the erection of a church.   The mound at St. Weonard's is of
very large dimensions, for its diameter at the base is,
as near as I could roughly measure and calculate it,
about a hundred and thirty feet, and its elevation
from the ground about, or somewhat more than,
twenty.   The summit forms a circular platform, of
about seventy-six feet in diameter, levelled in such a
manner that my first impression was that the tumulus
had been truncated.   The edge of this circular platform is planted round with large fir and other trees,
among which is a decayed yew tree, of very considerable antiquity, and a tall poplar stood exactly in the
centre.   I am informed that, until recently, the platform on the mound was the usual scene of village
fêtes, that it was the spot chosen especially for morris-
dancing, a custom which prevailed very extensively
in Herefordshire, and that the poplar in the middle
was used as the village maypole.   Nor could a spot
have been chosen more attractive for such purposes; for, placed itself on a bold isolated eminence,
the height of the mound gives to its summit a com-
manding prospect of a most extraordinary kind, extending in a vast panorama round the whole circuit
of the horizon.   Beginning with the west, we have
first the bold mountain of the Graig, in Monmouth-
shire; after which follow in succession the hills of
Garway and Orcop, that of Bagwy-Lydiatt, and

Tump.   There is a very large tumulus of this kind near the
church at Aston, on the northern border of Herefordshire;
and, in the twelfth century, one stood in the church-yard at
Ludlow.—(See my *History of Ludlow and the Border,* p. 14.)

the one known as the Saddlebow; to the north, the
wooded summit of Aconbury intercepts our view towards Hereford; while further eastward rise the hills
of Marcle and Stoke Edith, and behind them, in
greater elevation, the distant Malverns; then, in a
still more easterly direction, come Mayhill, in Gloucestershire, Penyard and the heights of the Forest
of Dean, among which the village of Ruardean, and
other well-known spots, are distinctly visible; these
are followed, as we turn to the south, by the hills on
the Wye, among which we trace Goodrich, Coppet-
hill, the Dowards, &c; and finally, the nearer hill of
Llanclowdy, cuts off our prospect in the direction of
Monmouth.

The purposes of these mounds have been the subject of different opinions, though the careful antiquary
never doubted their being sepulchral monuments.
Mr. Mynors had resolved, a few years ago, to open
the mound at Treago, and decide this question; and
it was finally arranged that I should pay a visit to
Treago, in the Easter week of the present year, (1855,)
to assist in carrying this design into effect.   Curiously
enough, the popular belief of the neighbourhood is
generally in favour of the sepulchral character of these
mounds, and at St. Weonard's it had been the tradition of some that the hermit himself was buried there,
and of others that some great chieftain had been interred in this "tump," and that he lies in a coffin of
solid gold.   This latter was the most difficult to deal
with, for it led to the apprehension that, when we
approached the centre, the eagerness of the country
people to secure the treasure might lead to the wan-
ton destruction of the deposit, during the night, and
before we should have time to examine it.

The mound appears not to have been raised originally on perfectly level ground, as those who elevated
it seem to have taken advantage of the natural rock
which crops out on the south-west side, and was made
to serve as a support.   The earth of which it is composed is the dry sandy soil of the neighbourhood.   The
south-eastern side of the mound was the most open

Opening of the Tumulus at St. Weonard's.

to approach, and, as it offered less incumbrance from
trees, and greater facility of disposing of the earth to
be carried out, it was determined to begin the excavation there.   Accordingly, on the morning of Tues-
day, the 10th of April, the men began their work at
this spot, with a cutting from eight to nine feet wide.
My first notion was to run a tunnel towards the centre;
but it soon appeared that the men were not accustomed to this kind of work, and it was found that we

should get on more rapidly by continuing the cutting, although rather deep; and this was done in the direction marked *a a* in the above plan. The manner in which this cutting was carried on, and the general outward appearance of the mound, are shown in the accompanying sketch. At about six feet above the level of the base of the tumulus there was an evident difference in the character of the soil, and the appearances were strongly in favour of the belief that this was the original surface of the ground, which must in that case have been very uneven. Acting on this belief, we took this as the level of our cutting, which was exactly fourteen feet deep from the top of the mound. On Thursday afternoon, when the workmen had arrived within about fifteen feet from the centre of the mound, they came upon what appeared to be the base of a heap of large flat stones (the sandstone of the spot, which breaks up into this form), rudely built up one over the other, and so completely free of earth within that we could thrust our arms in between them. My first impression was that we had come upon a cairn, occupying the interior of the tumulus, and I thought it advisable to clear away the earth from above, before removing the stones. This operation occupied the whole of the day on Friday. We found that, instead of being the base of a large cairn, the stones formed a small mound, and then sunk again; but we found also a layer of these large stones along the level of our cutting, until near the centre they began to rise again, and evidently reached a somewhat greater elevation than before. It was now thought advisable to carry the cutting to a little distance beyond the centre, and the poplar tree was sacrificed. It was not till Saturday night that this operation was

nearly completed, leaving uncovered a great part of
the heap of stones in the centre, which presented
the appearance of the exterior of a rude vault. On
Monday, the 16th, the stones in the centre were
cleared away, and within them appeared a mass of
much finer mould than that of the rest of the mound.
This mould also was cleared away to the level of the
cutting; but as yet no indications of a sepulchral
interment presented themselves, although the workmen were still of opinion that we were on the original
hard surface of the ground. But of the accuracy of
this opinion I now became very doubtful, and on the
following morning I directed the men to sink a pit
on the spot which had been covered by the vault of
stones. They had not proceeded far before they
came to a mass of ashes, mixed with pieces of charcoal and fragments of burnt human bones, which was
found to be about a foot and a half thick, and was
apparently about nine or ten feet in diameter. A
piece of thigh bone, part of the bone of the pelvis,
and a fragment of the shoulder blade, were picked
up here; and it appeared evident that the whole
of the ashes of the funeral pile had been placed on
the ground at this spot, and that a small mound of
fine earth had been raised over them, upon which
had been built a rude roof or vault of large rough
stones. No traces of urns, or of any other manufactured article were met with. Having been thus successful in discovering the central deposit, our attention was now turned to the first mound of stones, and
it was determined to clear those away and dig below
our level there also; and the result was the discovery
of another interment of ashes, also mixed with human
bones in a half-burnt state. This last operation was

performed on the morning of Wednesday, the 18th
of April; after which the excavations were discontinued.

The accompanying diagram, giving a section of the
mound in the direction of our cutting (which is shown

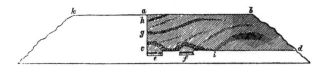

in the shaded part), will give the best notion of the
position of the two deposits at *e* and *f*, which represent the two pits dug through the ashes (represented by the black lines), to a small depth below.   One
of the most interesting circumstances connected with
the cutting itself was that of the regular discolora-
tions visible on the surface, arising, of course, from
the employment of different kinds of material, and
displaying in a most remarkable manner the mode in
which the mound was raised.   These are carefully
figured on the accompanying section.   As I have
already stated, the mass of the mound consists of a
uniform light-coloured sand; but from the point (*i*)
near where we first fell in with the stones, a narrow
arched stripe occurs of a much darker mould, as
represented in the cut.   Beyond this two or three
other bands of a similar description, but thinner, and
of lighter coloured soil, and, therefore, less strongly
marked, follow each other until, at *g*, we come upon
a narrow band of small stones, also represented in the
cut, and at *h*, near the summit of the mound, there is
another bed of similar stones.   It is evident, there-

fore, that when the small mounds roofed with stones
had been raised over the deposits of ashes, a circular
embankment was next formed round the whole, and
from this embankment the workmen filled up the
interior inwards towards the centre. When they
began filling in they appear to have fallen in with
some darker mould, which has formed the band at *i*,
and this dark band probably defines very nearly the
outline of the first embankment. The lighter shaded
bands show the successive fillings in towards the
centre, until at last the workmen made use of a quantity of stones and rubble, taken perhaps from the
quarry which furnished the large stones of the interior vaults. This bed of stones forms a kind of
basin in the middle of the mound. They went on
filling again with the sand till the work was nearly
finished, when they returned to the stony material
again, which appears at *h*. The length of our cutting from *c* to *d* was, as near as I could measure it
with accuracy, 64 feet 6 inches, and that of the surface, from *a* to *b*, was 46 feet 5 inches; as I have
stated before, the height of the cutting was 14 feet.
The distance from *a* to *k* was 29 feet 7 inches, making
therefore the diameter of the platform on the top of
the mound, in the direction of our cutting, exactly
76 feet. This I found to be rather the longest diameter, for the circle had not been quite a perfect one,
though very nearly so.

The result of this excavation has been so far satisfactory, that it has shown, beyond a doubt, that the
mound at St. Weonard's is a sepulchral monument;
but, unfortunately, nothing was met with calculated
to throw any light on the period to which it belongs;
so that at present it is left among that class of works,

which, as they are evidently not more modern than the Roman period, and have no decidedly Roman character, have been set down indiscriminately as British. One fragment of pottery turned up, found, I was assured, in the heart of the mound, which bears considerable resemblance to the coarse hard-baked earthenware of some of the Roman cinerary urns; but still, as it is just of that character that it is very difficult to decide its antiquity *per se*, I am by no means so convinced that it may not have fallen among the earth from the surface to venture to form an opinion upon it. It appears certain, however, that Roman coins have been dug up in the adjacent church-yard, which are now in the possession of Mr. Mynors; but having been accidentally mixed among a considerable collection of Roman coins, he is no longer able to identify them, or to ascertain to what emperors they belonged. I am inclined to suspect that this old road from Monmouth to Hereford, which is remarkable for its straightness, and which runs over hills that would now be avoided, was originally a Roman road from *Blestium* to *Magna;* and I shall not be at all surprised to hear some day of the discovery of further traces of Roman occupation in the neighbourhood of St. Weonard's.

V.

ON THE ETHNOLOGY OF SOUTH BRITAIN AT
THE PERIOD OF THE EXTINCTION OF
THE ROMAN GOVERNMENT
IN THE ISLAND.

N a paper read at the meeting of the British Association, in Liverpool in 1854, I endeavoured to show the error of the popular notion that there was anything like uniformity of race in the population of this island when it was first visited by the Roman arms, and the more than probability that it contained Teutonic as well as Celtic blood. Of the ultimate fate of this population we are left in great uncertainty, arising not only from the deficiency of direct information on the subject, but from the different applications of the name Britons in subsequent times, when it was usually applied to the Roman population of the island, but sometimes, when given to a people independent of the Roman power, to the Caledonians of the north, who alone continued in a state of hostility to the conquerors. I am not aware that in any instance in the later Roman historians the name of Britons is applied to the remains of the peoples who inhabited our island in the time of Cæsar; and I confess that I have serious doubts if there existed any representatives of the ancient Britons to whom that name could have been applied, unless it were the servile class which was attached to the soil, and which held no place in the political history of the country, except by occasional and partial insurrections into which they were driven by oppression or by the hope of plunder. Under the government of Agricola, as we learn from Tacitus, a policy of comparative gentleness and conciliation was adopted towards the Britons; but this appears to have been abandoned under his successors; and we have every reason to believe that the older population of the island was afterwards treated with an oppressive severity, the effect of which during four centuries may easily be imagined. Among the numerous Roman inscriptions which have been found of a date subsequent to the first century, commemorative of individuals, we never find the name of a Briton.

Britain, as a Roman province, had not only changed its population, but the forms of society had changed entirely. We may form a notion best and most correctly of the mode of life, and of the degree of civilization of the ancient Britons, by comparing them with what we know of those of the wild Irish and of the Celtic highlanders of Scotland in the middle ages. Living in septs or clans, each collected round a petty chieftain, who had his residence or place of refuge in the least accessible part of his little territory, they had no towns properly so called, and no tie of union, except the temporary one of war, or a nominal dependence on some powerful chieftain who had induced, by some means, a certain number of the smaller clans to acknowledge his sovereignty. Under the

Romans, on the contrary, Britain consisted politically
of a number of cities or towns, each possessing its
own independent municipal government, republican
in form and principle within themselves, but united
under the empire through the fiscal government of
the province to which they were tributary.   Each of
these cities, inhabited by foreigners to the island, was
expected to defend itself if attacked, while three
legions and numerous bodies of auxiliaries protected
the province from hostilities from without, and held
it internally in obedience to the imperial government.   The country was unimportant, and the towns
were everything.

It is not my object on this occasion to enter into a
discussion on the political constitution of the cities
and towns in Britain, but to speak of them merely
ethnologically.   In this particular case there is a
great difficulty in destroying the wrong impression
made by the terms which are necessarily employed in
history.   If we call the people Romans, the term is
correct politically, but incorrect ethnologically ; and
if we call them Britons, the name is incorrect both
politically and ethnologically, and correct only geo-
graphically.   The population of Britain during the
second, third, and fourth centuries of the Christian
era was neither Roman nor British, but an extraordinary mixture of all the different races who had been
reduced by the arms of Rome.   We have several
classes of independent evidence on this point.   First,
that important record, the Notitia Imperii, compiled
at the very close of the Roman period, gives us the
titles and country of the different garrisons of the
more important posts in the province at that time.
We learn there that Frisians held the town or station

of Vindobala on Hadrian's wall, and that Stablesians, believed to be a people from Germany, were stationed at Garriannonum in Suffolk. There were Tungrians at Dubræ or Dover, and at Borcovicus and Petriana on the wall; Lingones at Segedunum and Congavata on the wall; Nervii at Dictis in Westmorland, and at Aliona; Betasians at Regulbium; and Batavians at Procolitia; all from Belgium. We further find Gauls at the Portus Lemanis in Kent, at Vindolana in Northumberland, and at Glannibanta; different peoples from Spain and Portugal at Anderida in Sussex, at Magæ in Yorkshire, and at Condercum, Cilurnum, Æsica, and Axelodunum; Moors at Aballaba in the North, and another supposed African tribe at Arbeia in Westmorland; Thracians at Gabrosentæ on the wall; Dacians at Amboglanna; Dalmatians at Magna on the wall, at Branodunum in Norfolk, and at Præsidium in Lincolnshire; Fortensians, from Asiatic Sarmatia, at Othona in Essex; Crispians, from Pannonia, at Danum in Yorkshire; Solenses, from Cilicia, at Maglone.

Secondly, many inscriptions found on Roman sites in this island confirm the statements of the Notitia, and add names of other foreign races in different parts of Roman Britain. Thus we find, from these inscriptions, Lingones from Belgium, Gauls, and Dacians, in different parts of Cumberland; a people called Cavetii at Old Penrith; Spaniards, Dalmatians, and Betasians in the neighbourhood of Ellenborough; Germans at Brougham; Tungrians, Gauls, Spaniards, Thracians, Hamii (from the Elbe), Nervii, Belgians named Cugerni, and Germans, in different stations in Scotland; Vangiones, from the banks of the Rhine, at Risingham in Northumberland; Var-

duli, from Spain, at Riechester and Lanchester;
Thracians at Bowes in Yorkshire; Sarmatians at
Ribchester in Lancashire; Frisians at Manchester;
Thracians, again, at Wroxeter in Shropshire; and
Thracians and Indians at Cirencester. We further
learn from sepulchral inscriptions that one Dannicus,
who belonged to the Indian cavalry stationed at
Cirencester, was a citizen of Rauricum in Switzer-
land; that Sextus Valerius Genialis, of the Thracian
cavalry at the same town, was a Frisian; that Titus
Domitius Heron, prefect of the second cohort of
Gauls at Old Penrith in Cumberland, was a native of
Nicomedia of Bithynia in Asia Minor; that Crispinus
Æmilius, prefect of the Ala Augusta at Old Carlisle, came from Tusdrus in Africa; that Publius
Ælius, another prefect of the same Ala, was a native
of Mursa in Lower Pannonia; that Marcus Censo-
rius, prefect of the cohort of Spaniards at Ellenborough, came from Nîmes in Gaul; that an officer at
York named Lucius Duccius was a native of Vienna
in Gaul; that Flavius Longus, tribune of the twentieth legion at Chester, was a native of Samosata in
Syria; that Nominius Sacer, an individual buried at
Lincoln, was of the city of the Senones in Gaul; that
Caius Valerius, standard-bearer of the second legion
at Caerleon, was a native of Lugdunum in Gaul;
that Julius Vitalis, an officer of the twentieth legion,
buried at Bath, was a Belgian; that Caius Murrius,
of the second legion, also buried at Bath, was a native
of Forum Julii in Gaul; that Caius Cornelius Pere-
grinus, the tribune of a cohort at Maryport in Cumberland, was a native of Mauritania; that Cornelius
Victor, a soldier of the Gauls of Vindolana, was a
citizen of Pannonia; and that others mentioned in

the inscriptions were Greeks. It must be remembered that the information we thus obtain is very imperfect, and that we might perhaps have met with many other varieties of race in other places in this island, if they had found a place in the Notitia, or if other inscriptions had remained. Other evidence, of a different kind, but to the same purpose, such as inscriptions on pottery, &c. are also found. On a circular plate of earthenware found at Colchester we have roughly scratched the *cartouche* of the name of an Egyptian king, which would seem to show the presence there of Egyptians, and of an Egyptian who was acquainted with hieroglyphics.

The inscriptions, which are generally of much earlier dates than the Notitia, in combination with this record, prove that the same troops remained in each locality during the whole period of the Roman occupation; in fact that they were all virtually so many little military colonies. They show also that, whatever may have been the case at first, these different troops were not always recruited from the countries whence they were derived. It will be remarked, in the list given in the Notitia, that the Germans and Belgians together were far more numerous than the others; and many circumstances lead us to believe that even the troops, or colonies, which were named after other and more distant countries, were in later times recruited chiefly from the Teutonic tribes, which presented the readiest nursery of soldiers in the declining age of the Roman empire.

We are thus enabled to state that the "Roman" population of Britain consisted of a mixture of very different races, among which there was probably but little pure Roman blood and no British blood. This population was distributed in cities and towns with independent municipal governments, and most of the great landholders in the island were no doubt leading citizens in these towns.   They were bound together by a common language, that of Rome, and by the adoption of Roman manners, the result of which was the feeling of a new nationality.   Indeed we cannot give a better notion of what they were than by comparing them with the British settlements in America, while these remained dependent upon the mother country, bearing in mind that the variety of race was much greater in the one case (that of Roman Britain) than in the other.   Even the Roman legions, whose duty it was to keep the island in subjection, exhibited in later times the same diversity of race, and we find them actually making common cause with the towns, in their rebellions against the superior government.

One of the great vices of the Roman rule was the oppressive taxation of the provinces, which led not only to general rebellions of all the towns united, but apparently to frequent cases of resistance to the imperial authority by single towns, or by two or three towns in confederacy; and in such cases the rebels invoked the assistance of the German and Northern pirates, and even called in the aid of the still wilder peoples of Caledonia.   There was moreover hostility between different towns, arising sometimes from difference of race and partly from commercial or other rivalry, which doubtless contributed no little to the turbulence of this distant province.   In Gaul, the history of which is much better known, we trace more plainly these rivalries of the towns, and see how they sometimes degenerated into deadly hatred.   In Britain, unfortunately, in consequence of the very limited

I.   E

information which remains, we can only trace its existence by implication.   Thus, soon after the middle of the fourth century, when the island province was delivered from the ravages of the Picts, Scots, and Saxons, by the imperial general Theodosius, the way in which the historian Ammianus Marcellinus speaks of the event is such as to leave no doubt on our minds that the joint invasion had been encouraged, if not prompted, by the rebellious towns, and that the primary cause of their rising was the inattention of the emperor Valentinian to their complaints of oppressive taxation.   A few years later, in 383, the islanders entered into a still more formidable rebellion, and proclaimed Maximus emperor, who carried the troops of Britain over to the Rhine, where he was immediately joined by the Germans.   In the beginning of the fifth century, we again find the cities of Britain revolting, when they conferred the title of emperor on a man named Marcus, whom they slew in 407, and chose in his place a person named Gratian, who is distinctly stated by the historian to have been a *municeps*, or burgher of one of the towns of Britain. They let him reign four months, and then put him to death, and chose another man, named Constantine, to be emperor.   This man, possessed of more vigour and talent than his two unfortunate predecessors, imitated the example of Maximus, and, crossing over to the continent, found there sufficient sympathy to enable him to usurp for a time the empire in the West.   After this usurper's departure from the island with, no doubt, great part of the legionary troops, the towns in Britain governed themselves, and protected the province so effectually, that they drove away the Saxons, who had seized upon the occasion to invade it; and when the usurpation of Constantine was suppressed, the cities of Britain retained their independence.   Very soon after this, in the year 410, the emperor Honorius addressed letters to the cities of Britain, telling them to do what in fact they were already doing,—to provide for their own safety; and he thus acknowledged their independence.

The Roman population of Britain appears to have been, when united, capable of doing all that the letters of Honorius recommended to it, and the province does not appear to have been weakened by being cut off from the empire, or to have been immediately exposed to the attacks of external enemies.   But tradition confirms what appears to be implied by history, that the towns of Britain soon became involved in domestic dissensions and civil wars.   We are assured by the later Roman writers that the officers and leading men in the towns in Britain were remarkable for their ambition and love of intrigue; they had now the liberty as well as the inclination to act, and we can easily see, through the obscurity of history at that time, confederacies and counter-confederacies among the towns, in which the old commercial rivalries as well as ambition would play a part, and which led to civil wars and confusion; and it was then that the external enemies, as well Jutes, and Saxons, and Angles, as Picts, and Scots, and Irish, and others, were induced by the prospect of plunder or by the invitations of the contending parties to rush into the province.

The Roman towns were still strong, although they had lost the unity which made the strength of the island, and it took years to reduce them all under the power of the Teutonic invaders, who thus estab-

lished themselves gradually. The brief story of
the Saxon invasion told in the Saxon records is that
of the successive reduction, sometimes at rather distant periods, of the Roman towns to their obedience.
The Teutonic settlers were a race who, like the ancient Britons, were not accustomed to live in towns,
and were in fact prejudiced against them, and wherever they took one by storm, or entered it uncon-
ditionally, they plundered and destroyed it. But the
larger fortified towns were not easily taken, and the
greater number, after unsuccessful attempts at resistance in the field, appear to have yielded upon composition. The ambition of the great chiefs of the
conquering race, who soon became emulous of Roman
civilization, could not be otherwise than flattered at
possessing towns where the articles of Roman osten-
tation and luxury were manufactured, and, when they
aspired to form kingdoms, the prospect of an annual
revenue in the shape of tribute would restrain the
otherwise natural eagerness for present plunder.
Antiquarian discovery is continually confirming what
many circumstances would lead us to believe, that,
while the whole land without was distributed among
the Anglo-Saxon conquerors, the original Roman
population of which I have been speaking formed at
first from various races, but afterwards recruited
chiefly from Germany and Gaul, remained in the
towns, coexistent with the new Anglo-Saxon lords
of the soil, and still retaining their municipal forms
and institutions and their Roman manners, until these
became gradually more and more assimilated to those
of the Saxons—a change which would be facilitated by
the prevalence of Teutonic blood in the towns themselves. The natural antagonism which must have

remained between the townsmen and the conquerors continued to exist through the middle ages, and has even reached our own times in a certain sort of rivalry between town and country. I need only add, that to this preservation of the towns we owe our municipal corporations of the middle ages.

The conclusions I would draw from these considerations are, that, at the close of what is called the Roman period of the history of Britain, the remains of the original Celtic population were very small, and perhaps consisted chiefly or entirely of the peasantry who cultivated the land as serfs. Further, that the " Britons" who struggled against the invasions of the Picts and Scots and Saxons were a mixture of races foreign to the island, and lived congregated in towns, and that when the Anglo-Saxons at last obtained the ascendancy, the remains of this population continued to exist among them, and became part of the Saxon states, while the peasantry probably continued to exist in the same servile condition as before. In fact, that the popular story that the people who resisted the Saxons was the ancient Celtic population of the island, and that it retired before the conquerors until it found a last refuge in Wales, is a mere fiction. It may be added that these conclusions are in perfect conformity with what is known to have taken place in other countries similarly situated. If we cast our eyes over a map of Saxon England during the sixth or seventh century we shall see that the only towns of any importance then existing were actually the great Roman municipal settlements. To mention but a few, we have, first, the chief town in the island, London ; to the south-east of it, Canterbury and Rochester, with the old Roman port towns;

to the north-east and north, Colchester, Leicester, Lincoln, Doncaster, York, Carlisle, with one or two towns in Lancashire; and Chester. Westward and southward of London, we find the important towns of Chichester, Winchester, Old Sarum, Dorchester, Exeter, Bath, Cirencester, and Gloucester. Between the historical notices of the Saxon chronicle, and the known continued existence of these towns, we can trace the advance of the Saxons from town to town, as each submitted to their supremacy.

I cannot resist the occasion, while on this subject, of pointing out a circumstance connected with it, which has, I think, a meaning that has not yet been discovered. As we trace the advance of the three great divisions of the Anglo-Saxon race in their progress of conquest and settlement, and examine the Roman sites over which they passed, we perceive the smaller towns and the country ravaged and destroyed, while, as I have said before, the larger towns saved themselves from destruction. Now, if we look into Wales, which was certainly as completely subjected to the Roman government as any other part of the island, and which we find covered with Roman towns, roads, and settlements, which reached even into the wilds of Snowdon, the same scene of devastation presents itself—and to a greater degree; for while we find Roman towns scattered over Saxon England, we do not find that a single town to the west of the Severn escaped destruction. The strong town of Deva, or Chester, held its ground to the north, and Glevum, or Gloucester, survived, and a Roman town on the site of Worcester, may also have been preserved, but the line of strong towns between Gloucester and Chester—Ariconium, Magna, Bravinium,

Uriconium—a number of important towns in South Wales, with Isca, or Caerleon, the station of the second legion—and other no less important towns on the western and northern coasts and in the interior,— all these are found to have been utterly destroyed. As this destruction was certainly not the work of the Anglo-Saxons, although it must have taken place during the period of the Saxon invasion, to whom may we ascribe it? If, according to the common story, the "Ancient Britons," withdrawing from before the Saxons, had made their last stand in Wales, and found there a place of safety, it seems absurd to suppose that they would have destroyed the towns and country which were to have been their protection. In fact I think that the circumstance I have just mentioned is sufficient in itself to contradict the old story, and that it seems to imply that, contemporary with the invasions of the Saxons and Angles, and the irruptions of the Picts and Scots in the north, Wales itself was visited by a similar and even more fatal invasion. If we further compare the circumstances of the two cases, it seems to me that we are led very strongly to the supposition that the Welsh may be settlers on the ruin of the Roman province on their side of the island, just as the Saxons and Angles were in England, and the Northern invaders in the districts of the south of Scotland. I know that many will be startled at so bold a theory, but I would wish it to be clearly understood that I merely offer it as a suggestion arising out of the consideration of the circumstances of which I have been speaking, and as deserving a fair and careful examination. It may be asked, if the Welsh are not ethnologically what they are commonly represented to be, who are they, and whence did they come?

Our total ignorance of the history of the period to which this question refers, as far as regards them, renders it impossible to give any certain answer to it; but we might naturally turn our eyes towards Britany (Armorica), a country which in consequence of its physical character and condition, and from other causes, was never completely Romanized; in which, at the time of which we are speaking, there was apparently a tendency, if not a necessity, to emigrate; and the Celtic population of which, holding fiercely to their old nationality, were also, from that same position, accustomed to navigation, which was then equivalent to piracy. They might, likely enough, join in the scramble for the plunder of Britain.   It is unfortunate, for the clearing up of this question, that much of what is considered as the history of Britany during this period consists of mere modern interpretations of late legends.   At the beginning of the fifth century, the Armoricans had recovered their independence, resumed their ancient barbarism, which, indeed, they can hardly be said to have ever abandoned, and formed a sort of republic probably of chiefs of clans.   We have this information from the historian Zosimus.   We can, however, perceive, by the slight notices of the authentic chroniclers, that the Armoricans, become independent, joined in the general spirit of aggression which urged the barbarians to the invasion of the Roman province of Gaul, and that subsequently, when Aetius directed the Roman arms in Gaul, and just at the time of the Saxon invasion of Britain, the Armoricans themselves were closely pressed and partially subdued, and placed indeed exactly in that condition in which emigration would have attractions for its ambitious and turbulent chieftains.

Britain alone offered any field for their activity. Moreover, we suddenly discover at this time a more intimate
connection between Armorica and that island.

We can understand, if this were the case, why a
people who had far less intelligence for the application of the advantages of civilization than the Saxons,
destroyed all that remained of it, and, as settlers, took
to their own wilder way of living. I confess that
there are some difficulties in the way of this solution
of a very difficult question; but, at the same time,
if it could be proved to be the true one, it would
clear away other difficulties which are still more
embarrassing. People speak of the so close resemblance between the languages of Britany and Wales,
that I have seen and heard it stated, by men
who are understood to have known both languages
well, that a Breton of the present day might hold
conversation with a Welshman. Philologists know
that such a close similarity as this is hardly within
the range of possibility, after the natural changes
which all languages undergo in so great a length of
time,—if Welsh were historically the representation
of a language spoken in Britain in the time of Cæsar,
and Breton the similar representation of the language
of ancient Gaul. Whereas, if we could suppose that
Welsh was Breton, separated from it at the close of
the Roman period, and therefore not having experienced the long intervening influence of Roman civilization, the close similarity of the two languages is
much more easily understood. Moreover, I have
always felt convinced that the mediæval legends of
Wales were essentially Breton, and that all the
romance literature to which they gave rise was derived from Armorica, and at the same time felt the

E 2

difficulty of explaining a certain degree of relationship which they seemed to have with the minds and
sentiments of the Welsh themselves—a difficulty which
would disappear at once before such an explanation.
The legends connected with the romance-cycle of
king Arthur have always appeared to me to represent the mythic genealogy of the Celtic race as preserved in Armorica, and all our authentic information
on the subject represents it as being introduced from
thence into our island in the twelfth century. We
must not forget that the *Historia Britonum* of Geoffrey of Monmouth was avowedly founded upon a
Breton manuscript. Again, we know from what is
observed in other countries, where we are better
acquainted with the early social progress, how soon
a race in its emigration attaches to its new home the
legends and traditions which really belong to the
country it has left. These, combined afterwards
with a few traditions of a more historical character,
form what is usually called the fabulous or heroic
period of a nation's history.

However, the present is not the occasion for entering upon this part of the subject, and I shall content
myself with stating the suggestion, which appears to
me worthy of careful consideration. I will only add,
that a friend, who is profoundly versed in that part
of the subject, has remarked to me, since this paper
was first read, that he has always considered that a
class of inscriptions found in Wales, and belonging
apparently to the period subsequent to that of the
Roman occupation, which resemble nothing of the
sort found in other parts of England, present an
analogy with the inscriptions of the same kind found
in Britany, and with those only.

My object on the present occasion is more especially to enforce, as strongly as I can upon ethnologists,
the necessity of paying constant attention to the historical materials of their science.   That branch of it
which may be conveniently and properly termed crani-
ography is, at the present time, making great advances,
and at the same time it is a branch which requires to be
treated with extreme caution.   Of course we must find
our crania in the graves, or, as they are in our island
usually called, the "barrows," of the races which are
under our consideration.   When we have to deal
with the well-known burial places of particular races
the subject is clear and simple; but this is not always
the case, especially in Britain.   I have endeavoured
now to make clear to you the extreme diversity of
race which existed in this island under the Romans;
and, in a paper which I wrote on a former occasion,
and for another purpose, I gave reasons for believing
that there was far from uniformity of race before the
Romans placed their feet on our soil.   Nevertheless,
if we could place our hands on barrows or graves in
this country, and say with certainty that these belonged to the ante-Roman period, we might still
classify them according to their districts, and probably derive from the examination of them certain
ethnological facts.   But unfortunately this is not the
case; and I do not believe that there has yet been
found a grave in the island, to the south of the Forth
and Clyde, which you can venture absolutely to declare
to have been older than the Roman period, or even
to be that of a Celt.   It is true that there are one or
two localities, such as the downs of Wiltshire, in
which *probability* is in favour of the interments being
Celtic; but this is still far from certain, and it would

not be safe to found a system upon it. My own impression is, that we shall arrive at no important ethnological results from the mere examination of the skulls found in England in interments older than the Anglo-Saxon period; owing to the variety of races who had lived in the island contemporaneously or at different periods, and the impossibility of identifying the particular race to which any one interment belonged. With regard to the Anglo-Saxon cemeteries, there can be no doubt that they represent known races, and divisions of those races, and we can enter upon the investigation of them with certainty as to the foundation on which we build, and therefore with tolerable certainty as to the results. To these, therefore, as they may be rendered available to science in the course of future excavations, I would especially invite the attention of the craniographer, in the belief that his labours will not be altogether thrown away. The opportunity of observation has already been lost in too many cases, but I think that we may expect with certainty that, within a short period, new and favourable opportunities will occur, and I feel confident that they will not again be neglected. I trust that, now that the importance of such collections is becoming more generally known, many Saxon cemeteries from different parts of the island will pour in their contributions to our ethnological museums: while I would with equal care collect and examine the skulls from burials which are not Saxon, specifying their locality and the circumstances under which they were found, without calling them Celtic, or Roman, or by any other name, unless its appropriateness be very clearly ascertained.

VI.

ON THE ORIGIN OF THE WELSH.*

 FEEL that I might be considered as in some sort failing in my duty, or at least in what is expected from me, if I did not reply to the remarks of Mr. Basil Jones on my suggestions on this question, which were read at the Monmouth meeting of the Cambrian Archæological Association, and were published in the *Archæologia Cambrensis*, or I would hardly have taken up the subject at all at the present moment, when I must do it hurriedly, and in the midst of pursuits of a somewhat different description; and I hope this will be allowed me as an excuse for entering upon the question abruptly, and without any prefatory remarks.

* It was not to be expected that the suggestions relating to the origin of the population of Wales, offered in the preceding paper, would pass without exciting some controversy among the Cambrian antiquaries; and, accordingly, they were attacked, with some earnestness, in a paper, by the Rev. W. Basil Jones, read at the annual meeting of the Cambrian Archæological Association, held at Monmouth in the autumn of 1857, and printed in the *Archæologia Cambrensis* in April 1858. Mr. Basil Jones is a Cambrian scholar of very considerable learning and reputation, and any objections from him could not but deserve serious consideration. I have endeavoured to reply to them in the paper here printed, in which my notions on the origin of the Welsh are rather more fully developed than in the former.

Mr. Basil Jones has discussed the question in the tone of good feeling which ought to characterize all such discussions, and I should be very sorry not to follow his example. I shall only, therefore, endeavour to express rather more clearly some points which I think he has not quite clearly understood, and to set him right on those on which I think he may be misinformed. All that I can complain of in his general treatment of the question is, that he too often treats as mere theories what I have advanced as simple known facts, and that he then confronts them with mere vague hypothesis,—and I fear that after all he has done more to confuse and mystify the subject than to clear it up.

I would particularly insist on the necessity, in discussions of this kind, with regard to words especially, of keeping perfectly distinct the ideas attached to them at different periods, and under different circumstances; as, for instance, during the Roman period, during the middle ages, and in modern times, when old words are often applied technically. In a note on p. 138, Mr. Basil Jones remarks, that "there is no evidence that the Romanized provincials in Britain, or their descendants, were ever called *Romans*, as was the case in all other countries, and is so still in many parts of both the Eastern and Western Empire." I confess myself ignorant, at the present moment, of the authority on which it is stated that the provincials *were* called Romans in all other countries. An antiquary at present speaks of Roman Britain, or Roman Gaul, merely as a sort of conventional term for those countries during the Roman occupation or supremacy; but at that time I imagine that the term "Roman" would only be properly ap-

plied to people who were, or claimed to be, of Roman
race.   I do not at present recollect that the provincials of Gaul, as a people, were ever called Romans
any more than those of Britain; and with regard to
the latter province, after the earlier period of Roman
supremacy, the term " Britanni" was certainly not
used with any allusion to its old Celtic population,
but it was applied generally to the population of the
Roman province, of whatever race.   The very legions
themselves were called *Britons,* and the fleet, though
notoriously manned by Saxons and Franks, was
spoken of as British.*   The disregard of this fact has
caused great confusion among our historians.   But,
after the fall of the empire, during the mediæval
period, the term " Roman" was no longer applied to
race,† but to language, which was a characteristic by
which the races who had now made themselves mas-
ters of Europe most readily and naturally enough
distinguished those with which they came in contact.
During the middle ages the French language was
Roman, the Spanish was Roman, the Italian was
Roman; but we must not confound this mediæval
application of the word with that which it bore during
the Roman period.

In the same way we find that the Teutons had a
word in their own language which they appear to

* I may take this opportunity of remarking that the Anglo-
Saxon Latin writers affected to use Latin words in their ancient acceptation, and that it is under this influence that Bede
and others call the Welsh of their time Britons, on the supposition that they represented the population of the island in the
Roman period.   It was from them that the name *Bryttas,* or
Brettas, was taken into the Anglo-Saxon language.

† I am not speaking, of course, of the inhabitants of Rome,
or of the ecclesiastical use of the word.

have applied especially to those who spoke the language of Rome. I think that Mr. Basil Jones has not seized in its full bearing the question relating to the use of the word " Welsh," which was also evidently given by the Teutons to foreign peoples in reference to the language they spoke. In the mediæval literature of Germany, the term " *Wælsch*" or " *Welsch*" was applied always to the French, except when the writers, from a little pedantry or affectation, adopted the word by which the French designated their own language and literature, and called it Roman. Thus, the translators of the French mediæval romances or poetry into German always referred to their *Welsche* original. In modern German the word " *Wälsch*" is applied more especially to Italian. It may, however, be traced in mediæval German as applied to Italy, and to the other countries using the "Roman" dialects; and, as in the German popular feeling, Europe was divided among the peoples who spoke Roman, and those who spoke Teutonic, their poets were accustomed to use the phrase *in allen welschen und in tiutschen rîchen* (in all Welsh and Teutonic kingdoms) to signify everywhere. When we go farther into details, for which I have not space at present, we find that the term was applied to the inhabitants of different countries in Europe, but only to such as are known to have spoken or to speak Roman dialects. Mr. Jones has reminded me of the fact that even the Anglo-Saxons (as we find in the Anglo-Saxon Chronicle) called the French *Galwalas, i. e.* the Welsh of Gaul. Exactly in the same manner, in the earliest monuments of the old German language in which the word occurs, France or Gaul is called *Walho-lant, i. e.* the land of the Welsh. And

let not anybody suppose that the Germans might
have found any Celtic dialect spoken in the part
of Gaul which their Teuton brethren invaded and
conquered; for we have the strongest possible proof
of the contrary. During several centuries the Franks
in Gaul spoke their own language, although we know
that the conquered population spoke a different tongue;
this latter eventually gained the mastery, but, when
the German of the Franks at last disappeared, what
did the language of the Gallic population prove to
be? — not Celtic, but purely a Roman, or Latin,
dialect.

Now we know that the Anglo-Saxon writers often
speak of the inhabitants of this island, whom their
forefathers had conquered, by the name of Britons,
because they had learnt that name from the Roman
writers; but we also find that the term they especially applied to them in their own language was this
same Teutonic word, *Wælisc*, or *Wælsc*. I think it
perfectly fair to argue upon this, that the Teutons
who came into Britain applied the word in no different sense to that in which it was used by the rest of
their race, and that they, therefore, found the people
talking the language of the Romans. I believe, as
the result so far of my own researches, that this was
the case, and that if the language of the Anglo-Saxons,
like that of the Franks, had been superseded by that
of the conquered people, our language would then
have been simply a Roman dialect. The objections
to this view of the question are mere assumptions.
What right have people to say, " It is probable that
Britain was much less Romanized than Gaul," or " I
think" that such was the case? Perhaps I may be
allowed to speak of myself as one of the workmen in

this field, and say that we have dug, and excavated, and explored our country very considerably during some years past, and that I may venture to state, as facts, that the inscriptions of the Roman period are proportionally quite as numerous in Britain as in Gaul, that they are all purely Latin, without any trace of Celtic language or Celtic people; and, moreover, that these are found not in Kent, which Mr. Basil Jones thinks might have been as much Romanized as Picardy, but in the remotest parts of the island, in Northumberland, in Cumberland and Westmoreland, in Lancashire, not only on the borders of Wales, but in the very heart of that mountainous country, and even in its farthest parts, as at Luentinum, looking towards the Irish sea. I may add, that the whole of England and Wales is found to have been quite as thickly covered as the north of Gaul with Roman towns, and stations, and roads, and country houses, and every other mark of Roman cultivation. What room is there here for the assumption that it is probable that Britain was much less Romanized than Gaul? Nor do I think that anything is gained by the new hypothesis of Mr. Basil Jones that the Teutonic word " *Wälsch* " is equivalent with Gallic, and that the Germans applied it to the people speaking Latin, from a consciousness that they were descended from people of Celtic race, because this theory rests entirely upon an assumption, in which I cannot concur, that our wild and illiterate forefathers, at this remote period, were as profoundly learned in the science of ethnology, and as attentive and accurate ethnological observers, as Dr. Prichard himself. But I doubt very much whether the Teutonic *Wælsch*, and the name Gaul or Gallic, have any relation what-

ever to each other. People in the condition and at
the period to which these arguments refer did not
generally call other people by the names which those
people bore among themselves, or among still other
people, but by some term taken out of their own language, which, therefore, conveyed a distinct idea to
themselves. I would add, that the taking of resem-
blances of words for identities is one of the great
stumbling-blocks of the philologist and ethnologist.

Mr. Basil Jones has relieved my mind of some
doubts as to the close similarity between the languages
of Wales and Britany at the present day, although I
confess that his statement is quite contradictory to
those which I have heard and read as coming from
apparently good authorities. However, as he states
positively that the Welsh and Breton languages bear
only the same degree of similarity to each other as the
English and German, I will take it for granted that
such is the case. If an Englishman, who had never
heard any language but his own, were introduced to
a German who was similarly qualified, I believe that
an attempt at conversation would prove anything but
satisfactory. But I beg to say that this is not at all the
gist of my argument. I take the Welsh view of the
question, that the present Welsh language is derived
directly from that spoken by the Britons in this island
before the arrival of Cæsar, and that the language of
Britany is similarly derived from the language spoken
by the Armoricans at the same remote period, and
then I say that to suppose that, after the modifica-
tions which each must have undergone quite separately
and independently of the other during the whole period of Roman domination, joined with the changes
which even Mr. Basil Jones allows would have taken

place since the fifth century, the two languages should resemble each other as closely as they are acknowledged to do at present, is a simple absurdity in philology and ethnology. We are, therefore, thrown back upon the supposition, that about the time of the Anglo-Saxon invasion of Britain, either the Welsh went over to Gaul and became the Armoricans, or the Armoricans came over into Britain and became the Welsh. I put it in these general terms, because I have not been informed that there is any particular small portion of Britany in which the Breton tongue which resembles Welsh is talked, while the rest of the Bretons talk ancient Armorican; but it appears to me that if any part of the Bretons were emigrants from Wales, to judge by their unity of language, the whole of them must have been emigrants.

Now, although I must complain that Mr. Basil Jones has a great inclination to call my facts theories, and his theories facts, and that he shows rather too great a tendency, if I may use the popular phrase, to "chop logic" instead of investigating historical evidence, I am not at all alarmed at his threat of the *facile retorqueri.* He asks (p. 139) on what grounds I draw "a distinction between the condition of the two countries," *i. e.* Armorica and Wales. I thought that I had sufficiently stated this in the paper which has given rise to this, I hope not unimportant, controversy. Any one who has really studied the Roman antiquities of Wales must know that it was traversed in every direction by a multiplicity of Roman roads, which penetrated even into its wildest recesses; that it was covered in all parts with towns, and stations, and posts, and villas, and mining establishments, which were entirely incompatible with the existence at the same time of any considerable number of an older population in the slightest degree of independence. Now we know that the population of Armorica, long before the supposed migration either way could have taken place, was living in a state of independence, and even of turbulence, and that it was formidable in numbers and strength.   The Armoricans are believed to have been almost the heart and nerve of that formidable " Bagauderie" which threatened the safety of the Roman government in Gaul almost before the invasion of the Teutons became seriously dangerous. An attention to dates will put this part of the question more clearly before the reader.   The great and apparently final assertion of independence, or revolt from the Roman government, of the Armoricans, which Mr. Basil Jones quotes from Zosimus, occurred in the year 408 ; Honorius acknowledged the independence of the towns of Britain in 410; and I need hardly add that what is understood by the Anglo-Saxon invasion of Britain occurred many years subsequently.   During this period, when the towns of Britain must have been rejoicing in their independence, it is, I think, not probable that the people of this island would have migrated into Britany in such numbers as in a short time to supersede the Armoricans themselves, for I am not aware that there are any remains of an Armorican language in Britany distinct from the Breton. The subsequent history becomes obscure from the want of records ; but I venture to assert that it is evident, from the few historical notices we have, (I throw aside altogether the fabulous legends of a later date,) that the Armoricans were at this time a numerous and warlike people, that when the Saxon pirates entered the Loire they sometimes joined them in attacking the Gauls, (as the people of the Roman province were called,) and sometimes resisted them; that they were evidently no less piratical than the Saxons themselves, and in all probability possessed numerous shipping; that they did make war upon the Roman provinces just about the time that the Saxons were beginning to settle in Britain, and that they were driven back into their own territory by the governors of Gaul. Now I think there is nothing very extravagant in the supposition that the warlike energy of the Armoricans, having been repressed on the side of the continent, should have sought an outlet on the side of the sea, and that many adventurous chiefs may have collected their followers, taken to their ships, and, tempted by the known success of the Saxons, passed over into that part of Britain which the Teutonic invaders had not reached. I think, then, that the distinction which I have drawn between the condition of Wales and Armorica, at the time when the migration from one to the other is supposed to have taken place, is very plainly stated, and very fairly accounted for.

And now I beg to protest against the manner in which Mr. Basil Jones has decided the question of the authenticity of Gildas. " To those who believe," he says, in a note on p. 143, "*as most competent judges do*, in the genuineness of Gildas, the whole of this refutation will appear superfluous." I know not who form the majority of competent persons who have given this judgment; I plead guilty to having started the objections to Gildas,* and I know that many per-

---

* My opinions with regard to the authenticity of Gildas will be found in the *Biographia Literaria*, Anglo-Saxon period, pp. 120-29.

sons whom I consider competent have approved of
them; but I place reliance not upon this circumstance,
but upon the objections themselves, to which I have
seen no satisfactory answer, and the more I have examined them, the more I feel convinced of their force.
Space is not allowed me for entering far into this
question here, and I will merely state that some of
my leading arguments against the authenticity of
Gildas are, that the style of Latin in which the book
is written is not that which we might expect in the
fifth or sixth century, but rather that which came
from the school of Theodore at Canterbury in the
seventh century, when I suppose this book to have
been forged in order to cry down the Welsh Church;
that there are circumstances in it which are irrecon-
cileable with the character given to Gildas; and that
whoever wrote the book was entirely ignorant of the
condition of Britain at the period in which he is pretended to have lived, and of contemporary history.
This writer tells us gravely (§§ 15-19) that, when
the Roman legions left the island, they made a wall
from sea to sea to defend the Britons against the Picts
and Scots, but that, as this wall was only made of
turf, the northern barbarians easily broke through it,
and committed terrible ravages; that thereupon, at
the urgent entreaties of the Britons, the legions returned and built for the Britons a wall of stone and
mortar, extending from sea to sea, and fortified with
towers, and then departed finally from the island; and
that, after they were gone, the Picts and Scots returned, attacked the wall, fished down with hooks
the British soldiers who defended it, &c. Surely any
" Briton" living at this period, capable of writing and
apparently so knowing in the affairs of the end of

the Roman period, must have known perfectly well
that the wall of Hadrian was not built in the time
of the generations immediately preceding him, but
that it had stood there since the earlier part of the
second century, or, at all events, from time immemorial.   The whole story is, in fact, a mere legend
of the seventh century, invented (probably by the
Angles, a foreign people) to explain the co-existence
of the wall of Hadrian and its accompanying agger,
and the nonsense about hooking down the Britons is
no doubt of the same date.   Again, our so-called
Gildas, arriving at the Saxon invasion, tells us that
they came " tribus, ut lingua ejus exprimitur, cyulis,
nostra lingua longis navibus."   Pray how came this
worthy Briton, whether of the fifth or of the sixth century,* to have the Saxon word so glibly and correctly
on his tongue ?   It certainly sounds to me very much
like the oversight of a Saxon forger, who, familiar with
his own language and tradition, bethought him that
it was not the language of the Wælisc, but forgot that,
according to the opinion of some modern antiquaries,
the Britons of that time spoke not Latin, but Cymric !
It is a point of still greater importance, that Gildas
is made to describe the population of Britain at the
time of the departure of the Romans as being entirely
Christianized ; and, in lamenting over the ruin caused
by the Picts and Scots, he particularly mentions the
overthrow of the sacred altars (*sacra altaria*).   Now
I need not say that the numerous towns, and stations,
and villas, which have been excavated by antiquaries,
are found just in the state in which they were left

* The real date at which Gildas is *supposed* to have written
is very doubtful.   See my *Biographia Literaria*, Anglo-Saxon
period.

after their ruin by the barbarian invaders, and it is true that the altars are found overthrown and scattered about—but what are these altars? All absolutely heathen—Roman paganism and the paganism of the Roman auxiliaries—and among I believe I may say the hundreds of altars which have been brought to light, not the slightest trace of Christianity has yet been discovered. Some of these monuments of paganism, moreover, were evidently newly erected, or even preparing for erection, and in some cases not finished, at the time of the invasion. The same is the case with the equally numerous sepulchral monuments which have been found in various parts of Britain, the inscriptions on which are all unmistakably pagan. I am, indeed, entirely convinced that the picture of Christianized Britain at the close of the Roman period is a mere fable. And how, indeed, could it be otherwise, when in the opposite districts of Gaul Christianity was, to say the least, very imperfectly known? Of this we might adduce abundant evidence. A few years ago excavations near one of the sources of the river Seine brought to light the ruins of a Roman temple dedicated to the goddess of that river—*Dea Sequana*—which had evidently been overthrown in the invasion of the barbarians, and they show that the worship of the goddess had been at that time in full vigour. Among numerous objects of interest found in this temple were an extraordinary number of *ex voto* offerings, made by individuals who believed that their health had been miraculously restored to them by the intervention of the goddess, and an urn full of money, with an inscription stating that it had been offered to the *Dea Sequana* by an individual named Rufus. These coins ranged from Augustus

to the usurper from Britain, Magnus Maximus, so
that some of the offerings must have been given at
the very close of the fourth century, or very near, or
even at, the time when Britain was cut off from the
Roman Empire.   An equally interesting fact remains
to be noticed.   In the noble museum of Mr. Mayer,
of Liverpool, may be seen, among the antiquities of
the Faussett Collection, a sepulchral urn of the Anglo-
Saxon period, on which is incised with great neatness
the following inscription, beginning with the well-
known heathen invocation, *Diis Manibus :*

D. M

LAELIAE

RVFINAE

VIXIT.A.XIII

M.III.D.VI

intimating that it contained the ashes of a young girl,
named Lælia Rufina, whose age was thirteen years,
three months, and six days.   This interesting monument, which appears to have come from an Anglo-
Saxon Cemetery in Norfolk, was perhaps deposited
there many years after what is called the departure
of the Romans, and proves, what I have always in-
sisted upon, that the Roman population of Britain
remained probably through several generations coexistent with the Teutonic settlers.   None of our readers
will, I am sure, discover in the character of this inscription anything Christian, or anything Cymric.*
   I have mentioned these facts chiefly to show the
great importance of excavations in clearing up the

---

* I may state that a correct engraving of this interesting urn
is given in the fifth volume of Mr. Roach Smith's valuable
Collectanea Antiqua, with that scholar's remarks upon it.

mysteries of this period of the history of our island. The objects thus brought to light are at all events truthful. The written testimony of the old historians, even when it is authentic, is that of persons who were often prejudiced, or credulous, or mendacious, and who always gave at least a colouring to the facts they recorded; but the relics which we disinter from our soil have no colouring but their own, and their evidence, if not always complete, is at least faithful.

I will not trespass on our space by entering into any further discussion of the question of the destruction of the Roman towns in Wales and on the border, or of one or two remarks which I think Mr. Basil Jones has made hastily, and perhaps he might withdraw them on further consideration. For instance, I can hardly think him serious when he says (p. 137), —" Mr. Wright appears to assume that the Roman towns in this part of Britain were of equal importance with those to the east of the Severn. But as we find no large towns in Wales now, and *as like causes produce like effects*, it seems probable that the Roman towns of Britannia Secunda were generally small and insignificant as compared with those in the more advanced parts of the island." I cannot imagine anything more unlike than the local causes which influenced the comparative magnitude of towns in Roman Britain and in modern England; and, to return always to facts as the best arguments, surely Mr. Basil Jones must be aware of the extent of the walls of Wroxeter, of Kenchester, of Caerleon, of Caerwent, and I think of other Roman towns to the west of the Severn, which certainly had no claim to be called insignificant. I cannot say that I understand the reason of his exceptions of towns from the list of those which I consider to have been destroyed, nor have I seen anything yet advanced to shake my belief that the destruction of Roman towns in Wales and on the border was at least as general, if not much more general, than in the districts of Britain conquered by the Angles and Saxons.*

In conclusion, I confess that I am rather at a loss to understand the tone of triumph with which Mr. Basil Jones treats the hasty remarks I had made in a previous number of the *Archæologia Cambrensis,* on the question which had been raised with regard to the ethnology of Cumberland. I do not exactly understand how a "reason" can take off the edge of a "fact," but the reasons here employed are certainly not likely to have that effect. He says (p. 149):—" The occupation of a frontier, designed for the protection of the interior, is not of that orderly and peaceful kind

---

* I would remark that the destruction of a town, and the abandonment of a town, are two different things. In some cases, when a town was destroyed, the whole of the inhabitants were massacred, or carried away, and the place was never inhabited again, as happened probably at Verulamium, and no doubt at Uriconium. But in other cases, the remains of a municipal population, which was always strongly attached to its locality, returned and re-established themselves either outside the ruins of their former habitations, or, if they found a portion of the interior easily cleared, commenced rebuilding there. The latter perhaps was the case with Caerleon, although I am rather inclined to think that the modern Caerleon was a later settlement. As ground was of little value in the ages which followed the fall of the Roman power, people did not take much trouble to clear sites, but they gladly settled near old buildings, in order to obtain the materials. The mere existence, therefore, of a modern town at or near the old site, does not of itself prove that the ancient town was not destroyed; but we must look to other circumstances.

which is most likely to change the character of a people."

In reply to this remark, which by no means applies to the case in question, or to my arguments upon it, I can only invite Mr. Basil Jones to study without bias the Roman antiquities of Northumberland, Cumberland, and Westmoreland. But he adds, immediately afterwards:—" It is no more evident that the Brigantes of Ireland and the Brigantes of Britain were kindred tribes, than that the Cumbri of the North and the Cymry of Wales were so."

I beg to say that this is a very inaccurate comparison, and not very sound logic. Mr. Basil Jones has before (p. 144) quoted the Saxon Chronicle very incorrectly, as mentioning the " Cymry" in the north in A. D. 945. It is true that record tells us that in that year king Edmund harrowed all *Cumbra-land*, meaning, of course, the district which we now call Cumberland; but this word is always considered to have had, in the mouth of an Anglo-Saxon, a simple meaning, *the land of vallies*, and every one knows that this is an accurate description of the country itself.* I do not deny that it may mean the land of the Cumbras; but neither Mr. Basil Jones, nor anybody else, has adduced the slightest evidence that there ever was a people there bearing such a name. The Latinized forms *Cumbria* and *Cumbri* only occur at a later period, and were, no doubt, invented merely to represent *Cumberland* and the Cumberlanders, and I believe have nothing whatever to do with these

* We must not forget that the next county was called West-meraland (Westmoreland), an Anglo-Saxon word formed in the same way, and equally significative—the land of the western lakes, or the land of lakes in the west.

imaginary Cymry. The very improbable story of these Cymry having given their territory to the Scots, and retired into Wales, belongs also to a later period, and was an invention of the Scottish kings, who, having got possession of Cumberland during the confusion of the Danish invasions, wanted an excuse for retaining it under the Normans. What I meant to say about Carlisle was simply this. I believe it is the prevailing notion that this name—in its older form, *Caerluel*—was that given by the Celtic Britons to the town which the Romans called Lugubalium, and at the close of the empire, Lugubalia.* Now what I said was, that it was evident from the passage in Bede, which I think is the earliest mediæval mention of this town, that the natives of the place still knew their town by its Roman name of Lugubalia; that Bede tells us expressly that *Luel* was the form

---

* I think Mr. Basil Jones passes too slightingly over my suggestion that Carlisle was "still Roman." Bede speaks of several places by their ancient Roman names, as here of Carlisle, which he calls Lugubalia, acknowledging that that was not the name given to it by the English population in his time. How did Bede know that this place was Lugubalia? At the present day it requires a considerable degree of antiquarian research to identify a Roman site with its ancient name, and there was none of this antiquarianism in Bede's time, even supposing (which is not very probable) that he had the *Itinerary* of Antoninus to employ it upon. I can only answer the question by supposing, as I have always supposed, that the town continued to be occupied by the descendants of the original population, and that they continued to call it by its Roman name. The other circumstances of the anecdote support this view of the case. I will add here, that I think I could gather many circumstances from the Anglo-Saxon writers which tend to show that there must have been an extensive knowledge of the Latin language in England under the Anglo-Saxons at an early period (*i. e.* before their conversion).

to which the name had been corrupted by his countrymen the Angles, *not by the Celtic inhabitants of Cumbria* (I never supposed anybody would think I gave
the words in italics as Bede's); and that the word
caer was not then prefixed to the word, though I
thought it might easily be accounted for. Mr. Basil
Jones " wishes I would account for it;" and I have
no objection to try. *Caer*, he says, is not Gaelic;
I believe it is as little Cymric as Gaelic, but that it
is a mere abbreviation or corruption of the Roman
word *castrum*, which the Saxons, with a somewhat
different organic conformation, reduced into *caster* or
chester. I see no reason whatever why the word
might not have taken this same form among a Gaelic
population, who had the Roman fortresses among
them, and knew them by their Roman name, as well
as among Cymry in the same circumstances, and it
is evident that it did sometimes take this name over
the extreme northern districts of England and the
south of Scotland, as we have not only Carlisle, but
Carvoran, on Hadrian's Wall, Caerlaverock, in Dum-
friesshire, and I believe some other instances. It is
a curious circumstance that the Saxon *caster*, or *chester*, occurs here in the same districts where we meet
with the *caer*, or *car ;* of two neighbouring Roman
stations on the wall, not more than three miles apart,
Magna and Æsica, the former is called *Car*voran,
and the latter Great *Chesters*. I can only account
for this circumstance by supposing that, from a very
early period, the Angles lived intermixed with a previous population of this district, perhaps in a position
of greater relative equality than was the case with
the Saxon and Roman population in other parts of the
island ; that perhaps, in this instance, an Angle family

or clan was settled at Æsica, and a family of this older population at Magna; that while the one spoke of their *chester*, the other spoke of their *caer;* and that the population in general accepted the names severally as the inhabitants of the particular locality pronounced them; but it does not follow at all that the previous population were Cymry, or Welshmen.

I will now resume the principal heads of the suggestions which I had ventured to make on the subject of the settlement of Wales, which are briefly these:—

I.—It appears to me, from what I learn of the similarity between the modern languages of Wales and Britany, that the one people must have been separated from the other at a period subsequent to the Roman period.

II.—From a consideration of the Roman antiquities of Wales, it does not appear probable that there was at the close of the Roman period any independent population there, speaking Celtic, likely to have migrated into Britany, and to have transplanted their language thither.

III.—On the other hand, the known circumstances of Britany at that time are such as would very well account for an emigration into our island.

IV.—The general destruction of the Roman towns and settlements in Wales, and on the Welsh border, which must have occurred during the period of the Anglo-Saxon invasion of the other parts of the island, seems to imply an invasion and settlement from abroad at that time.* A previous population of Wales, or

* I return to this question of the destruction of the towns to make a remark which I fear may be thought rude, but which certainly is not intended to merit that designation. It would be much for the interest of science if nobody would hazard an

of Britons retiring into Wales before the power of
the Saxons, would not have destroyed their own

opinion for or against any question until he has duly made himself
acquainted with that question, and with all the circumstances
connected with it. It often happens that questions, otherwise
simple enough, are only made more confused and obscure by
voluntary contributions of this kind, which are perhaps quite
ungrounded. A suggestion has been offered from several quarters, which I think Mr. Basil Jones seems inclined to adopt,
that the towns may have been destroyed in the wars of later
times. Now this suggestion rests only on the assumption that
the remains of the towns, when excavated, present no evidence
in themselves of the period at which the destruction took place.
This, as every experienced antiquary knows, is not the case.
All the sites of ruined Roman towns with which I am acquainted
present to the excavator a numerous collection of objects ranging through a period which ends abruptly with what we call
the close of the Roman period, and attended with circumstances
which cannot leave any doubt that this was the period of destruction. Otherwise, surely we should find some objects which
would remind us of the subsequent periods. I will only mention one class of articles which are generally found in considerable numbers, the coins. We invariably find these presenting
a more or less complete series of Roman coins ending at latest
with the emperors who reigned in the first half of the fifth century. This is not the case with Roman towns which have continued to exist after that period, for there, on the contrary, we
find relics which speak of the subsequent inhabitants, early
Saxon and mediæval. I will only, for want of space, give one
example, that of Richborough, in Kent. The town of Rutupiæ
seems to have capitulated with the Saxon invaders, and to have
continued until its inhabitants, in consequence of the retreat of
the sea, gradually abandoned it to establish themselves at Sandwich. Now the coins found at Richborough do not end with
those of the Roman emperors; but we find, first, a great quantity
of those singular little coins which are generally known by the
name of *minimi*, and which, presenting very bad imitations of the
Roman coinage, are considered as belonging to the age immediately following the Roman period, and preceding that of the
earlier Saxon coinage. These coins commemorate no individuals, and are probably the coinage of the towns themselves

F 2

towns; and, moreover, such a population would, as far as we can judge from known facts, have spoken the Latin language.

V.—That such a relationship between the populations of Britany and Wales is consistent with the relationship between the literature and legends of Wales and Britany and those of mediæval Europe.

I beg again that it may be understood that I only give these as suggestions, though I think there is good evidence in favour of them; I do not bind myself to them, if they are proved to be ungrounded. But I think that each of these heads requires a careful and candid investigation—or rather, that it wants continued research to furnish further facts towards clearing it up. I assure Mr. Basil Jones that I object to no kind of direct evidence, but I can only take that evidence strictly for what it can be proved to be worth.

after the quantity of Roman money in circulation became inconveniently small. We also find at Richborough a certain number of Anglo-Saxon coins of a later date. We find, moreover, at Richborough, articles of purely Anglo-Saxon character, as fibulæ, and other personal ornaments, such as are found in the early Anglo-Saxon cemeteries. Nothing corresponding to these coins, or other objects, has been found at Caerleon, or Caerwent, or on the other sites in Wales, or on the Border.

VII.

ON ANGLO-SAXON ANTIQUITIES, WITH A PARTICULAR REFERENCE TO THE FAUSSETT COLLECTION.

HERE is scarcely any part of our islands in which we do not find, here and there scattered over the surface of the ground, artificial mounds, or tumuli, of various elevations, from one foot, or even less, to more than a hundred. It has been long known that these tumuli covered the last remains of the different peoples who ·lived here in the ages preceding the introduction of the Christian faith, subsequent to which the interment of the dead was differently regulated. Accidental discoveries must often have brought this truth to light, if the knowledge of it, or at least the belief in it, had not been, as I think there is every reason for believing that it was, handed down to us traditionally from the time at which they were made. In fact, it is no unfrequent occurrence, when we open a tumulus which, as far as we could judge from its outward appearance, cannot have been touched for many ages, to find that at some remote period it had been broken into and its contents either abstracted or broken and scattered about. Great numbers of such tumuli have been destroyed unobservedly in the va-

rious processes of agriculture or in the adaptation of
their site to modern purposes. Others have been
opened through mere motives of curiosity, or even of
superstition, and any object of interest they contained
was carried off under the indefinite character of an old
relic. It has only been in more recent times that
these monuments have been explored with care and
order, in the hope that an intelligent examination and
comparison of their contents might make us acquainted
with peoples and races concerning whom we learn
little from the pages of written history.   Thus has
the practice of " barrow-digging "—to use the phrase
which has become popular within the last few years
—passed through three distinct phases; during the
first long-extending period its object was mere plunder, consequent on the knowledge that articles of
value were often deposited with the dead; during an
intermediate period, its object was curiosity; and
during the third period, it was knowledge, or, to use
at this meeting the more appropriate word, Science.
It is this latter period alone with which we are at
present concerned.

The difficulties with which sound English archæology has had to contend in its beginning, arose chiefly
from the vague spirit of curiosity which preceded it.
Instead of the careful and extensive comparison, from
which alone we can hope to deduce facts of importance, people looked at each article only with regard
to itself; and, for the course of inductive reasoning
which science requires, they thoughtlessly substi-
tuted mere irrational conjecture.   This had become
a sort of habit.   People assumed, without knowing
why, that the tumuli of which I have been speaking
covered the remains of battle-fields, and never ques-

tioning the fable or tradition which made the heroes
of these battles Danes or Britons, Saxons or Normans,
(popular tradition knew little of Romans,) they followed that tradition in calling whatever articles were
found in them Danish or British, or Saxon or Norman. It is quite wonderful, when we look back
into the writings of the old antiquaries of note, how
few escaped from the influence of such popular
errors. Although accustomed to classification in
other branches of science, they seem never to have
thought of applying it to this; and museums were
simple collections of curiosities, instead of being the
materials for scientific investigation. It may be said
to have been in the Anglo-Saxon tumuli of Kent
that a better spirit of investigation first showed itself,
and that the foundations were laid for the higher cultivation of archæological science which now happily
prevails.

There are various circumstances characteristic of
the Anglo-Saxon interments, which contributed much
towards this result; because they led people almost
necessarily to follow a new course of reasoning. The
larger and more remarkable tumuli, those which are
known to be Roman, and those which are believed or
supposed to be British, were in general found singly
by themselves, or in a group of not more than two
or three; they were probably memorials of respect
or attachment to persons of distinction, while people
in general were buried in a less ostentatious or less
durable manner. As the interments had in most
cases been preceded by cremation, it was only in
particular instances that the contents offered anything remarkable or characteristic. On the contrary, the Anglo-Saxon tumuli are arranged in ex-

tensive groups, forming regular cemeteries, each probably belonging to a sept or to a district. Each grave contains almost invariably a considerable number of articles of very different descriptions, so that the abundance of the objects alone invited to comparison. Another circumstance also has contributed to their preservation. In the Anglo-Saxon interments the body, with the objects accompanying it, were laid in a grave, at some depth below the level of the ground, so that the plunderer who sought objects of value, or the collector who sought curiosities, found nothing in the mounds they opened to encourage their researches. From these circumstances, the first correct principles of our national archæology were obtained in the investigation of the Anglo-Saxon cemeteries; and it adds considerably to the interest of the extensive and valuable collection now exhibited to us, that they not only form the finest collection of Anglo-Saxon antiquities of the pre-christian age ever yet made, but that they are those upon which the foundations of our present knowledge were laid.

The Rev. Bryan Faussett, of Heppington near Canterbury, to whom we owe the formation of this collection, had passed the greater part of his life in a district peculiarly rich in Saxon remains; for the succession of chalk downs stretching out from Canterbury towards the east and south are remarkable for the numerous groups of Saxon barrows, or rather the Saxon cemeteries, which are found on their slopes and summits. In the year 1730, one of these groups, situated on a high part of Chartham down, somewhat more than three miles to the south-west of Canterbury, was partially excavated by Charles Fagg, esq., of Mystole, in Chartham parish. These excavations were carried on, in a very unsatisfactory manner,

under the immediate personal direction of Dr. Crom-
well Mortimer, the secretary of the Royal Society;
and so little was then known either of the character
of the cemeteries, or of the objects they contained,
that the learned secretary of that celebrated scientific
body actually wrote an elaborate paper on them, in
which he arrives at the conclusion that they were the
graves of the soldiers slain in a battle fought here
between Julius Cæsar and the Britons. Bryan
Faussett, at this time only about ten years old, is
said to have been present at the opening of these
graves, which excited in him an interest that clung
to him during the remainder of his life. He was subsequently curate of Kingston, about five miles to the
south of Canterbury, from 1750 to 1755, and while
resident there his attention was forcibly riveted on
a very remarkable and extensive group of barrows
in his own parish, on the brow of the hill near Ileden.
Still possessed by the notion that these barrows or
tumuli marked the site of a battle between Cæsar
and the Britons, Bryan Faussett was anxious to open
them, but the permission to do so was refused by the
owner of the land, Thomas Barrett, esq., and Mr.
Faussett's curiosity remained unsatisfied. At length,
in 1757, Mr. Faussett was enabled to gratify his
spirit of research in commencing a series of excavations in a cemetery on a spot called Tremworth down,
in the parish of Crundale, which however proved to
be Roman. His excavations on this site were continued in the year 1759. In 1760, 1762, and 1763,
he pursued his researches in the very rich Saxon cemetery at Gilton in the parish of Ash, near Sandwich, where he opened no less than a hundred and
six tumuli or graves, which enriched his collection
with a number of interesting objects. In 1767, Mr.

Faussett's attention was again called to the barrows
in Kingston parish, and the land having passed by
the death of its former owner and the marriage of his
daughter to a personal friend, he obtained at last full
liberty to excavate. He was soon convinced of his
error in supposing that they had any connection with
Cæsar or the Britons, and he obtained from them
many of the most precious articles which are now
found in his collection. During the autumn of the year
just mentioned Mr. Faussett opened fifty-four tumuli
on this site. His further researches here were interrupted, for some reason or other, from the September of 1767 to the middle of July, 1771, when he resumed his labours on the same spot, and during that
and the following month opened a hundred and sixty-
five barrows. In August and October, 1772, he
opened thirty-four more tumuli on this spot; and in
the August and September of the following year, he
examined forty-five more; making in all three hundred and eight separate interments in one cemetery.

Although with Bryan Faussett, the notion that
these tumuli covered the remains of Cæsar's soldiers
was now entirely exploded, he fell into another opinion equally erroneous, and of which he seems never
to have divested himself. He found Roman coins,
and he concluded very hastily that the date of their
deposit must have been the reign in which they were
struck; he found fragments of Roman pottery in
comparative abundance; he found a small number of
urns containing calcined bones, which he, unable to
discriminate the character of the pottery, imagined
must have been deposited at a date anterior to that
at which the Romans abandoned the practice of cremation. Against these circumstances, Mr. Faussett

had to place the absolute uniformity of character of the interments as he found them; and he explained this anomaly by supposing that the coins, urns, &c., were the remains of previous Roman burials, which had been broken up, at a later period, in order to use the old graves for a new interment. From these circumstances Faussett concluded that "this spot" had been "no other than a κοιμητήριον, or common burying-place; of Romans, no doubt, (and that, too, from a very early period;) but not of those alone, but also, if not chiefly, of Romans Britainized, and Britons Romanized (if I may be allowed the use of these expressions), even till long after the Romans (properly so called) had entirely quitted this isle. In short," he adds, "my opinion of this matter is, that this spot was a burying-place not only, at first, for the Roman soldiers who may be supposed to have kept garrison in some of the many intrenchments and look-outs in this neighbourhood, but that, afterwards, it served for such of the inhabitants of some one or more of the adjacent villages; which we may very reasonably presume were latterly inhabited by what I have presumed before to call 'Romans Britainized and Britons Romanized,' i.e. by people of both nations—who, having mixed and intermarried with each other, had naturally learnt, and in some measure adopted, each other's customs. The ossuaries, or bone-urns, here found, will sufficiently prove that this place was used as such in the time of the higher empire, i.e. before the custom of burning the dead ceased among the Romans; and the coins of Gallienus, of Probus, of Carausius and Allectus, and of the Constantine family, will be ample evidence of its having continued to be used as such in the time of the lower empire. How much longer it was put to that use it is impossible for me to determine from anything yet found there; but my conjecture is that it served for that purpose (I mean, a burying-place for some neighbouring village, or perhaps villages), long after the Romans (*i.e.* those properly so called) had entirely evacuated and quitted this isle." Mr. Faussett adds that, from the circumstance of a cross-shaped fibula being found in one of the graves, it is plain that the wearer of it was a Christian, and therefore that this cemetery may have been in use until the time when Archbishop Cuthbert, who came to the see of Canterbury in 741, ordered that the burials should take place in cemeteries adjacent to the churches.

I have quoted the whole of this statement of Bryan Faussett's opinions in order to show you how imperfect the science of archæology was in this country only eighty years ago, and how apt people were to build theories upon what they believed to be facts, merely because they did not themselves know the contrary. Mr. Faussett was ignorant that the Roman coinage of all dates was in general and extensive circulation among the Anglo-Saxons; that great quantities of Roman pottery were in use among them; that the practice of cremation did exist among the Teutonic settlers in this island; that the bone-urns which he dug up were all of Saxon, or rather perhaps of Frankish, manufacture; and, finally, that the cross-shaped ornaments are so common, and occur under such circumstances, that we cannot possibly take them as any evidence that the skeletons with which they were found were those of Christians.

The years 1772 and 1773 were those of Mr.

Faussett's most active researches. In the July of the former of these two years he began to open a rather extensive cemetery, or, more accurately speaking, two cemeteries, on Sibertswold down, about half way between Canterbury and Deal. During the summers of this and the following year he opened a hundred and eighty-one Anglo-Saxon graves, many of which contained objects of the greatest interest. During the July and August of 1772, Mr. Faussett also opened forty-eight graves in a smaller cemetery on Barfreston down, in the immediate neighbourhood of that at Sibertswold.   During the summer months of the year 1773, Mr. Faussett opened forty-four Saxon tumuli in a cemetery in the parish of Beakesbourne, about four miles to the south-east of Canterbury; and in the autumn of the same year, returning to the scene of his earliest antiquarian impressions, he opened fifty-three graves on Chartham downs, in the same cemetery which had, in 1730, occupied the attention of Mr. Fagg. and Dr. Mortimer.   With these excavations Bryan Faussett's labours seem to have closed.   He was probably hindered from continuing them by declining health, as we know that he died within three years after, in 1776.

Bryan Faussett had a successor in these researches, in the Rev. James Douglas, who, in the years 1779 and 1780, assisted in opening a number of graves in a Saxon cemetery on Chatham lines, which was cut through in the course of the military works there.   In 1782, Douglas opened some Saxon barrows at St. Margaret's on the Cliff, near Dover; in 1783, he opened a group in the parish of Ash near Sandwich; and in 1784, he explored a small group in Greenwich park.

The researches of Douglas were far less extensive than those of Bryan Faussett, but they have been better known through the circumstance that the former, towards the end of the century, published the result of his inquiries in a folio volume which has long been advantageously known to antiquaries by the title of *Nenia Britannica*. In attempting to appropriate these remains, Douglas erred in the opposite direction from Bryan Faussett. The latter imagined that they belonged principally to a population which preceded the Anglo-Saxons. Douglas seems himself to have set out with this notion; but he soon relinquished it, and he went so far right that he ascribed them to the Anglo-Saxons themselves. Douglas, however, laboured under certain prejudices and vulgar errors. He imagined that the Saxon settlers, before their conversion to Christianity, were mere barbarians—that they were totally unacquainted with art—and that they were neither capable of making, nor likely to possess, the numerous articles, rich in material and ornamentation, which were found in these cemeteries. Further, he fancied that there was a Byzantine character in the ornamentation, and he immediately concluded that it must be the work of artificers who came to England along with Theodore the Greek in the year 668. He therefore adopted the very untenable theory that these were the graves of Christian Saxons; and that they belonged to the period which intervened between the conversion of the Anglo-Saxons at the close of the sixth century and the middle of the eighth century, when the cemeteries were ordered to be attached to the churches. Nothing can be more evident to the unbiassed observer of these interments than the pagan character of them all.

I have dwelt the more upon the opinions of these investigators, because in science the history of error is often as instructive, to the student at least, as the declaration of truth; inasmuch as it teaches him the necessity of caution, especially in a science, like British archæology in its present condition, where there is much room for speculation. From the time of Douglas to our own days no further researches were made in the Anglo-Saxon cemeteries, and no one attempted to correct or to build upon his labours. Those of Bryan Faussett, which had not been published, remained unknown, except by a few articles engraved in the plates to the Nenia; Douglas himself having had access to the Faussett collection. So little indeed were the correct principles of archæology understood in this country that a diligent, if not a very correct, collector of facts, Sir Richard Colt Hoare, who made an unwise attempt at an arbitrary classification of barrows by their outward forms, actually set down the contents of Saxon tumuli as British, although he might have corrected himself by a simple glance at the then very well-known work of Douglas. In 1841, and during several subsequent years, Lord Londesborough (then Lord Albert Conyngham), who was residing at Bourne near Canterbury, and had a rather extensive cemetery in his own park, opened at different times a considerable number of barrows there, at Wingham near Sandwich, and on Breach down in the parish of Barham, about four miles to the south of Canterbury. His lordship was accompanied, at most of these excavations, by Mr. Akerman, Mr. Roach Smith, or myself, and I believe that Mr. Akerman and Mr. Roach Smith, in giving accounts of those and other disco-

veries in the same neighbourhood, *first* stated clearly
and distinctly to what people these remains belonged,
namely, to the Anglo-Saxons of the period previous
to the introduction of Christianity; or from the
middle of the fifth century to the end of the sixth,
and in some parts probably, where Christianity had
penetrated more slowly than in others, to the middle
of the seventh. The interest excited by these discoveries called much attention to the subject, and it
was soon known that several Anglo-Saxon cemeteries had been partially opened by accident in other
parts of Kent, and that the contents had either been
scattered abroad and lost, or preserved by private
individuals who were not aware of their peculiar character. Thus, a rather extensive cemetery had been
opened at different times from 1825 to 1828 at Sittingbourne, and many of the articles found in it were
preserved by Mr. Vallance. Mr. Rolfe, of Sandwich, had already begun to form his valuable collection from the cemeteries and barrows of Gilton,
Coombe, Woodnesborough, and other places, which
has been since so much enriched from his excavations
at Osengall.* Saxon cemeteries of great interest have
been also excavated at Strood and Rochester; another
has been cut through by the railway at Northfleet;
and traces of several others have been noticed in
different parts of Kent.

You have now before you, in the Faussett collection alone, the contents of between seven and eight
hundred graves, and you will see that, as I have
already intimated, they furnish an almost indefinite
variety of articles; and this variety would no doubt

---

* Mr. Rolfe's collection now forms part of the museum of
Mr. Mayer, in Liverpool.

have been greatly increased but for the perishable
materials of which many of those placed in the graves
were composed.   There are, however, certain classes
of articles which are more numerous than the others,
and to which it may be well to call particular attention.

The Anglo-Saxon grave forms generally a very
regular parallelogram, with a floor carefully smoothed,
and sometimes of rather large dimensions in propor-
tion to the magnitude of the interment.   In some
instances I have met with square holes at each
corner, apparently intended to receive the ends of
beams of wood, as though some sort of framework
had been raised over it at the time of interment.   In
the parish of Adisham, in Kent, Faussett opened a
very curious grave, the form of which will be best
understood by the accompanying cut, and he thus

Cruciform grave, at Adisham, Kent.

describes it in his manuscript account of his explora-
tions:—" The grave," he says, " which was cut very
neatly and exactly out of the rock chalk, was full five

feet deep; it was of the exact shape of a cross, whose legs pointed very minutely to the four cardinal points of the compass; and it was every way eleven feet long, and about four feet broad. At each extremity was a little cove, or arched hole, each about twelve inches broad, and about fourteen high, all very neatly cut, like so many little fire-places, for about a foot beyond the grave, into the chalk. It is impossible to say for what purpose, or under the influence of what caprice, so singular a form was given to a human grave."*

The body was usually laid on its back in the middle of the floor of the grave. In the MS. account of his diggings, Faussett frequently mentions traces of the existence of a coffin, but, as far as my experience goes, I am led to think that the use of a coffin was not common. Where the body was that of a man, we almost always find above the right shoulder the iron head of a spear, and in general we may trace, by the colour of the earth, the decayed wood of the shaft, until near the foot of the skeleton lies the iron-spiked ferule which terminated it at the other end. We sometimes also meet with one or more smaller heads of javelins, or arrows; for I disagree entirely with a statement which has been made lately and adhered to, that the bow was in discredit

---

* Since this lecture was delivered, Faussett's manuscript has been printed in a large 4to. volume, in 1856, under the title of *Inventorium Sepulchrale*, at the expense of its proprietor Mr. Mayer, and under the editorial care of Mr. Roach Smith. Mr. Smith, in a note upon the grave described above, suggests that it may have been a grave cut across an older one; but I think that several circumstances connected with it, and especially that of the "little coves," being found at all the four extremities, militate against this supposition.

among the Anglo-Saxons as a weapon.* Closer to the side of the skeleton lies usually (though not always) a long iron broad-sword, not much unlike the claymore of the Scottish highlander, of which it was perhaps the prototype. Its most usual form is that represented in the annexed figure. The sheath and

2. Sword, from Barham Down.

handle appear in most cases to have been made of perishable materials, and we seldom find more than the blade with the spike by which it was fixed into the handle. The tip of the sheath, however, is some-times met with, having been made of bronze or other metal, and also at times, the handle of the sword, which has been found of silver.† A usual form of the top of the handle is represented in Figure 3.

Another article, pecu-liarly characteristic of the Saxon interments, is the knife, the length of which is generally about five or six inches, although at times it extends to from ten to eleven inches, and then from its shape it must have been a very formidable weapon, in-

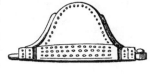

3. Top of the handle of a Sword, from Kingston Down.

* See on this subject the note at the end of this paper.

† Fine examples of the handle of the Anglo-Saxon sword will be found in the engravings to Mr. Smith's *Collectanea* and Mr. Akerman's *Pagan Saxondom*.

dependent of its utility for other purposes. It has
been pretended that it was from the use of this instrument, called in their language a *seax*, that our
forefathers derived their name of *Saxons*.   Another
weapon, the axe, is found at times in the Saxon
graves, but it is of very rare occurrence, and was
probably not in general use in this island.   The accompanying group of weapons were taken from one
grave on Kingston Down; they consist of two swords
of rather different form to that represented above (2
and 8); of the head (3) and the ferule (6) of a spear;
of smaller javelins or arrow-heads (1, 7); and of
knives large and small (4, 5.)*

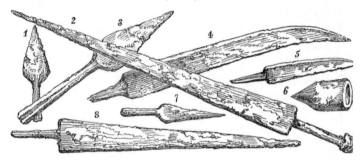

4. Weapons, from Kingston Down.

Over the breast of the Saxon warrior is generally
found the iron umbo or boss of his shield.   Its shape

* Mr. Akerman, *Pagan Saxondom*, p. 48, has given his
opinion that the sword was not an ordinary weapon of our
Anglo-Saxon forefathers, and states that its occurrence in the
grave is an exception. I have remarked, in more than one
instance, that the sword was entirely decayed in the same grave
where the spear-head was very well preserved, and this to
such a degree that it required close observation, and an experienced eye, to detect in the colour of the earth the traces of

is not always the same, as will be seen by the examples
now exhibited, but there
is a general character
about this part of the
accoutrements of the
Anglo - Saxon which
makes it perfectly inex-
cusable for any one who
pretends to the character

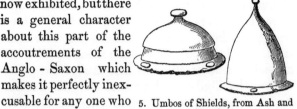

5. Umbos of Shields, from Ash and
Chartham.

of an archæologist to misappropriate it, as has been
done in a recent publication which I regret to say
contains too many errors of this kind, I mean Wilson's
" Archæology and Pre-historic Annals of Scotland."
Beneath the boss of the shield is usually found a
piece of iron which is best
described by a drawing,
and which no doubt was
the handle by which the

6. Handle of Shield.

shield was held. Douglas, who had not observed
carefully the position in which it is found, imagined
it to be part of a bow, and called it a bow-brace.
The shield itself, as we know from the Anglo-Saxon
writers, was of wood, generally of linden, and has
therefore perished, but we find remains of nails, studs,
and other iron work, belonging to it.

---

its former existence; and I am not aware whether highly tempered steel undergoes more rapidly the effect of decomposition
than steel less highly tempered, or than common iron. But
there is another cause of the rarity of the sword; it was, no
doubt, the weapon on which the Anglo-Saxon set the greatest
value, and was much more richly ornamented than the others;
and a dying warrior is described not unfrequently as be-
queathing his sword to a friend, or to a brave relative. This
circumstance would be enough to explain why the sword was
not so frequently buried with the dead.

Such are the more common arms which we find, without much variation, in the graves of our Anglo-Saxon forefathers, of the period to which these cemeteries belong.   The miscellaneous articles are so varied, that I can only enumerate them rapidly.   Of personal ornaments, the first that attract our attention are the fibulæ, or brooches, and the buckles. The latter are usually of bronze gilt, and are often very elaborately ornamented, as will be seen by the numerous examples in the Faussett collection.   From the position in which they are found, it is evident that they formed, most generally, the fastening of the girdle.   The forms of these buckles are varied.   The two first examples here given (7) are of a form which is not uncommon.   Sometimes they are square, instead of round, as in the example No. 8.   Two small

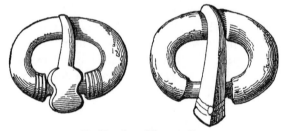

7. Buckles, from Kingston Down.

8. Buckle, from Kingston Down.

buckles, found at Gilton Town in the parish of Ash,

near Sandwich, are represented, of the size of the
originals, in our cuts, Figs. 9
and 10; the first made of
brass, the second of iron.
The buckle is very com-
monly only the extremity
of a bronze ornament, more
or less elaborate. No. 11

9 and 10. Gilton Town, Kent.

is a small and very plain buckle of this kind. Nos.
12 and 13 are buckles of ornamental
forms, which occur not unfrequently both in the Faussett collection, and in other collections
made from the Kentish graves.

11. Buckle, from
Kingston Down.

They are some-

13. Buckle, from
Sibertswold.

12. Buckle, from Kingston Down.

times very massive, the larger ones apparently belonging to the male, and the smaller ones to the

female costume.   The four following cuts represent
varieties of buckles of this class.   Fig. 14 is a
buckle made of brass, found on Barfriston Down,
near Sandwich.   Fig. 15 is another example, of

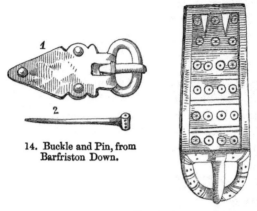

14. Buckle and Pin, from
Barfriston Down.

15. Buckle, from Barfriston Down.

the same material, and found in the same place.   In
Fig. 16, the buckle numbered 1, which is of brass,

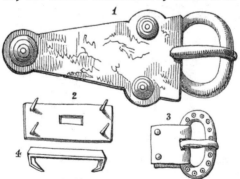

16. Buckles, from Kingston Down.

was found in the cemetery on Kingston Down.   No.

3, found in another grave in the same cemetery, is of the same material, but here the shank is simply formed by a piece of brass doubled, and riveted on the strap.* Examples of this latter method of attaching the buckle are common enough, and the brass which holds it is not unfrequently ornamented by cutting or stamping. An example is given in Fig. 17, found in the Saxon cemetery at Chessell Down, in the Isle of Wight. These figures are all represented of the size of the originals. The buckles of this latter class

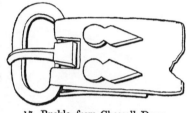

17. Buckle, from Chessell Down, Isle of Wight.

are sometimes found of very large dimensions, and elaborately ornamented. This is especially the case in the Frankish examples found by the Abbé Cochet in Normandy.

Many of the fibulæ which are found upon male skeletons, as well as females, are extremely rich and beautiful. In the Kentish tumuli the prevailing form is circular, and they are often of gold, profusely ornamented with filigree work, and with garnets or other stones, or sometimes with glass or paste, set usually upon chequered foils of gold. The use of this fibula appears to have been to fasten the mantle over the breast, where it is most commonly found. Some of

* The 2nd and 4th figures in this group represent a small plate of brass with a rectangular hole in the middle, which had been riveted on wood, but the object of which is uncertain; and one of a number of small brass staples, all found in the cemetery on Kingston Down.

the finest examples of the Saxon gold fibulæ occur in
the Faussett collection.   Their general size is from

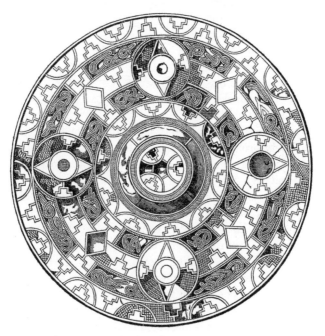

18. The great Fibula, from Kingston Down, with section.

an inch and a half to two inches in diameter; but the
Faussett collection possesses one of considerably
larger dimensions, which was found in the grave of

an Anglo-Saxon lady, on Kingston Down. This
magnificent ornament is no less than three inches and
a half in diameter, a quarter of an inch thick at the
edges, and three quarters of an inch thick at the
centre, all of gold, and weighing between six and
seven ounces. It is covered with ornaments of
filigree work, in concentric circles, and is set with
garnets and with pale blue stones. The acus or pin
on the back is also
ornamented and set
with garnets. It was
found high on the
breast, near the right
shoulder. Other ex-
amples of the circu-
lar gold fibula will
be seen in the Faus-
sett collection, and
they are met with
in almost every col-
lection of Anglo-

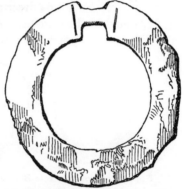

19. Plain Fibula, from Kingston Down.

Saxon remains from the Kentish barrows. Fibulæ
of plainer forms are also of common occurrence,
sometimes consisting of a mere circle of bronze, like
the example here figured.

Other jewellery, such as rings, bracelets, neck-
laces of beads, pendants to the neck and ears, &c.
are found in abundance, and in a great variety of
form. The ear-rings are very diversified in form,
but they often consist of a plain ring with one or two
beads on it. The second object in the group, Fig. 20,
was perhaps an ear-ring; it is of brass, with a small
brass spangle strung on it. The first object in this
group is a small bulla, or pendent, of silver, found,

like the other, in the cemetery on Kingston Down.

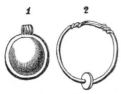

20. From Kingston Down.

Gold coins are sometimes fitted up as pendent ornaments. The most common material of beads is glass or variegated clay, the latter made with great skill, and often exhibiting pleasing patterns. The two beads of this description represented in Fig. 21, found in the cemetery on Barfriston Down, are of this material, and from the rings attached to

21. Ear-rings, from Barfriston Down.

them, may have been ear-rings. They belong to a class of manufacture which has continued to exist in this country down to a recent period. Another common material of beads was amber, and we some-times find small lumps of amber which have been merely perforated, in order to be attached to the person by a string. It must be observed that we sometimes find a string of beads round the neck of a man, and other circumstances show that there were Saxon *exquisites* who were vain enough of their personal adornments. It is a very usual thing to find one or more beads of amber near the neck in cases where there can be no doubt that the deceased was a man; but this circumstance is explained by a

widely prevailing superstition in the middle ages,
that amber carried on the person was a protection against the influence of evil spirits.
Large hair-pins, usually of bone or bronze,
and more or less ornamented, are generally
found near the heads of skeletons of females,
in such a position as leads us to conclude that
the Saxon ladies bound up their hair behind
in a manner similar to that which prevailed
among the Romans. The general form of
these hair-pins is represented in Fig. 22, which
is one of the least ornamental examples.

The interments of the Anglo-Saxon ladies
are generally accompanied with a number of
articles of utility, as well as of ornament.
By a lady's side we usually find the remains,
more or less perfect, of a bunch of domestic
implements, somewhat resembling the article brought
into fashion a few years ago, under the name of a
châtelaine. To these were hung, among other

22. Hair-
pin, from
Kingston
Down.

23. Tweezers, from Kingston Down.

articles, small tweezers, intended for the eradication
of superfluous hairs, which are so common, that it is
evident that the practice of depilation prevailed generally among the Anglo-Saxon ladies. Other instruments have evidently served for ear-picks and tooth-
picks. The tweezers so closely resemble those found
on Roman sites, that we can hardly doubt that it was

from the Romans the Anglo-Saxons originally de-

rived them. The cut given as an example is represented here of its natural size. The next, Fig. 24, represents examples of what are believed to have been ear-picks, tooth-picks, &c. as they were found attached to the châtelaine in a grave at Si-bertswold. Combs also are found very frequently, not only in the graves of women, but in those of men—a proof that the latter, which in fact was the case among all the branches of the Teutonic race, paid great atten-tion to their hair. Those which are preserved are usually of bone, and they are, as at pre-sent, sometimes single, and sometimes double. The ex-ample, Fig. 25, is curious on account of the two guards for

24. Châtelaine, from Kingston Down.

the protection of its teeth from damage when not in

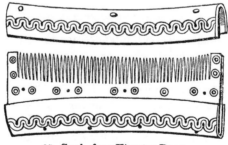

25. Comb, from Kingston Down.

use. It is more than probable, that in many of the
graves in which little is found, there were originally
combs and other articles of wood, a material which of
course has perished long ago, even where it existed in
much greater masses. It appears that there was
often attached to the châtelaine, or suspended by the
side of it, a bag of some kind, containing other articles
used by the ladies, for we frequently find on the spot
where it has lain a heap of small articles, which are at
times tolerably preserved, but in others the iron is so
much oxidized, as to present a mere confused mass of
fragments. In these groups, which differ much, both
in the number and in the character of the articles
which compose them, we usually find one or more
small knives, and a pair of scissors. The Anglo-
Saxon scissors of this early period resemble in form
the shears of modern times, though we have found
one or two examples of scissors formed like those now
in use. We have also pins, and needles, and keys,
and other small articles, which I will not now attempt
to enumerate. I will mention, however, that you
find in the Faussett collection a curious example of a
supposed fork, found in one of the graves on Kingston Down. It is represented in the next Figure (but
not quite correctly, as it should be longer in form,
and not bent, but straight). It constitutes another
example of the necessity for careful and extensive
comparison before we hazard opinions on the purposes
of many of the objects found in the Anglo-Saxon
graves. I have been convinced, by Mr. Roach
Smith, that the object in question is not a fork, but
a totally different thing,—in fact, that it is part of the
metal tag at the end of the belt. The forked part,
fitted in between two small plates of metal, forming

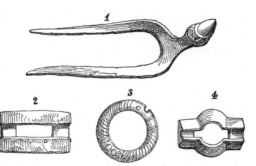

26. Tag of a belt, and other articles, from Kingston Down.

the two sides, and the small knob remained as the

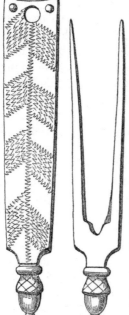

27. Tag of a belt, found in London.

termination of the belt. A better example is here given, Fig. 27, from the museum of Mr. Roach Smith, with and without its casing. The construction of this object appears to have been borrowed from the Romans, for among several examples in Mr. Smith's peculiarly rich Museum, one which is in a very perfect condition was found with Roman remains, and others have a mediæval character. A fork, however, has actually been found in one of the early Saxon graves on Harnham Hill, near Salisbury; and the museum of Lord Londesborough possesses a very curious Anglo-Saxon fork of a later date (the ninth cen-

tury). These examples have been supposed to dis-
prove the commonly received opinion that forks
were not used in eating at table before the six-
teenth century; but I think it more than probable
that these single examples of forks furnished from
Anglo-Saxon times, as well as others which are
mentioned incidentally at a somewhat later period of
the middle ages, were not used for eating, but merely
for serving out of the dish some articles of food which
could not be so conveniently served with any other
implement. The other Figures (2, 3, 4) in the cut
No. 26, are supposed to be parts of a small lock or
fastening to a box. Mr. Faussett found several
examples of an object which is represented in the
annexed Figure, and which, from its general appearance, seems to have been an internal bolt of a box.

28. Bolt, from Kingston Down.

Another kind of implement, of which, though there
are some varieties, the one represented in the figure,
No. 29, is a common form, is also found frequently,

29. Supposed Key, from Kingston Down.

and can only at present be explained by supposing it

to be a key. These were perhaps used to fasten or un-
fasten internal bolts in boxes like those just mentioned.

Faussett found in the cemetery on Sibertswold

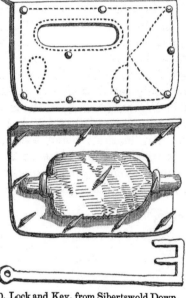

Down the remains
of a small wooden
box, with its brass
lock attached to it,
both sides of the
latter of which are
represented in the
cut, Fig. 30. The
object represented
below, which was
found with it, is
perfectly identical
with that repre-
sented in our pre-
vious cut, and there
can hardly be a
doubt that it was
the key belonging
to the lock. The

30. Lock and Key, from Sibertswold Down.

lower figure of the
latter represents the bolt, similar to that represented
in Fig. 28, in the position in which
Faussett imagined that it had been
placed. This lock is two inches and
a half in length, and the key is three
inches and a half long. Keys of the
more common forms are also found,
imitations, no doubt, of Roman
models. That represented in Fig. 31,
though found in an undoubted Anglo-

31. Key, from
Chartham Down.

Saxon grave, appears to be of Roman

workmanship. The remains of cylindrical locks are
also found in the Anglo-Saxon graves,
not unlike similar ones in use in modern
times. One of these, formed of brass,
and found in a grave on Sibertswold
Down, is represented, the size of the
original, in Fig. 32.

A great variety of household utensils, of different kinds, are also found
in the Anglo-Saxon graves. The

32. Lock, from Si-
bertswold Down.

pottery, when not Roman, is of a rude construction,
and, in fact, it is not very abundant, for our Anglo-
Saxon forefathers, for several ages after their settlement in this island, seem to have used principally
pottery of Roman manufacture. I would merely call
your attention to the particular character of several
earthenware urns, found in Kent, which Bryan Faussett supposed to be early Romano-British, and of
which I shall have to speak again further on. But
if the Anglo-Saxon earthenware was rude and coarse
in its character, the case was quite different with the
Anglo-Saxon glass, which is rather common in the
graves of Kent. The glass of the Anglo-Saxons is
fine and delicately thin. It is found chiefly in drinking cups, though a few small basins and bottle-shaped
vessels of glass have been found. The drinking cups
are in shape either pointed at the bottom, or rounded
in such a manner that they could never have stood
upright, a form which it is supposed was given them
to force each drinker to empty his glass at a draught.
This practice is understood to have existed down to
a much later period, and it is said to have given rise
to the name *tumbler*, applied originally to a drinking
glass which was never intended to stand upright.

The ornamentation of the Anglo-Saxon glass generally consists either of furrows on the surface, or of
strings of glass attached to the vessel after it was
made.   Both these ornaments seem to come fairly
under the epithet " twisted," which is often applied
to drinking cups in the earliest Anglo-Saxon poetry
that has been preserved.

Bowls, large basins, and dishes, of metal, are not
unfrequently found in these graves, of such elegant
form that we can hardly help supposing them to be of
Roman manufacture; and in one instance a bowl of
apparently Roman workmanship was found mended
with what were as evidently Saxon materials.
Others, however, seem to be Saxon, and prove certainly that the Anglo-Saxons had skilful workmen.
These bowls, basins, and dishes, are usually of bronze,
and are often very thickly and well gilt.   The metal
is generally thin, and it may be remarked, as a particular character which distinguishes Anglo-Saxon
workmanship from Roman, that the substance is
usually thin instead of being massive.

There is another domestic implement which requires
particular notice, and which is not uncommon in the
Kentish Saxon graves.   I mean a bucket, of which,
as it has been made generally of wood, there seldom
remains more than the hoops, and other bronze or
iron work.   One, engraved by Douglas, seems to
have been composed almost entirely of brass, or
bronze, and iron.   The use of these buckets has been
the subject of conjecture and of very contrary
opinions; but I am inclined to believe that it was
the vessel called by the Anglo-Saxons a *fæt*, or vat,
and that its use was to carry into the hall, and convey
into the drinking cups of the carousers, the mead, ale,

or wine, which they were to drink. These buckets generally possess too much of an ornamental character to have served for any purpose of a less honourable description. The early Anglo-Saxon poem of Beowulf, (1. 231,) in describing a feast, tells us how

| byrelas sealdon | cup-bearers gave |
| win of wunder-fatum. | the wine from wondrous vats. |

These vats or buckets are never large. The one engraved by Douglas was only seven inches and a half high; another found in Bourne park, the largest I have seen, was about twelve inches high.*

* I believe I first suggested, in the *Archæological Album*, this use of the bucket, and it seems to have been generally adopted since; but it has been very recently disputed by Mr. Akerman, in his *Pagan Saxondom*, p. 56. "These vessels," Mr. Akerman remarks, "have been supposed to have been used to hold ale or mead at the Anglo-Saxon feasts, an opinion to which we cannot subscribe. It has been conjectured that the passage in Beowulf—

| byrelas sealdon | cup-bearers gave |
| win of wunder-fatum, | wine from wondrous vats, |

alludes to them; but it is difficult to conceive how the term 'wondrous' could apply to utensils of this description, while the huge vats of the Germans are to this day the wonder of foreigners."

One would really imagine that Mr. Akerman was joking with my very literal translation of the passage in the Archæological Album; he certainly has taken a wrong impression of the meaning of the original, by arguing on the common modern usage of the English words. *Wunder-fatum* is certainly represented word for word by *wondrous vats*, but the "vats" of the Anglo-Saxon poet were not such implements as we call by that name now,—*fæt* was the term applied very generally to almost any kind of vessel. Neither would the Anglo-Saxon *wunder* have presented any difficulty to those who are acquainted with the Anglo-Saxon language, and more especially with its

I will only mention, as a further illustration of the great variety of articles which are found in these Anglo-Saxon graves, and which show us how little we have hitherto really understood of the degree of civilization existing among the Anglo-Saxons before their conversion to Christianity, that with one interment has been found a pair of compasses. A small

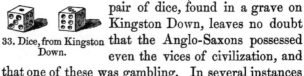 pair of dice, found in a grave on Kingston Down, leaves no doubt

33. Dice, from Kingston that the Anglo-Saxons possessed
Down. even the vices of civilization, and

that one of these was gambling. In several instances

poetry : it simply indicated something excelling in beauty, or form, or some other qualities, the common examples of the same article, and the real meaning of the words might be given in the English " very beautiful vessels," or " very elegant vessels," which, according to Anglo-Saxon notions of beauty and elegance, is a sufficiently exact description of the buckets of which we are speaking. One thing is certain, that the Anglo-Saxon poet who wrote these lines never imagined that he would be taken as intimating that every time the cup-bearers went round to pour liquor into the cups of the guests, each carried a duplicate of the great tun of Heidelberg in his hand.

Mr. Akerman goes on to say :—" In a recent communication with which we have been favoured by the Abbé Cochet, he mentions the fact of his finding in the cemetery of Envermeu a bucket containing a glass cup, and hence concludes that the problem of the use of the former is solved, and that they are, in fact, drinking cups. With all deference for his opinion, we have arrived at a different conclusion. In the Frank graves at Selzen, glass drinking cups were found, protected in a similar manner, but does it not lead to the inference that the larger vessel was intended to hold *food* and not drink ? From the circumstance of their being discovered in the graves of either sex, it seems highly probable that these buckets were used for *spoon-meat*, and are, in fact, porringers."

I must confess that I cannot at all understand the train of

scales and weights have occurred. Mr. Rolfe obtained from the interesting cemetery at Osengell a pair of delicately formed bronze scales, with a complete set of weights, all formed from Roman coins. You may observe a set of such coin-weights in the Faussett collection, and other examples have been found. This leads me to recur to a former statement of the not unfrequent occurrence of Roman coins in these Anglo-Saxon graves, and we have other reasons for believing that Roman money was long in circulation after the Romans relinquished the island. Coins even of the eastern emperors were brought hither, perhaps by traders, long after the fall of the empire of the west. In one of the graves at Osengell was

reasoning by which Mr. Akerman arrives at these inferences and probabilities, which appear to me to be mere gratuitous assumptions. He seems to argue, moreover, as though the worthy and learned Abbé and I had supposed that these buckets were drinking vessels, which is not the case; but I must say, that until I see better reasons against it than are advanced here, I feel inclined to adhere to the explanation I have suggested, which seems to me a very natural and reasonable one. I agree with the Abbé Cochet that the finding of the drinking glass in the bucket is to some degree a confirmation of my opinion, as it seems to imply a connection between the uses of the two articles. Mr. Akerman should have given us some authority for believing that the Anglo-Saxons did eat *spoon-meat* in the way he seems to suppose, or that any people in Western Europe ever eat out of buckets. I have been reminded that the practice of serving out the ale or other liquor in vessels closely resembling the Anglo-Saxon buckets still prevails in England, with the only difference that these vessels are made of tin, and that, instead of being named buckets or vats, they are simply called cans. (I may add, that Mr. Akerman has since conjectured that they may be holy-water vessels, supposing that the graves containing them were those of Christians, which I think less happy than the former explanation.)

found a gold coin, in a very perfect condition, as though it had not long left the mint, of the emperor Justin, who reigned at Constantinople from 518 to 527. We know that the early Anglo-Saxon coins, known as *sceattas*, were copied from the Roman coinage, principally from the coins of the Constantine family, which were so largely circulated in this country. These *sceattas*, which were of silver, have been found in the Kentish graves. In a grave opened by Lord Londesborough's directions, on the Breach Down, the remains of what appeared to be a small purse presented themselves, among which were four silver *sceattas*. Coins of the Merovingian dynasty of the Franks are also found, and in the Faussett collection there was one of Clovis. Setting aside all other evidence of the date to which these interments belong, the comparison of these coins is decisive. Having alluded to the presence of coins which must have been brought hither from Constantinople, I must also mention the by no means unusual occurrence of an article which we should certainly not have expected to find there, namely, cowrie shells, which I believe are only found on the shores of the Pacific. Several of these will be observed in the Faussett collection.

You will bear in mind that all I have yet said relates to the contents of the Anglo-Saxon cemeteries found in Kent, and I must now recall your attention to the particular construction of the Anglo-Saxon grave. The barrows of other peoples are generally raised above ground, without any, or with very slight excavation, and the interment was usually placed on the surface of the ground. The Anglo-Saxons, on the contrary, dug a rather deep rectan-

gular grave, sometimes small, but often of considerable dimensions; that from which Mr. Faussett
procured his largest gold fibula was six feet deep, ten
feet long, and eight feet broad, and one, at the opening of which I assisted, in Bourne park, was fourteen
feet long, more than four feet deep, and about eight feet
broad; the deposit was laid on the floor of the grave,
which was then filled up with earth, and a mound
raised above it. The pagan Saxon graves were in
fact exactly the type of our ordinary churchyard
graves, except that the mound was circular and generally larger. The circumstances of the interment are
often interesting, though they have been hitherto
less noticed than the articles found in the grave. In
general, each grave contains only a single skeleton,
but this is not always the case; and in some of the
graves at Osengell, in the Isle of Thanet, which I
assisted in opening with Mr. Rolfe, a grave contained
two, or even three, bodies. In the arrangements of
such interments I remarked evidences of domestic
sentiment of the most refined character. Where
two bodies were laid in one grave, they were generally those of a male and female, no doubt of a man
and his wife, and they were usually laid side by side,
and arm in arm, with their mouths turned towards
each other, and close together, as though taking a
last embrace. In one grave I found the bodies of a
man and his wife, and daughter, a little girl, as
appeared by the remains of her personal ornaments.
The lady lay in the middle, enfolding in her right
arm the left arm of her husband, and holding with
her other that of her daughter. We are led almost
naturally to ask, what event can thus have swept
over the homestead, to have destroyed perhaps whole

families together? for, from the appearances of the
grave, I am satisfied that in each case the whole
interment was made at once.   Perhaps it was a de-
structive pestilence ; or, when we consider that this
cemetery crowned an extensive down which overlooked the sea, it may have been equally ruthless
pirates, who, in their sudden descents on the coast,
spared neither age nor sex, leaving, on their departure,
husbands, and wives, and children, to receive interment together from the hands of those who had
escaped the scourge under which they fell.

There is another circumstance which I have remarked not unfrequently in the Kentish cemeteries,
where the mound was of any magnitude.   When the
workmen opened the mound, human bones appeared
here and there scattered about in it in a manner
which led us at first to suppose that the grave had
been opened before, and almost caused us to desist
from exploring it further.   When, however, we
opened the grave itself, we found that the original
deposit had not been disturbed, and that the few
bones found in the mound must have been deposited
there quite independent of it.   This has occurred to
me so often, that I think it cannot be accidental, and
I am inclined to believe that, at all events in certain
cases which we have not the means of knowing, it
was the practice to kill a slave or a captive, and
throw his remains into the mound as a sacrifice to
the spirit of the tenant of the tomb below.

The cemeteries in eastern Kent, lying generally
upon downs which had never been cultivated, and
where, except at Osengell, the mounds still remained
over the graves, are easily discovered, and attracted
early attention.   But in other parts of the kingdom,

where the ground has long been under the process of agriculture, and the mounds thereby entirely cleared away, the existence of Anglo-Saxon cemeteries can only be brought to light by accident. Thus, although single articles which we now know belonged to the period of the Anglo-Saxon pagan interments were met with from time to time, and found their way into museums, as odd things which nobody clearly understood, the existence of the numerous cemeteries which have since been discovered was not even suspected. When, however, the researches of Lord Londesborough called more attention to the subject, closer observation soon led, not only to the knowledge that such cemeteries had been found and destroyed, and slightly or imperfectly recorded, but to the discovery of a number of others which had never been touched. Several had been discovered years ago in Leicestershire, and a few articles found in them were engraved by Nichols. More recently, a very extensive cemetery had been broken into and destroyed at Marston Hill, in Northamptonshire, some of its contents being fortunately preserved; and previous to this, a less extensive one had been broken into at various times at Badby, in the same county. An account of the cemetery found at the former place has since been published in the " Archæologia " by Sir Henry Dryden. An extensive burial site, of a similar character, was explored by Mr. Dennett, on Chessell Down, in the Isle of Wight.

In the year 1844, a cemetery was discovered at the village of Kingston, near Derby, where, in every case, cremation had preceded interment, and where consequently, all that remained to identify the people to whom these belonged, was the pottery of the sepulchral

I.   H

urns, which was itself of an unusual character.   It was supposed generally to be British, but Mr. Roach Smith immediately suspected and afterwards satisfied himself that it was Saxon; yet I believe that for some time Mr. Smith and myself were alone in asserting its Saxon character, and even those whose belief in its British character was shaken, could only be induced to yield so far as to call it " supposed British." Subsequent comparison, however, and especially the discoveries of the Hon. Mr. Neville, have left no doubt whatever of its being purely Anglo-Saxon. This pottery, which will be best understood by the figures, is peculiar in form, and ornamented with circles, stars, lozenges, and other marks, stamped on

34. Urn, from Marston Hill,   35. Urn, from Cestersover,
        Northamptonshire.   Warwickshire.

the surface in regular order, as though with the end of a stick, and it is especially characterized by bulges or protuberances on the sides.   It has since been found more or less in most of the cemeteries in East Anglia, and it is a curious circumstance that, in Beowulf, which is understood to have been originally an Angle poem, the heroes are represented as burning their dead; so that cremation was probably the practice originally of that Teutonic tribe at least, if not of the others. A cemetery discovered near Newark contained, like that near Derby, nothing but urn-burial, and similar deposits of the Anglo-Saxon period have been found in Warwickshire.

Among the more interesting of recent discoveries I must particularise the small cemetery at Fairford, in Gloucestershire, opened by Mr. Wylie, and the very extensive ones at Great and Little Wilbraham opened by Mr. Neville. But such discoveries have become now so numerous, that it will be sufficient on this occasion to give a bare enumeration of them. We will begin with the extensive cemeteries at Great and Little Wilbraham, in Cambridgeshire; at Linton, in the same county, and at Stowe Heath, near Icklingham, in Suffolk, and others of various extent which have been opened or traced at Staunton, Aldborough, Ixworth, and Eye, in the county last mentioned; at Walsingham, and near Swaffham, in Norfolk; and at Sandby and Shefford in Bedfordshire. All these belonged to the kingdom of the East Angles. In the extensive inland district occupied by the Mercians, who were chiefly of the Angle race, cemeteries have been found at Caenby; at Castle Bytham, near Stamford; in the neighbourhood of Newark; and at Searby, near Caistor, in Lincolnshire; near Cottgrave, in the county of Nottingham; at Kingston, and in parts of the Peak, in Derbyshire; at Ingarsby, Great Wigston, Queenboroughfield, Rothley Temple, and Billesdon, in Leicestershire; near Warwick, at Churchover, and Cestersover, in Warwickshire; at Marston Hill, Badby, Hunsbury Hill, and Barrow Furlong, in Northamptonshire. Others, found near Abingdon, and at Long Wittenham and Blewbury, in Berkshire; at several places in Hampshire; at Harnham Hill, and near Devizes, in Wilts; and probably those at Fairford, and elsewhere, in Gloucestershire; at Mentmore, and Dinton, in Buckinghamshire; and at Souldern, and Cuddesden, in Oxfordshire; belong to the West Saxons. Of the Northern Angles we know only a very interesting cemetery at Driffield, in Yorkshire, and a few scattered remains which have been dug up from time to time in the north-eastern counties of England, and in the Lowlands of Scotland. A few Anglo-Saxon remains have been found in the neighbourhood of Colchester, and in some other spots in Essex, which we must, of course, ascribe to the East Saxons.

It will be seen at once by this enumeration, comparing it with what has been found and what is daily being found in the county of Kent, that there must be a great number of Anglo-Saxon cemeteries scattered over this island of which we yet know nothing. It is desirable, therefore, that we should spread abroad, as much as possible, the knowledge of these, which may only be called *our* national antiquities. From the circumstance I have impressed upon your attention,—that the discovery of a spear-head, or a sword, or of the boss of a shield, or of any other article which you know to be Saxon, is not the mere obtaining of that article itself, but is probably the indication of an extensive field of discovery, whoever finds that indication should, if possible, carefully mark the spot, and cause the ground to be trenched. It is desirable, for reasons I am going to show to you, that we should extend our knowledge of this class of antiquities as much as possible.

We learn from our oldest authority on this subject, the historian Bede, that the Teutonic settlers in this

island consisted of three different branches or tribes
of that race; the Jutes, who established themselves
in Kent, in the Isle of Wight, and on a part of the
opposite coast of Hampshire; the Saxons, who
formed the three small states of the East Saxons, the
Middle Saxons, and the South Saxons, and the far
more extensive one of the West Saxons; and the
Angles, who, as East Angles, Mercians, and North-
umbrians, occupied a still larger portion of the surface
of modern England. It becomes interesting to us to
know if there are peculiarities in the remains found
in the Anglo-Saxon graves which correspond with
the ethnological division given us by the historian,
for it is in this manner that the science of archæology
becomes serviceable to ethnology and to history.
This question will only be fully ascertained by more
extensive researches, and by careful observation;
but certain peculiarities have already been remarked
which lead us to expect that such researches will be
ultimately crowned with important results.   I have
already stated that the practice of cremation of the
dead and urn-burial distinguished the Anglian race
from the Kentish Jutes, and apparently from the
Saxons.   This practice seems, among the Angles
themselves, to have prevailed in particular districts
more than in others, which perhaps indicates smaller
divisions of race, a subject into which I will not
attempt at present to enter. You will observe in the
collection before you, that the fibulæ of the people of
Kent were almost all round, the few examples of
fibulæ of other forms found in the Kentish graves
being evidently importations. Now, when we turn
to the collections made from the graves of East
Anglia, such as that of Mr. Neville, we find the

fibulæ assuming a totally different form, which has

36. Large Fibula, from Stow
Heath.

37. Large Fibula, from Little
Wilbraham.

been termed cross-shaped, because the general out-

line is that of a single or double cross. There is a marked difference between two varieties of this fibula, the larger ones and the smaller ones; the former are sometimes of extravagant dimensions. I believe examples have been met with, nearly, if not quite, a foot in length. Both are made of bronze or copper, and the large ones, at least, have in general been highly gilt. The round fibula is rarely found in an East Anglian grave. As far as ob-

38. Small Fibula,
from Stow Heath.

servation has yet gone, these cross-shaped fibulæ prevail wherever the

Angle race settled. They were used in Mercia
certainly; indeed, some of the finest examples of the
large cross-shaped fibula have been found in Leicestershire. We are as yet but little acquainted with
the Northumbrian graves, but, as far as our knowledge goes, these same cross-shaped fibulæ, identical
both in make and ornament, are found there also.*
Again, when we look to the collections from the
graves in the West of England, from Hampshire to
Gloucestershire, we find a round fibula prevailing,
but differing in character from anything we have
seen before. From its form it has been called cup-

39. Fibulæ, from Fairford, Gloucestershire.

shaped, but saucer-shaped would perhaps give a
better description of it. It is usually of copper, gilt,
and the field is variously ornamented, not unusually
with a rude figure of a human face in the centre.

Thus we observe at the first glance, in one article
alone, a very remarkable variation in form, extending
exactly over the districts which the early historians

* Excavations made in the Isle of Wight by Mr. Hillier,
since the above was written, show that the Saxon population of
that island used a cross-shaped fibula; but it differed from that
of East Anglia, a little in the character of its ornament, and
entirely in its material, all the examples found by him being of
silver, gilt.

give as the limits of the three great branches of the
Anglo-Saxon race ; the elegantly ornamented round
fibula of gold and precious stones of the Jutes of
Kent, the cross-shaped fibula of the Angles, and the
cup-shaped fibula of the Saxons of the West. I have
no doubt that we shall gradually discover differences
in other articles equally distinctive; for as yet we
have much to learn in this class of antiquities. Several
articles have already been found of which the exact
purpose is not yet clear, and will only be ascertained
by more extensive comparison, and by the results of
future excavations. Of these I will only allude to
one, which shows us the necessity of caution in
guessing at the meaning of things we do not understand. A curious implement had been from time to
time found with Anglo-Saxon remains in different

40. Object, from Little
Wilbraham.

parts of Anglia and Mercia.
It was conjectured that these
articles might be latch-keys,
and they were commonly set
down as such; but there is
nothing in their appearance
to lead us to any distinct
notion of the purpose for
which they were intended,
and they had been obtained
so carelessly that it was not
observed that they usually
occur in pairs. At length
a discovery was made at
Searby near Caistor, in Lincolnshire, which at least
helped us forward a step in
explaining it. Two of these so-called latch-keys were

found fixed together with a bow of metal. From this moment it became quite evident that they were not keys. Numerous pairs of these articles, one of which is represented in the annexed figure, have since been found at Little Wilbraham, and may be seen in Mr. Neville's (now lord Braybrooke) Museum, and from the position in which they appear to have lain, and other circumstances connected with them, I believe that Mr. Roach Smith has hit upon the right explanation, namely, that they are the tops or handles to bags or purses, or to *châtelaines,* which were pendent to the girdles of the Anglian and Mercian ladies. Here, then, we have another article of costume peculiar in form to the Angles, and not found in the same shape among the Jutes or the Saxons.

It is thus that, in these researches, as new discoveries are made, we arrive step by step at truth. I will mention one other, and a very remarkable instance of the errors which are apt to arise from careless observation, and of the necessity of extensive comparison. On the Continent, as in England, Teutonic graves had from time to time been accidentally opened, and articles taken from them had found their way singly into museums, where they were looked upon as a sort of nondescripts. A Prussian collector named Houben, at Xanten, the site of a

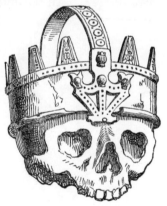

41. From Xanten, in Prussia.

Roman station in the Rhenish provinces, in a book
on the antiquities of that site published in 1839,
engraved a skull with the brow encircled by a bronze
crown, which had been found in a grave with articles of undoubted Teutonic character.   There was
something so romantic in the idea of this grim old
king of the Teutons, whose love of royalty was so
great that he carried his crown with him even into
the tomb, that no one dreamt of doubting the truth
of Houben's statement.   So much indeed were scholars thrown off their guard by it, that one of the
most distinguished of the French antiquaries of the
present day, the Abbé Cochet, having obtained from
a Frankish cemetery in the valley of the Eaulne a
hoop of a not dissimilar character, was inclined at
first to adopt the explanation hazarded by the person
who took it out of the earth, that it was a " *coiffure
ou couronne.*" The correct explanation, however, had
already been given by Mr. Roach Smith in his *Collectanea Antiqua.*   All the different parts of the sup-

posed crown and coif-
fure had indeed been
found in Anglo-Saxon
graves   in   different
parts of England, and
all more or less con-
nected with the re-
mains of buckets.   In
fact you will recognize
the principal ornament
of   Houben's   crown
among the fragments
in the Faussett collec-
tion, in a portion of a

42. From Kingston Down, Kent.

bucket found in a grave on Kingston Down, repre-

sented in Fig. 42. A similar ornament was pointed out
by Mr. Roach Smith as
having been found on
Stowe Heath; and one
still more closely re-
sembling it, found in a
Frankish grave at Douv-
rend, in the department
of the Seine-Inférieure,
is given by the Abbé
Cochet, and is repre-
sented in our Fig. 43.
In the learned Abbé's
later work, *Le Tombeau
de Childéric I*er,—a book
which ought to be in the

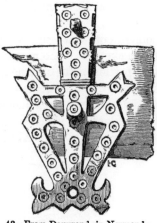

43. From Douvrend, in Normandy.

hand of every student of our national antiquities,—he

44. From Envermeu, in Normandy.

has given us another example, found in a Frankish
cemetery at Envermeu in Normandy, and represented
in our cut, Fig. 44.   Other examples have since been
pointed out, which shows that this ornamental part of
the bucket was by no means uncommon. Lastly, another portion of the ornamentation of Houben's crown,
the triangular ornaments round the rim, were pointed
out by Mr. Smith in a bucket found at Wilbraham in
Cambridgeshire, which is represented in our cut, Fig.
45. More recently, the Abbé Cochet has entirely satis-

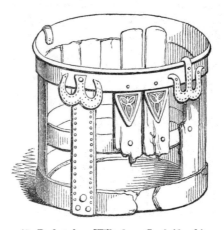

45. Bucket, from Wilbraham, Cambridgeshire.

fied himself of the correctness of Mr. Roach Smith's
explanation, by the discovery, in a Frankish grave at
Envermeu in Normandy, of a bucket nearly entire,
with precisely the same ornament as that of the supposed coiffure found in the valley of the Eaulne.
The Abbé has given an engraving of this bucket in
the second edition of his most interesting and valuable work, *La Normandie Souterraine,* which by his

kind loan I am enabled to reproduce here, (Fig. 46.)

46. Bucket, from Envermeu, Normandy.

A comparison with the Teutonic remains in our
island has thus solved the riddle.   This crown of
the German king, this *coiffure* of the Frank, were
neither more nor less than the rims of buckets, such
as are found not uncommonly in the cemeteries of
Kent and East Anglia.   One of Houben's diggers
had no doubt put the rim of the bucket on the skull,
to mystify his employer.

Unfortunately, until very recently, scarcely anything has been done in investigating the remains of
the Teutonic tribes on the Continent which answer
to those of the Anglo-Saxon cemeteries.   The barrows of the districts which were occupied by the
Jutes, Saxons, and Angles, before they came hither,

and which therefore must possess so great an interest
for us, are I believe altogether unexplored.   For
Germany, the only book to which I can point, which
is a very valuable one, is the account of the Teutonic
cemetery at Selzen on the Rhine, published by the
brothers Lindenschmit in 1848.   A similar cemetery
near Lausanne in Switzerland has been explored by
M. Troyon; and we have been made acquainted with
the contents of the Frankish cemeteries in France
by the labours of M. Baudot, Doctor Rigollot, and
especially by the Abbé Cochet in his work, *La Normandie Souterraine,* already mentioned.   The discoveries of the brothers Lindenschmit and of the Abbé
Cochet are of particular interest to us in regard to
our Anglo-Saxon cemeteries, with which the interments at Selzen are as nearly as possible identical.
I will merely observe that, if there had remained
any doubt as to the pottery found near Derby and
in other parts of Mercia and East Anglia being of
the Saxon period, it would have been entirely dis-
pelled by a comparison with that found at Selzen;
and point out the complete identity between the
Saxon and German glass.   The various forms of
drinking cups, as well as their ornamentation, are the
same in England and in Germany.   The example to
which I will call your attention is one of a very remarkable kind.   In several parts of England, examples have been found of a singularly shaped glass
vessel, ornamented externally with knobs of the same
material.   One of these has been found by Mr. Wylie,
in Gloucestershire, and is figured in his book on the
Fairford Graves; another has been found in the
county of Durham; and Mr. Joseph Clarke has the
fragment of a third found in Hampshire.   There is a

fourth in the Faussett collection; and a fifth, which was found near Reculver, in the museum at Canterbury. One of these same glasses was found in a Teutonic grave at Selzen; and another, engraved by

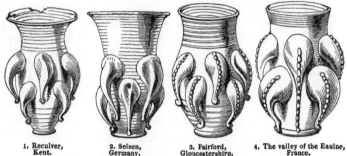

1. Reculver, Kent.   2. Selzen, Germany.   3. Fairford, Gloucestershire.   4. The valley of the Eaulne, France.

47. Anglo-Saxon, Old German, and Frankish Glasses.

48. From Ashford, Kent.

the Abbé Cochet, was met with in the Frankish cemetery in the valley of the Eaulne. Another example, of much larger dimensions, and much longer in its proportions,—for it is nine inches and a half high, by three and three quarters at the top, and only one and three quarters at the bottom, was found at Ashford, in Kent, and is represented in our cut, Fig. 48. The identity of these glasses, as well as of the drinking glasses of the more usual forms, is so complete, that I believe they must have all come from the same manufactories; and I think it probable that the Anglo-Saxons and the Franks at this early period ob-

tained their glass from works at Mayence and along
the Rhine.   I would further observe that I have
seen vessels of glass which were dug up at Mayence,
and were evidently of very late Roman manufacture,
which displayed many of the peculiar characteristics
of the glass found in the Teutonic graves.   On the
other hand, the cemetery at Selzen presents examples
of jewellery and goldsmith's work of such a character
as would lead us to suppose it was brought from
Kent.   The Frankish cemeteries are interesting to
us because they show us whence a few articles of
rarer occurrence in the Kentish graves were procured, such as the battle-axe, or *francisque*, a particular shaped long fibula, and the few examples of
burial urns.   I give here an example of the form of

49. Battle-axe, from Londinières, Normandy.

the first of these articles which seems to have been
most common among the Franks—it was found by
the Abbé Cochet at Londinières on the river Eaulne.
Axes identical in form with this have been found in
Kent; but they are of rare occurrence, and evidently
could not in this country be called a national weapon.
The fibulæ to which I allude are very peculiar in
form, and evidently belong to the Continent, though
a small number of examples have been found in England, chiefly in Kent.   One of the examples here
given (1) is from Osengell in the isle of Thanet; the
other (2) is from Selzen in Germany.   Their identity

of character strikes us at once; and it is remarkable

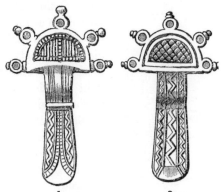

1.   2.
50. Fibulæ, from Osengell and Selzen.

that this is a prevailing form of fibula in the Frankish graves. I have already alluded to the urns in
the Faussett collection; a comparison of the examples found by the Abbé Cochet in the cemetery
in the valley of the Eaulne, will enable us to satisfy
ourselves of their perfect identity with the few Kentish urns, and it is probable indeed that the latter
were imported from France. At all events, they
differ much from the Anglian urns, of which we have
given examples before. In these Frankish urns we
can trace an evident, though rude, attempt to imitate
the ornamentation of Roman pottery, and in some
instances we have even a copy, more or less perfect,
of the well-known egg-and-tongue pattern. The latter is sometimes intermixed with other forms in a
very incongruous manner, as will be seen in an example which I give (Fig. 51) from Mr. Roach Smith's
Collectanea Antiqua. All these circumstances can
leave no doubt in our minds of the intimate intercourse between the Franks and the Kentish Saxons.

To return, then, to Kent, and to the collection which is now before us, —as little as the subject has yet been really studied, it already begins to throw a considerable light on the condition of the Anglo-Saxons in England before the period of their conversion to Christianity; after which, only, we begin to know them from history.

51. A Frankish Urn.

The Kentish graves, abounding in ornaments of gold and silver and other jewellery, and containing many articles indicating social refinement, show a people who were rich and powerful, far more so than the other Anglo-Saxon states, where the precious metals are rarely found, and the gold ornaments are replaced by gilt bronze; and this explains to us the high position held by Kent towards the other states at the dawn of our Anglo-Saxon history. Cowrie shells, brought from the Indian ocean, money from Constantinople and from France, glass from the interior of Germany, all these prove an extensive commerce, the origin and accompaniment of national prosperity.

I need not say, after these considerations, that the study of the interesting objects now exhibited to you is one of national importance, and that the collection made by Bryan Faussett ought to be considered as, in the highest sense of the term, a national monument. I cannot therefore help sharing largely in the regret, felt by I believe every Englishman who has reflected on the subject, at the manner in which this collection has been rejected by the trustees of our great national museum, and for the sort of an excuse which was made for that rejection, when its propriety was questioned in the House of Commons. It was not only from being transferred to the Continent, or from passing into the hands of some other collector, that this collection was saved by the intelligent zeal of Mr. Mayer; for I have reasons to believe that Mr. Mayer actually stepped in between the British Museum and a public auction room, and that if he had not purchased them, the whole collection might now have been scattered in small lots, all over the world. I must add that we are about to receive from that gentleman a benefit for which we might probably have looked in vain but for the chance which threw the collection into his hands.* Mr. Mayer is already proceeding with the publication of the whole of the Faussett manuscripts, to be illustrated with engravings of the articles forming this collection, and he has wisely placed it under the editorial care of an antiquary whom I consider as the most capable of all our scholars to perform such a task effectually, Mr. Roach Smith. The study of Anglo-Saxon antiquities, and consequently the knowledge of the subject, are evidently extending themselves, and several works of great interest on particular cemeteries have been published by the zeal of individuals. I need only mention the " Fairford Graves," by Mr. Wylie, and the cemetery of Great Wilbraham, by Mr. Neville. I will take this opportunity, too, of calling attention particularly to the

* Now published; see before, the note on p. 120.

praiseworthy undertaking of one of our well-known
antiquaries, Mr. Akerman, who is publishing in numbers, under the title of " Remains of Pagan Saxondom," a series of miscellaneous articles from cemeteries in different parts of the country, which is highly
deserving of the encouragement I trust it has received, and will form a very useful collection of examples.   But all these works sink in importance
before Bryan Faussett's Journal of his Excavations.
Whatever his antiquarian knowledge may have been,
Faussett was a most careful observer and most faithful recorder of what he observed; and I can venture
to announce that everybody who understands the
subject will be astonished at the quantity of valuable
facts which will be placed before the world by the
publication of these manuscripts.

SUPPLEMENTARY NOTES TO THE FOREGOING ESSAY.

NOTE (to p. 121) ON THE USE OF BOWS AND ARROWS AMONG THE ANGLO-SAXONS.

IN a paper in the 34th volume of the Archæologia, Mr. Aker-man has stated the opinion that the bow was a despised im-plement among the Anglo-Saxons, and that they did not use it as a weapon of war; and as on other occasions he has since re-peated this, as though it were an acknowledged fact, and the statement appears to a certain degree under the authority of the Society of Antiquaries, perhaps I may be permitted to offer a remark or two on the subject. In the first place I would observe, that I cannot understand any people despising or neglecting so formidable a weapon as the bow if they were acquainted with the use of it, and that it was well known to the Anglo-Saxons we can have no doubt, since our English names, *bow* and *arrow*, are words belonging to the Anglo-Saxon language; and the fact of these words having been preserved in the language shows that the use of the things they designate was derived from the Saxons and not from the Normans, other-wise we should doubtless have called them *arks* and *fletches*.

Mr. Akerman quotes the following lines from the celebrated Exeter Book (p. 341, Thorpe's edit.), where they form part of a collection of gnomic verses—

scyld sceal cempan,	a shield shall be for the soldier,
sceaft reafere,	a shaft for the robber,
sceal bryde beag.	a ring for the bride.

And he seems to imagine that this proves that the Saxons held the arrow in contempt, as a weapon only to be used by robbers. Mr. Akerman also gives from the same book several passages, illustrating, as he supposes, the use of the Saxon *gar* as a javelin thrown by the hand. One of these, taken from a religious poem (p. 42), runs as follows—

þon gar-getrum	when the gar shower
ofer scild-hreadan	over the shield's defence
sceotend sendað.	warriors send.

I will only remark on the first of these passages, that, although no doubt the bow was the best weapon for a robber, who naturally wished to kill his victim at a distance, yet it does not at all follow as an inference that it must be despised by other people. If we alter the words to make the sentiment applicable to modern times, and say, " a pistol for the highway-man," which would be equally true, should we be justified in inferring from this that the pistol is a weapon that Englishmen hold in contempt?

In the second of these extracts, Mr. Akerman has been led into an error by Mr. Thorpe's English translation. It is true enough that the Anglo-Saxon *sceotend* may be translated in general language a *warrior*, but it signified a warrior of a par-ticular class; in fact it is the substantive of the word *sceotan*, to shoot, and is the Anglo-Saxon word for *an archer.* Moreover, Mr. Akerman has given us, somehow or other, a mutilated sentence, the remaining words of which would have gone far towards setting him right. The passage should have been read and translated thus :—

þonne gar-getrum	when the shower of shafts
ofer scild-hreadan	over the shield's defence
sceotend sendaðˇ,	the archers send,
flacor flan-geweorc.	quivering arrow-work.

Indeed, I can hardly imagine anybody reading the poetry of the Exeter Book, even slightly, and leaving it with anything but the conviction that the people for whom it was composed were well acquainted with the use of bows and arrows. It must be remembered that the language of this poetry is often figurative, and in such language the images are naturally taken from objects with which people were most familiar. It is sin-gular enough, that in the same gnomic poem from which Mr. Akerman takes the first of the foregoing extracts, and only a few lines further on (p. 343), the poet, speaking of the natural fitness of things to each other, says—

| boga sceal stræle, | a bow shall have an arrow. |

Again, in a poem on the endowments of men (p. 296), we are told that

| sum biðˇ rynig, | one is a runner ; |
| sum ryht scytte. | another a sure archer. |

And a little further on we are informed that another

.... scyldes rond	.... the disc of a shield
fæste gefegan	makes firmly
wið flyge gares.	against the arrow's flight.

I think there can be little doubt that these terms *quivering* or *flickering*, and *flying*, have reference to the feathers on the arrow. The idea found in other passages, of the arrows coming in *showers*, will be well understood as applied to a discharge of archery in a battle. The epithets in the following passage (from the Exeter Book, p. 326), are expressive and peculiarly characteristic of an arrow's flight—

Ful oft of þam heape	full oft from that troop
hwinende fleag	whining flew
giellende gar	the yelling arrow
on grome þeode.	on the fierce nation.

Again, in the same religious poem from which Mr. Akerman gives the second illustration I have quoted from him, and only a little further on (p. 47), we meet with the following passage :—

He his áras þonan	He his angels thence
halig of heahðum	holy from above
hider onsendeð,	will send hither,
þa ús gescildaþ	who shall shield us
wið sceþþendra	against the enemies'
englum earhfarum ;	noxious quivers;
þi læs unholdan	lest the fiends
wunde gewyrcen,	inflict a wound,
þonne wroht-bora	when the accuser
in folc Godes	among God's people
forð onsendeð,	sendeth forth
of his brægd-bogan	from his bended bow
biterne stræl ;	the bitter arrow ;
forþon we fæste sculon	therefore we should firmly
wið þam fær-scyte, &c.	against that sudden shot, &c.

Here we have a distinct image of hostilities in which one party drawing their arrows (*gares*) from their quivers (literally, arrow-cases), shoot them from bended bows into the midst of the other party—which in fact is exactly analogous to the passage immediately preceding, taken from a poem describing historical events (the song of the scop or minstrel). I will only give one other example—it is taken from the Legend of St. Guthlac (p. 170), and is part of the description of the progress of a mortal disease—

com se seofeð́a dæg	The seventh day came
ældum andweard	present to mortals
þæs þe him ingesonc,	since that into him penetrated,
hat heortan neah,	hot near the heart,
hilde scurum	in battle showers, (i.e. *showers of arrows such as occur in a battle*,)
flacor flan-þracu.	the quivering arrow's force.

Surely, with these extracts taken only out of one volume, nobody will tell us again that the Anglo-Saxons were not well acquainted with the use of bows and arrows in war. I may add that Alfric, in his Vocabulary, gives, among his list of arms (*nomina armorum*), *fla* (an arrow), *boga* (a bow), and *boġanstreng* (a bow-string). I have no doubt whatever that some of the smaller iron blades we find in Saxon graves are the heads of arrows—they are too small for javelins; but all doubt is quite set at rest by the recent researches of Mr. Hillier in the Anglo-Saxon cemetery in the Isle of Wight, where he has found not only unmistakeable arrow-heads, but the remains of the bows. A bundle of arrow-heads, I believe about a dozen, was found in one grave opened by Faussett.

NOTE (to p. 147) ON THE ETHNOLOGY OF THE ANGLO-SAXONS.

The Anglo-Saxon historians have left us a very straightforward account of the great ethnological divisions of their race, and as far as we have yet gone in this line of research the difference in the articles found in Anglo-Saxon cemeteries, in different parts of the island, corresponds with it; but the exact geographical limits are not so easily fixed, and, in fact, they no doubt varied at different periods. The limits of the Kentish Jutes are clearly defined, and the same may be said of the South Saxons, the Middle Saxons, and the East Saxons; and to some degree of the Northumbrian Angles. It would not, however, be so easy to fix the exact boundary line inland of the East Angles or of the Middle Angles of Lincolnshire; and the

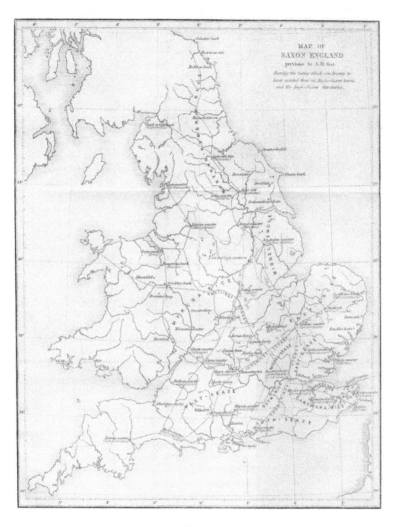

The material originally positioned here is too large for reproduction in this reissue. A PDF can be downloaded from the web address given on page iv of this book, by clicking on 'Resources Available'.

boundary of the Mercians was continually varying. It must be
understood that I am speaking of the Mercians of the age
previous to their conversion, of the history of which we are
really ignorant. We learn from the Saxon Chronicle, that in
the year 571, the west Saxons under Cuthwulf took from the
Britons the towns of Bedcan-ford (Bedforda), Lygean-byrg
(Lenbury), Ægeles-byrg (Aylesbury), Bænesing-tun (Benson),
and Egonesham (Eynesham); that in 577, under Cuthwine
and Ceawlin, they defeated the Britons at Deorham, and
obtained possession of Bath, Cirencester, and Gloucester; that
in 584 they defeated the Britons at Fethan-lea (which has
been conjectured to be Frethorne, on the Severn), and
took "many towns;" and we know that they subsequently
extended their conquests to the Wye. It is not till 628
that we find the Mercians invading the frontiers of the
West Saxons, and fighting a battle with them at Cirencester.
I think, therefore, that in treating of the pagan period we may
consider the kingdom of Wessex as including the modern
counties of Bedford, Buckingham, Oxford, and Gloucester, and
perhaps also part of Worcestershire and Herefordshire, and
that the population of those districts are really Saxon and not
Angle. This is a consideration which must not be lost sight
of in our classification of the early Anglo-Saxon remains; and
it is upon it that I have given the limit between the west
Saxons and the Mercians in the map of Saxon-England during
the pagan period which accompanies this paper. The Mercians
appear to have pushed forth from Lincolnshire in a western and
south-western direction, and so to have reached the borders of
Wales at a very early period, after which they began to extend
their conquests towards the south.

The distribution of the cemeteries, as marked by the small
crosses in this map, is far from uninteresting; but the discoveries hitherto made have been in most cases so accidental,
that it would be premature to draw any inferences from it.
However, as I suspect the presence of these cemeteries marks
generally the seat of what we might, perhaps, call the more
aristocratic part of the race, that is, of those who were buried
together with the greatest ceremony, their position has, to a
certain degree, an historical importance. As far as we yet
know, the mass of the great cemeteries of the Jutish race lay in
east Kent, on the sea-coast from Hythe to Ramsgate, and along
the banks of the Thames; the cemeteries of the east Angles lay

in and on the borders of Cambridgeshire ; those of the Mercians especially in Leicestershire. It is rather a peculiarity of the Peak of Derbyshire that the Saxon barrows there are not found in cemeteries, but in single scattered tumuli, and that district may have been occupied by a peculiar tribe, or by a mining people, who, though not Saxons, adopted Saxon manners. They have been found rather in a similar way scattered over the Downs of Sussex. The discoveries in other parts of the country are as yet too few to allow us to form any judgment of the peculiarities in their position. The following is, as nearly as I have been able to make it, a complete list of the Anglo-Saxon cemeteries of the pagan period which have hitherto been discovered. The numbers refer to the map.

KENT.

1. Chartham Down.
2. Kingston Down.
3. Gilton, in the parish of Ash.
4. Coombe, in the parish of Wednesborough.
5. Sibertswold.
6. Barfreston Down.
7. Wingham.
8. Minster, in Thanet.
9. Osengell, in Thanet.
10. St. Margaret's, near Dover.
11. Between Folkestone and Dover.
12. Folkestone.
13. Barham.
14. Bourne Park.
15. Sittingbourne.
16. Chatham Lines.
17. Rochester.
18. Strood.
19. Northfleet.
20. Greenwich.
21. Reculver.

EAST SAXONS.

22. Colchester.

EAST ANGLES.

23. Linton Heath, Cambridgeshire.
24. Great Wilbraham, Cambridgeshire.
25. Little Wilbraham, Cambridgeshire.
26. Stowe Heath, Suffolk.
27. Staunton, Suffolk.
28. Aldborough, Suffolk.
29. Tostock, near Ixworth, Suffolk.
30. Eye, Suffolk.
31. Near Bungay, Suffolk.
32. Near Swaffham, Norfolk.
33. Walsingham, Norfolk.
34. Markeshall, near Norwich.

WEST SAXONS.

35. Harnam, near Salisbury.
36. Roundway Down, near Devizes, Wilts.
37. Fairford, Gloucestershire.
38. ———, Gloucestershire.
39. Near Abingdon, Berkshire.
40. Long Wittenham, Berkshire.
41. Blewbury, Berkshire.
42. Cuddesden, Oxfordshire.

WEST SAXONS (*continued*).

43. Souldern, Oxfordshire.
44. Mentmore, Buckingham-
shire.
45. Dinton, Buckingham-
shire.
46. Sandby, Bedfordshire.
47. Shefford, Bedfordshire.

ISLE OF WIGHT.

48. Chessell Down.
49. ————

MERCIA AND THE MIDDLE
ANGLES.

50. Caenby, Lincolnshire.
51. Castle Bytham, Lincolnshire.
52. Near Newark, Lincoln-
shire.
53. Searby, near Caistor,
Lincolnshire.
54. Syston Park, Lincoln-
shire.
55. Near Cottgrave, Not-
tinghamshire.
56. Kingston, near Derby.
57. Winster, in the Peak.
58. Middleton Moor, Peak.
59. Haddon field.
60. Brassington, Peak.
61. Standlow, near Dovedale.
62. Cowlow, near Buxton.
63. Ingarsby, Leicestershire.

MERCIA AND THE MIDDLE
ANGLES (*continued*).

64. Great Wigston, Leicestershire.
65. Queenborough field, Leicestershire.
66. Rothley Temple, Leicestershire.
67. Billesdon Coplow, Leicestershire.
68. Husband's Bosworth, Leicestershire.
69. Parish of St. Nicholas,
Warwick.
70. Near Warwick.
71. Cestersover, near Rugby,
Warwickshire.
72. Churchover, Warwickshire.
73. Marston Hill, Northamptonshire.
74. Badby, Northamptonshire.
75. Hunsbury Hill, Northamptonshire.
76. Barrow Furlong, Northamptonshire.
77. Welford, Northampton-
shire.

THE ANGLES NORTH OF THE
HUMBER.

78. South Cave, Yorkshire.
79. Great Driffield, Yorkshire.
80. Near Rudstone, Yorkshire.
81. Castle Eden, Durham.

VIII

ON THE TRUE CHARACTER OF THE
BIOGRAPHER ASSER.

N using Asser's "Life of king Alfred" as the groundwork of a biographical sketch of that monarch, some doubts arose in my mind as to the authenticity and character of that well-known work, which were communicated to the Society of Antiquaries in the following paper. It is an important question, because it affects one of the most interesting periods of our national history; and I hope that these observations may lead to a more thorough investigation of the question. It will be borne in mind that the book in question purports to be a life of king Alfred, written in the 45th year of his age (*i. e.* A.D. 893 or 894), by his intimate friend bishop Asser.

I think no person can read Asser's "Life of Alfred" without observing that it consists of two distinct parts; of a chronology of events arranged year by year, on which are engrafted a few anecdotes of Alfred's private life, and of an eulogy of his character. The first of these portions, which is the strictly historical part, will be found on comparison to be nothing more than a translation of the Saxon Chronicle. I

ON THE BIOGRAPHER ASSER.   173

might point out, as remarkable examples of this fact, the entries in the years 867, 869, 870, 871, &c.; but I will only instance here the brief entry in the year 874, which stands as follows in the Chronicle :—

An. DCCCLXXIV.   Her for se here from Lindesse to Hreope-dune, 7 þær winter-setl nam, 7 þone cyning Burhred ofer sæ adræfden, ymb twa 7 xx. winter þæs þe he rice hæfde, and þ lond eall ge-eodon.   And he for to Rome, and þær ge-sæt to his lifes ende, and his lic liᵹ on sc'a Marian cyrican on Angel-cynnes scole.   And ᵹy ylcan geare hie sealdon Ceolwulfe, anum unwisum cyninges þegne, Myrcna rice to heal-danne, and he him aᵹas swor, and gislas seald, þ hit him gearo wære swa hwilce dæge swa hie hit habban woldon, 7 he gearo wære mid him sylfum, 7 mid eallum þam þe him læstan woldon, to þæs heres þearfe.

"Here went the army from Lindesse to Hreope-dune, and there took its winter-quarters, and *they drove over sea the* king Burhred, about two-and-twenty years after he had the kingdom, and overcame all that land.   And he went to Rome, and there remained till his life's end, and his body lieth in St. Mary's church in the school of the Angles.   And the same year they gave to Ceolwulf, *an unwise thane of the king,* the kingdom of Mercia to hold, and he swore oaths to them, and gave hostages, that it should be ready for them *on whatever day they would have it,* and that he would be ready with himself, and with all that would remain with him, to be at the service of the army."

In Asser's Latin the entry for the same year is as follows :—

"Anno dominicæ incarnationis 874, nativitatis

autem Ælfredi regis 25, supra memoratus sæpe exercitus Lindissig deserens, Merciam adiit, et hyemavit in loco qui dicitur Hreopedune. Burghredum quoque Merciorum regem regnum suum *deserere et ultra mare exire* et Romam adire contra voluntatem suam coegit, 22 regni sui anno. Qui postquam Romam adierat, non diu vivens ibidem [de]functus est, et in schola Saxonum in ecclesia sanctæ Mariæ honorifice sepultus adventum Domini et primam cum justis resurrectionem expectat. Pagani quoque post ejus expulsionem totum Merciorum regnum suo dominio subdiderunt. Quod tamen miserabili conditione *cuidam insipienti ministro regis* (ejus nomen erat Ceolwulf) eodem pacto custodiendum commendaverunt, *ut qualicunque die illud vellent habere* iterum, pacifice illis assignaret, quibus in eadem cognitione obsides dedit, et juravit, nullo modo se voluntati eorum contradicere velle, sed obediens in omnibus esse." p. 8.

It is, I think, impossible to deny that one of these accounts is taken verbatim from the other. It is improbable that Asser should be the original, because in his narrative the yearly entries contain many things which are irrelevant to the subject, and they have there a remarkable appearance of " patch-work," while in the Saxon Chronicle they are perfectly in their place, in entire harmony with what goes before and with what follows.

Now if these entries are taken from the Saxon Chronicle, it is impossible that they can have been written so early as 894, because by the most favourable supposition that has been hazarded on the antiquity of this part of the Chronicle, it was not composed before the beginning of the tenth century, and it is more than probable that it is a work of a later period.*

With regard to the other portion of the work, the biographical matter interwoven with the chronological entries, I confess that it does not appear to me to embrace the kind of information to be expected from Alfred's friend and contemporary. Let any one read Eginhard's "Life of Charlemagne," and compare it with the dry chronicles of the time, he will find facts told by the biographer with the vigour and spirit of a man who was active and interested in them, accompanied with vivid sketches and clear views of the policy and character of that great monarch. When we turn to Asser, we seem to have a writer who would fain imitate the biographer of the Frankish emperor, but who only knows the history of his hero from one bare chronicle, and depends upon popular traditions for his views of his personal character.

There is clearly much that is legendary and not historically true in Asser's account of Alfred. I am inclined to doubt the truth of the alleged neglect which, according to Asser, had been shown to Alfred's education in his infancy. We know that his father king Ethelwolf was an accomplished scholar, that he had been an ecclesiastic before he came to the throne, that his friends and advisers were ecclesiastics, such as Swithun and Alstan, the former of whom at least was a scholar, that he was a great patron of the clergy

* I do not think that there is any substantial reason for attributing a part of the Anglo-Saxon Chronicle to Plegmund. But, even supposing the entries during the greater part of the reign of Alfred to have been contemporary, it is quite improbable that such a man as Asser should use them in the way they are used in the "Life of Alfred."

and of the church, that Alfred (his favourite child) was twice carried to Rome before he was six years of age:—is it probable that under such circumstances the royal youth would be left to pick up his first scraps of learning, after he was advanced beyond the common age of receiving such instruction, by the caprice of accident? or is it not much more likely that he derived the thirst for knowledge, which distinguished his after life, from the teaching and example of the learned men whom he had seen at his father's court?

At page 5, the writer of this book quotes the oral authority of Alfred, in a very ostentatious manner, for the story of Offa's wife Eadburgha, which must have been familiar to the ears of every inhabitant of Alfred's dominions. Yet a little further on, when he arrives at what was one of the most important events of Alfred's life, his pretended destitution in the isle of Athelney, which one would suppose Asser must have had many occasions of hearing from the king's own mouth, all that he has to add to the words of the Saxon Chronicle he professes to take from a legendary life of St. Neot! I am aware that the passage relating to the adventure of Alfred with the neat-herd's wife is considered to be an interpolation, and that it was omitted in what appears to have been the oldest MS. But by giving up the passage omitted in the manuscript, we do not get rid of the allusion to the story, or of the reference to the authority of St. Neot's life, for the oldest MS. contained the words, " Et, ut in vita sancti patris Neoti legitur, apud quendam suum vaccarium," and there is, moreover, in this book a second reference to the same authority. Now it is my opinion that no life of St. Neot existed in the time of the real Asser, but that the lives of that Saint were first composed later on in the tenth century, perhaps not till his name was made famous by the violent dispute about the possession of his relics, at the time of their felonious translation from Cornwall to Huntingdonshire, in the year 974.

The second reference to the authority of the Life of St. Neot also relates to what is perhaps a legendary part of Alfred's history, namely, the unknown disease under which he is said to have laboured. At page 12, the writer, with the Life of Neot before him, states that he suffered under this disease from the twentieth year of his age until he had passed his fortieth year—"quod (proh dolor!) pessimum est, tantam diuturnitatem a 20 ætatis suæ anno usque 40 et eo amplius annum per tanta annorum curricula incessanter protelasse,"—at which time, when hunting in Cornwall, he came to the shrine of St. Neot, where he humiliated himself in prayer, and was miraculously and *radically* cured—" Sed quodam tempore divino nutu antea cum Cornubiam venandi causa adiret, et ad quandam ecclesiam orandi causa divertisset, in qua sanctus Gueryr requiescit, et nunc etiam sanctus Neotus ibidem pausat, sublevatus est. . . . . Oratione autem finita cœptum iter arripuit, et non multo post tempore, ut in oratione deprecatus fuerat, se ab illo dolore medicatum esse divinitus sensit, ita ut *funditus eradicaretur.*" Yet, after so explicit a statement that the king had been cured of his disease, we find the writer a little further on, at page 17, asserting that he still laboured under it at the time the book was written, and that he had never experienced even a short intermission of relief.— " Nam a 20 ætatis anno usque ad 45 *quem nunc agit,* gravissima incogniti doloris infestatione incessanter fatigatus, ita, ut *ne unius quidem horæ securitatem habeat,* qua aut illam infirmitatem non sustineat, aut sub illius formidine lugubriter prope constitutus non desperet." I can with difficulty be brought to believe that king Alfred's friend bishop Asser could have made so much confusion.

With the few contemporary documents preserved from the ravages of time, it is impossible to test in a satisfactory manner the historical accuracy of that part of the account of Alfred which we owe solely to the writer of this book. I think it would not be difficult to point out one or two passages which are of a kind to excite suspicion, but I will only mention one. Under A.D. 877, Asser says: " Tunc rex Ælfredus jussit cymbas et galeas, id est, *longas naves,* fabricari per regnum : "—I suspect that this is an allusion to the *long ships* which Alfred caused to be constructed, not in 877, but in 897, (as we learn from the Saxon Chronicle,) long after the book from which we are quoting is supposed to have been written. I would add, that I think I can sometimes detect the writer forgetting his assumed character for a moment, and speaking of things as though he were living long after the time at which they occurred. At the period when the book is pretended to have been written, Alfred must have been occupied in the midst of all the reforms he was introducing into his kingdom, and particularly those which affected the administration of justice : I can hardly think that a person writing at the time, and avowedly closing his work with that time, and, moreover, *addressing it to Alfred himself,* would have written thus :—" *Erat* namque *rex ille* in exequendis judiciis, sicut in cæteris aliis omnibus

rebus, discretissimus indagator; nam omnia pene
totius suæ regionis judicia, quæ in absentia sua *fiebant,*
sagaciter investig*abat,* qualia *fierent,* &c." I think it
impossible that a person would speak of a king of the
country in which he was writing, during his reign,
and in a work addressed to that king, as *rex ille.* It
would be used rather by a person who was speaking
of a king long since dead, and who would distinguish
him from those who came before or after him.

Many of Asser's anecdotes are not only evidently
legendary, but they are extremely puerile. When
we are expecting some remarkable proof of the great
genius of Alfred, this writer tells us seriously that
the pious monarch, long grieved that the candles
offered in his churches should not burn steadily because the wind penetrated through the crevices of
the doors and windows, and caused a current of air
in the interior, at length hit upon the *wonderful* idea
of making horn lanterns to put over them!—" ex-
cogitavit, unde talem ventorum sufflationem prohibere
potuisset, consilioque *artificiose* atque *sapienter* invento, lanternam ex lignis et bovinis cornibus pul-
cherrime construere imperavit. *Bovina namque cor-
nua alba, ac in una tenuiter dolabris erasa, non minus
vitreo vasculo elucent.* Quæ itaque lanterna *mira-
biliter* ex lignis et cornibus, ut ante diximus, facta,
noctuque candela in eam missa, exterius ut interius
tam lucida ardebat, nullis ventorum flaminibus im-
pedita; quia valvam ad ostium illius lanternæ ex
cornibus idem fieri imperaverat."

There is another remarkable circumstance connected with Asser's narrative,—he says nothing of
Alfred's writings. Yet it was probably between 890
and 894 that the king translated the Pastorale of St.

Gregory into Anglo-Saxon, and distributed it among his bishops, in the preface to which work he says he translated it "sometimes word for word, sometimes meaning for meaning, even as I learnt them of Pleg- mund my archbishop, and of *Asser my bishop*, and of Grimbold my mass-priest, and of John my mass- priest,"—Swa swa ic hi ge-leornode æt Plegmunde minum ærcebiscope, 7 æt Assere minum biscope, 7 æt Grimbolde minum mæsse-preoste, 7 æt Johanne minum mæsse-preoste.

It is clear, from what has been just said, either that Alfred's translation of the Pastorale was made after the year 894, or that the writer of " Asser's Life of Alfred " believed such to have been the case, for it is not possible that, if Asser's book be authentic, and the Pastorale had been translated before the time in which it was written, Asser should have been ignorant of so important a circumstance.   Now Asser (pp. 18, 19) gives the story (which appears to have been pre- valent at a later period, as it is alluded to under different forms by historians of the twelfth century) of the murder of John the " presbyter," by some of his monks, after he had been made by Alfred abbot of Athelney ; and he introduces it as a thing which had occurred some time before—(facinus quoque in eodem monasterio *quodam tempore* perpetratum muti taciturnitate silentii oblivioni traderem . . . . nam *quodam tempore*, cum instinctu diabolico quidam sacerdos et diaconus . . . . contra suum abbatem præfatum Johannem nimium latenter in tantum *amaricati sunt*, &c.)—and which he was going out of his way to mention.   Yet Alfred himself, in the passage above quoted from the preface to the Pastorale, speaks of the same John as being not only alive then,

but as being a simple presbyter, and not an abbot
("my mass-priest," not "my abbot"). This appears
to me sufficient in itself to destroy our faith in the
book; and I have no doubt if we had contemporary
documents of the proper kind we should find numerous similar mistakes. I am inclined to think that the
story concerning Alfred's school for the children of
the nobles, where they were to be instructed in the
English and Latin languages, (Asser, p. 13) had no
other foundation than the words of the king in the
same preface—for-þi me þingð betere, gif geow swa
þincð, þ we eac sume bec þa þemed beþyrfysta syn
eallum mannum to witanne, þ we þa on þ ge-þeode
wendon þe we ealle ge-cnawan mægen, 7 ge-don swa
we swiðe eaðe magon mid Godes fultume, gif we þa
stylnesse habbað, þ eall seo geoguð þe nu is on
Angel-cynne freora manna, þara þe þa speda hæbben,
þ hi þam befeolan mægen syn to leornunga oðfæste,
þa hwile þe hi nanre oþerre note ne mægen, oð fyrst
þe hi wel cunnen Englisc ge-writ arædan. Lære
mon siððan furðor on Leden ge-þeode, þa þe man
furðor læran wille, 7 to herran hade don wille—
("therefore it appears to me better, if it appear so
to you, that we also some books which are judged
most needful for all men to understand, that we
translate them into that language which we all know,
and bring to pass, as we very easily may with God's
help, if we have quietness, that all the youth that
now is in the English nation of free-born men, who
have the means to maintain them, may be set to
learning, while they are capable of no other occupation, *until first they know well to read English writing.*
Let them be afterwards taught further in the Latin
tongue, whom one will teach further, or one designs

for a higher degree.") We have here an indirect re-commendation of a certain mode of instruction, which was to be the result of the English translations of Latin books, but no indications of any schools having been established for the purpose.

We are accustomed to consider Asser as having been made by Alfred, *bishop of Sherborne* (though this is not stated in Asser's work). It is rather sin-gular that the original copy of Alfred's translation of Gregory's Pastorale in the Public Library of the University of Cambridge (apparently the one from which Matthew Parker printed the Introduction), is addressed to Wulfsige bishop of Sherborne, although in the same introduction Asser is spoken of as being a bishop. Perhaps the Asser of history was made bishop of Sherborne towards the end of Alfred's reign, or in that of his successor, having previously been bishop of some other see. The list of the bishops of Sherborne in Godwin is confused; a better list is found in the Cottonian Manuscript, Tiberius B. v., written about the year 993, where they stand thus, Ealhstan, Heahmund, Æthelheah, *Wulfsige, Asser*, Æthelweard, Waerstan, Æthelbald, Sigelm, Ælfred, Wulfsige, Alfwold, Æthelsige. The Saxon Chronicle gives us the bare statement that Asser bishop or Sherborne died in 910 (nine years after king Alfred). And Asser biscop ge-for æfter þam, se wæs æt Scireburnan biscop.

I think that the writer of the book (supposing it to be a forgery) did know that Asser was a bishop, although his information is not easily reconciled with history. After giving a somewhat ostentatious and suspicious account of the favours which he had re-ceived from Alfred, and telling us that the king

made him in one day abbot of the two monasteries of
Angresbury and Banwell, at the same time promising
greater gifts at a future period, he adds, that the
king afterwards gave him " Exeter, with the whole
parochia which appertained to it in Saxony (Wessex)
and in Cornwall,"—nam sequentis temporis successu
ex improviso dedit mihi Exanceastre, cum omni parochia quæ ad se pertinebat in Saxonia et in Cornubia (p.
15). I believe that among the Anglo-Saxon writers
the word *parochia* (our *parish*) was used invariably
(according to its Greek root) to signify an episcopal
diocese; * and that Asser (or the person who took on
himself to represent him) intended to say that the
king made him bishop of Exeter. I am not aware
that there was a bishop of Exeter before the reign
of Edward the Confessor, when (about A. D. 1049)
the see of Crediton was removed to Exeter by Leofric.
I at first thought that the book of which we are speaking might have been fabricated towards the end of
the tenth century; but the mistake just pointed out,
would bring it down as low as the reign of the Confessor. At either of those periods, traditionary anecdotes of king Alfred, the " darling of the English,"
as he is called in the popular poetry even of the

* Thus, to quote the first example which comes to hand, in
the list of Bishops of the end of the tenth century in MS. Cotton.
Tiber. B. v., it is said of Wessex, in duas *parrochias* divisa est,
altera Uuentanæ ecclesiæ, altera Scireburnensis ecclesiæ . . . .
Uuentania ecclesia in duas *parrochias* divisa est tempore
Friðestan . . . . deinde in tres *parrochias* divisa est, Wil-
tunensis, et Willensis, et Cridiensis ecclesiæ . . . . Provincia
Merciorum *duos episcopos* habuit Headden et Uulfridum, postea
Wilfrið electus et Headda præfatus regebant *ambas parrochias*,
&c. &c. (See Reliquiæ Antiquæ, vol. ii. pp. 169, 170, where
this valuable document is printed).

twelfth century, must have been very abundant, and in everybody's mouth. At both periods it may have had a political use, either as intended to encourage the Anglo-Saxons in resisting the Danes, or in supporting the English party headed by earl Godwin against Edward's Norman and French favourites. For this purpose, some monk appears to have conceived the idea of forming a life out of the traditions, and to have taken for his groundwork a copy of the Saxon Chronicle (perhaps mutilated and ending with the year 894) and the legendary life of St. Neot; and, in order to give greater authority to his book, he pretended that it was written by Alfred's friend Asser. This would also account for the writer's dwelling so much on Alfred's patriotic love for the popular poetry of his native land, which must have been a peculiarly gratifying theme to the Anglo-Saxons in the tenth and eleventh centuries. The writer's ignorance with regard to the see of Exeter is not greater than several historical blunders in the life of St. Neot. There appeared another edition of the life of Alfred, with the addition of the translation of the entries of the Anglo-Saxon Chronicle previous to Alfred's birth, and a short continuation from the same source. It was printed by Gale, and goes under the name of Asserii Annales; but its more proper title is said to be the Chronicle of St. Neot's, it having been written there. This circumstance, and the use made of the " Life of St. Neot,"* lead me to suggest that the writer of the life of Alfred was a monk of that house. It does not appear, on an in-

* Leland mentions the Chronicle alluded to, and two different lives of the saint, as being in the library of St. Neot's in Huntingdonshire.

vestigation of the subject, that any person has ever seen a MS. of Asser which can safely be assigned to an earlier date than the eleventh century.

These are the grounds on which I was led to suspect the " Life of Alfred " attributed to Asser. It is a subject which requires further investigation; but I must acknowledge that whatever further attention I have given to the subject has only confirmed the suspicions I had been thus led to entertain.

IX.

ANGLO-SAXON ARCHITECTURE, ILLUSTRATED

FROM ILLUMINATED MANU-

SCRIPTS.*

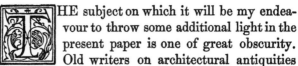HE subject on which it will be my endea-
vour to throw some additional light in the
present paper is one of great obscurity.
Old writers on architectural antiquities
carelessly jumbled together almost all monuments distinguished by the absence of the pointed arch under
the title of Saxon. Some more recent antiquaries
have gone into the opposite extreme of asserting that
there are now remaining no specimens of Anglo-
Saxon buildings. The difficulty attending this question arises from the absolute impossibility of identifying existing structures of an early period with
historical dates. This difficulty has been increased

---

* This paper was written at the commencement of the
Archæological Association, and was printed in the first number
of the Archæological Journal, published in March, 1844. It
was, I believe, the first attempt to throw light upon the history
of this early period of our national architecture by a comparison of the drawings in contemporary illuminated manuscripts.

by the adoption of several general assertions, which I am inclined to believe altogether incorrect. It has been stated that parish churches were very rare among the Anglo-Saxons, that they were small unsubstantial buildings, and even that they were built of nothing but wood. I think the notion that Anglo-Saxon churches were all built of wood will now hardly find supporters. We know that there were structures of this material; a few wooden churches are mentioned in Domesday Book; Ordericus Vitalis mentions a wooden chapel on the banks of the Severn, near Shrewsbury, which was probably built a very short time before the Norman conquest;* and there was a wooden church at Lytham in Lancashire, which was destroyed, and a stone church built by its Norman lord, as we learn from Reginald of Durham.† This last writer, only two pages after, mentions a church of stone at Slitrig in Teviotdale, although only a chapel dependent on the church of Cavers, and which must have been older than the Conquest, for in the twelfth century it was a roofless ruin.‡ The notion that the Anglo-Saxon churches were few and small, is chiefly founded upon some general assertions of the Anglo-Norman monkish chroniclers, on which we ought to set very little value; for not only was it the fashion, for at least two centuries after the

---

* Illic nimirum lignea capella priscis temporibus a Siwardo Edelgari filio, regis Edwardi consanguineo, condita fuerat.— Ord. Vit. ed. Le Prevost, vol. ii. p. 416.

† Nam prædicti militis avus ecclesiam præfatam, quondam asserum viliore compage constructam, a fundamentis diruerat; pro qua et aliam lapideam in honore sancti confessoris, licet non omnino in eodem loco confecerat.—Reginald. Dunelm. (Surtees' Publication), p. 282.

‡ Reginald. Dunelm. p. 284.

Conquest, to speak contemptuously of everything Saxon, but general assertions of the old monkish chroniclers are seldom correct. It is my belief that a careful perusal of the early chroniclers would afford abundant proof that churches were not only numerous among the Anglo-Saxons, but that they were far from being always mean structures. It is not the object of the present observations to enter into this part of the subject, but I will cite two passages which offer themselves almost spontaneously on accidentally opening two well-known writers. Ordericus Vitalis, speaking of the state of England in 1070, only four years after the Conquest, says, " Fiebant et *reparabantur basilicæ*, et in eis sacri oratores obsequium studebant Deo debitum persolvere."* Churches to be repaired at this time must have been Saxon, and I think of stone; if they had been mean structures, and in need of repairs, it is more probable that the Normans would have built new ones. There can be no doubt that the Anglo-Saxons paid much less attention to architecture than the Normans. William of Malmesbury,† speaking of the laxity of manners among the Anglo-Saxons in the age preceding the Conquest, says, " Potabatur in commune ab omnibus, in hoc studio noctes perinde ut dies perpetuantibus, *parvis et abjectis domibus* totos sumptus absumebant, Francis et Normannis absimiles, qui *amplis et superbis ædificiis* modicas expensas agunt." And a few lines after he adds, " Porro Normanni . . . . domi *ingentia ædificia* (ut dixi) moderatos sumptus moliri." This passage must not be taken as a proof of the meanness of Anglo-Saxon architecture in general; it is merely a

* Orderic. Vital., vol. ii. p. 215.
† De Reg. Angl., lib. iii. p. 102. ed. Savile.

somewhat indefinite statement of a well-known fact, that the Saxon nobles did not establish themselves in vast feudal castles like those of the Anglo-Normans. William of Malmesbury goes on to describe the change among the clergy under the Normans, and observes, " Videas ubique in villis* ecclesias, in vicis et urbibus monasteria, *novo ædificandi genere* consurgere." The expression, *a new style of building,* is important in two points of view: the way in which it is introduced shows that churches in another style of building were in existence, and that they were numerous, for William of Malmesbury (who is good authority on this point) does not tell us that the number of churches was at first multiplied greatly by the Normans; and, secondly, it proves that there was a marked difference of style between the ecclesiastical buildings of the Anglo-Saxons and those of the Anglo-Normans. Recent antiquaries have accordingly found architectural remains in several parish churches where other parts of the building are Norman, differing so remarkably from the Norman parts

* The meaning of the word *villa* at this period is fixed by the following passage of Ordericus Vitalis, vol. ii. p. 223. Gaufredus Constantiniensis episcopus . . . . qui certamini Senlacio fautor acer et consolator interfuit, et in aliis conflictibus . . . . magister militum fuit, dono Guillelmi regis ducenas et octoginta *villas* (quas a manendo *manerios vulgo vocamus*) obtinuit. It is said of Lanfranc (A.D. 1070—1089) in MS. Cotton. Claud. C. vi. fol. 168. v°. (written in the twelfth century), In *maneriis* ad archiepiscopum pertinentibus *multas et honestas ecclesias* ædificavit. We might expect to find good specimens of the *earliest* Norman in some churches in Kent, in the estates which formerly belonged to the archbishop of Canterbury. It is not probable that the churches built by Lanfranc would need rebuilding before the thirteenth or fourteenth centuries. We may identify these estates by Domesday Book.

of the same building, and from Norman architecture in general, that they have not hesitated to attribute them to our Anglo-Saxon forefathers. These characteristics are chiefly observed in massy steeple towers, such as those of Sompting in Sussex, and Earl's Barton in Northamptonshire; and it is probable that the tower was the strongest and most durable part of an Anglo-Saxon parish church, and would therefore be most likely to be preserved amid Anglo-Norman repairs.

There is a source of information on the subject of Anglo-Saxon architecture which has hitherto been neglected, and which has always appeared to me to be of great importance. I mean, *illuminated manuscripts;* and it is the object of the present essay to show how remarkably they support the belief that the remains just alluded to are Anglo-Saxon. Illuminated manuscripts are, for the middle ages, what the frescoes of Pompeii and Herculaneum, and the paintings of the Egyptian pyramids, are for more ancient times: they throw more light than any other class of monuments on the costume and on the domestic manners of our forefathers. These manuscripts, which extend through the whole period of the middle ages, are full of architectural sketches. At the time when they are most abundant, *i. e.* subsequent to the twelfth century, these sketches are of less value in an architectural point of view, because the monuments themselves are numerous, and their dates more easily established; still they afford much information on domestic and military architecture. But at an earlier period, they furnish data which we have no other means of obtaining. It may be observed that the mediæval artists,

whatever subject they treated, represented faithfully
and invariably the manners and fashions of the day ;
and that from the language and character of the
writing we are enabled to fix their date with great
nicety.   The manuscript to which attention is now
called, is a fine copy of Alfric's Anglo-Saxon translation of the Pentateuch, preserved in the British
Museum, MS. Cotton. Claudius B. IV.   It was
written in the closing years of the tenth century, or
at the beginning of the eleventh, *i. e.* about the year
1000 or very shortly after, and is filled with pictures,
containing a great mass of architectural detail.   The
proportions are often drawn incorrectly, (the universal
fault of the Anglo-Saxon artists,) but the architectural character is perfectly well defined.

The cut, Fig. 1, presents some of the characteris-

1. Arcade, MS. Cotton. Claud. B. iv. fol. 36. v°.

tics of most frequent occurrence in this manuscript.
It represents an arcade, with a door under one of the
arches.   Columns and capitals of this simple form are
most common, and the arches, when round, are all re-

productions of this type.   It has not been thought
necessary to give in our cuts the figures of personages with which all these drawings are accompanied
in the originals.   Under the arches and door-ways
we not unfrequently observe kings and ministers
seated, and distributing justice, in the manner represented in our cut, Fig. 2, where a messenger is entering, the bearer of intelligence, through the triangular-

2. Arches, from the same MS., fol. 37. v°.

headed door-way on the left.   The manner in which
the messenger places his hand at the top of one of the
columns must be accounted for by the unskilfulness
of the artist and his ignorance of perspective.   The
compartments of the walls which are lightly shaded
in the engraving, are in the original painted yellow.

Polychromy is observable in all the architectural subjects throughout the manuscript; the arches, and even the mouldings and different parts of the columns, are painted of various hues. The colours most frequent are yellow and blue. It may perhaps be doubted how far we may depend on the strict truth of the colours employed by the early artists, for in some instances they seem to be extremely fanciful. I have met with pictures in which men's hair was painted of a bright blue; but it is not impossible that at some period it may have been the custom to stain the hair of that colour. However, be the colours true or not, these drawings appear to establish the fact, that the Anglo-Saxon buildings were painted in this variegated manner.

The figure given above contains other characteristics of importance, which frequently recur in the manuscript, especially the baluster columns. Many other instances of similar pillars are found in the manuscript, and here again in the original the different members of the columns are coloured. These are precisely the kind of columns which are still found in some remains of buildings supposed to be of the Saxon era. They occur in the oldest parts of the church of St. Alban's, where we find also the same triangular-headed arches which occur so frequently in our manuscript. A series of the baluster columns at St. Alban's are engraved from drawings by Carter, in the plates published by the Society of Antiquaries (Muniment. Antiq., vol. i. pt. 15.), from which the example given in the present page, Fig. 3,

Fig. 3.

I.   K

is copied. These columns are characterized by the same double and treble band mouldings, in the different parts of the column, as appear in our cut, Fig. 2. I see no reason for disbelieving that the baluster columns and triangular-work may be parts of a church of St. Alban's built early in the eleventh century with the Roman materials which had been collected from the laborious and continued excavations of many years, by abbots Ealdred and Eadmar, among the ruins of the ancient city of Verulamium, described in a paper in the former volume of these essays.* Most of the church-steeples supposed to be Anglo-Saxon, contain belfry windows with columns of this description. For the sake of comparison, I give two examples (Figs. 4 and 5) from the towers of Earls

Fig. 4, Earl's Barton, Northamptonshire.

* It has been observed, I think by Rickman, that the great quantity of tiles observed in the old parts of St. Alban's church renders it probable that they were not taken from older Roman buildings, but made for the occasion. I think, however, that this assumption is by no means of sufficient strength to outweigh the distinct testimony of the old chronicler relating to the excavations carried on during the lives of the two successive abbots, both of whom, he says, collected in this manner the tiles and stones for the building: of abbot Ealdred, he states,

Barton church in Nor-
thamptonshire, and St.
Benet's in Cambridge.
They have only that dif-
ference in design from
the specimens in the Cot-
tonian manuscript, which
we might expect to find
between the columns of
a small window in a pa-
rish church-steeple, and

Fig. 5, St. Benet's Church, Cambridge.

the larger ornamental columns of a doorway.

One of the most striking, and constantly recurring
characteristics of the architecture of our Anglo-Saxon
manuscript, is the triangular-headed door-way. We
have already seen an instance in Fig. 2. The arrangement of apparently two slabs of stone leaning together
at an angle, and supported over a doorway on two
columns, is frequently repeated in the manuscript: the
chief ornament being apparently the different colours
with which it is painted. This simple arrangement
is sometimes varied by architectural accessories, such
as placing a round arch within an angular arch, or
filling up the triangle with an entablature or tympanum, or giving ornamental capitals to the columns,
the latter evident imitations of Roman capitals. In

Tegulas vero *integras* et lapides quos invenit aptas ad ædificia
seponens, ad fabricam ecclesiæ reservavit (M. Paris. Hist. Abb.
p. 40); and of his successor Eadmar, Et cum abbas memoratus
profundiora terræ ubi civitatis Verolamii apparuerunt vestigia
diligenter perscrutaretur, et antiquos tabulatus lapideos cum
tegulis et columnis inveniret, quæ ecclesiæ fabricandæ fuerent
necessaria, sibi reservaret, &c. (p. 41). It may be observed
that the Anglo-Saxon *tegel*, our *tile*, signified tiles and bricks of
whatever description (if made of baked earth): *hrof-tegel* was
the term used for the tiles used to cover roofs of buildings.

Fig. 1, we have seen a low round arch within a triangle. In Fig. 6, we have a double arch, joining in a sort of pendant, similarly placed within a triangle. Fig. 7. represents a triangular tympanum. The first of these two last-mentioned figures appears, by the capitals, to be intended as part of a more richly decorated building than that to which the other belonged.

Fig. 6, MS. Cotton, fol. 64. v°.   Fig. 7, fol. 65. v°.

I have already stated that triangular arches are found in the oldest parts of the abbey church of St. Alban's. They occur as windows in most of the steeple-towers of the character supposed to be Saxon, and are also found in some instances as door-ways. We have a door-way of this description in Barnack church, Northamptonshire, and another in Brigstock church, in the same county. Windows of this description are still more common. Of the following cuts, Fig. 8. represents a doorway in the church of Barnack; Fig. 9. a very curious belfry-window in the church of Deerhurst, in Gloucestershire; and Fig. 10. a window from the tower of Sompting church in Sussex.

The church of Sompting presents a very interesting specimen of what appears to be an Anglo-Saxon

Fig. 8, Barnack.   Fig. 9, Deerhurst, Gloucestershire.

steeple, and one which seems to have preserved its
original form, even to the roof. It
is joined to a church of late Norman style, but apparently containing also some relics of an earlier
building.   From the difference of
the stone, and its much greater
corrosion by the atmosphere, in the
steeple, we are at once led to believe

Fig. 10, Sompting.

the latter to be at least more than a century (perhaps
two) older than the body of the church; and it is remarkable that Domesday bears witness to the existence
of a church in this parish in the time of William the
Conqueror, which must then have been old, to need
rebuilding so soon as the middle of the twelfth century,
which appears to be about the date of the body of the
present church.   There can be little doubt that the
present steeple belonged to that older church, which
was standing here at the time of the conquest.   It is
very much to be desired that a list should be made of
all the parish churches mentioned in the Domesday

survey, and that the churches now existing in the
same places should be carefully examined. Among
the illuminations of the manuscript of Cædmon, pl.
59, as published in the Archæologia, vol. 24, there is
a rude but curious figure of an Anglo-Saxon church,
the steeple of which bears considerable resemblance
in form to those of which we are speaking. The date
of Deerhurst tower appears also to be justly fixed to
a period antecedent to the Norman conquest. The
original inscribed stone is still preserved among the
Arundelian marbles at Oxford, which states that the
church of Deerhurst was consecrated on the 11th of
April, in the fourteenth year of the reign of Edward
the Confessor, which would be A.D. 1056, or 1057,
according as the regnal year may have been counted
from Edward's accession, or from his coronation. A
new steeple could hardly have been wanted during
the Anglo-Norman period; and as the one now standing cannot have been built at a later period, we seem
justified in concluding that it was the original Saxon
tower.

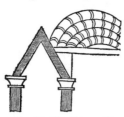

Fig. 11. represents another of these triangular-
headed door-ways from the Cot-
tonian manuscript. It is accompanied with what is intended to represent a dome.
Domes occur frequently in the
manuscript, and form a con-
necting link between Anglo-
Saxon and Byzantine architecture. The dome represented
in our cut appears to be covered in a very singular
manner with parallel semicircles, apparently of tiles;
the form which occurs more generally in the manu-

Fig. 11, MS. Cotton, fol.
38. v°.

script has a knob or ball at the summit, from which, as a centre, the rows of tiles radiate. It may be observed, also, that in these drawings the roofs are generally covered with tiles which, in form and arrangement, bear a close resemblance to the scales of a fish. They are, in fact, the representatives of the lozenged-shaped slating of the Roman period.

The capitals of columns in this manuscript are also deserving of attention. Several examples have been given in the cuts which illustrate the preceding pages : the following additional varieties are selected from different parts of the volume.

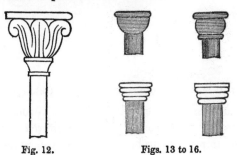

Fig. 12.   Figs. 13 to 16.

The most simple and common form is that which has been represented in Figs. 1, 2, 7, and 11. The capitals more richly ornamented are generally formed of leaves, as in Figs. 6, 12, and 17. The foliated capitals, of course imitated from the older Roman, are charac-teristic of the Byzantine and Ro-

Fig. 17.

manesque styles. I think they are not found in early Norman, but begin to be introduced towards the period of transition. Foliated capitals of a pecu-

Fig. 18, Sompting Church.   Fig. 19, Corhampton.

liar and elegant description (Fig. 18.) occur in the
door-way of the tower of Sompting church. An arch
in Corhampton church, in Hampshire, rests upon
imposts bearing a very close resemblance to the
rudely drawn capitals of the manuscript represented
in our Figs. 15, 16. The manuscript presents
some other architectural characteristics, and especially
several figures of fonts, all of one form, a plain basin
on a shaft, somewhat resembling an egg-cup. But
enough has been said for the object I had in view.

We have then, in the manuscript under consideration, a series of architectural drawings which are
purely Saxon, and of the date of which there can be
no doubt. They present a number of characteristics
which are sufficient to distinguish a peculiar style,
which probably was the general style of Anglo-

Saxon buildings. It is certain that the old artists produced little on parchment which was not modelled on what really existed before their eyes. I would add, that although illuminated manuscripts become more numerous after the Conquest, I never met with one of a later date exhibiting any of the peculiar characters mentioned above. We find a similar style on parts of existing buildings which are evidently of a very early date, and which therefore, as it appears to me, we are justified in attributing to the same age as the manuscripts, in the same way that we should ascribe an unknown effigy to the age in which its costume is found to prevail in similar illuminations. It remains for further examination to show how far we ought to refer every example of this style to the same age of the Saxon period. The dates of early buildings appear to have been often fixed too arbitrarily.

X.

ON THE LITERARY HISTORY OF GEOFFREY OF MONMOUTH'S HISTORY OF THE BRITONS, AND OF THE ROMANTIC CYCLE OF KING ARTHUR.

HE history of Britain, during the latter years of its existence as a Roman province, is that of a series of rebellious usurpations in opposition or rivalry to the wearer of the imperial purple at Rome; and the manner in which these usurpations were carried on proves not only how the Romano-British population of this island had become essentially Roman in its character, but that the imperial power was fast drawing towards an end. Towards the middle of the fifth century, as the communications with Rome were cut off by the inroads and conquests of the barbarians in the other provinces, another race, of whom we are in the habit of speaking collectively as the Saxons, who had certainly been settled on the eastern coasts of Britain for years, and who had joined in supporting the Romano-British usurpers, began to contend for mastery in the island. In the dim cloud that envelopes the subsequent history, we can just trace the faint outlines of civil contention, until, in the course of the latter half of the fifth century, the different tribes of

Germanic invaders had established their power over the greater part of what is now called England.

In authentic history this period is nearly a blank. A writer of a very suspicious character, who passes under the name of Gildas, but whose book, the more I read it the more I am convinced, is the forgery of some Saxon ecclesiastic of the seventh century,* and whose information is probably the record of Saxon legends, has preserved a story (which cannot be authentic in its details) that when the usurper Maximus, towards the end of the fourth century, had carried away the insular legions to war against the legitimate emperor in Gaul, the Romano-British population, without defensive troops, were exposed to the ravages of the Picts and Scots of the north. In this dilemma, they humbled themselves to Rome, and petitioned for help.   A Roman legion was sent, drove the Scots and Picts back to their own mountains, constructed a new wall to confine them within their limits, and returned to Gaul.   Their departure was the signal for a new invasion and new ravages, which were only checked by the return of the Roman troops, in consequence, we are told, of a new application for aid on the part of the inhabitants of this distant province.   Towards the middle of the fifth century, as I have already observed, the Roman troops were finally withdrawn; a new irruption of their northern enemies reduced the Romano-Britons to the utmost distress, and, a last and touching appeal to Italy having been made in vain, the ruler or usurper of the power in Britain (for the island had

---

* See what I have said of this writer in the " Biographia Britannica Literaria, Anglo-Saxon period," p. 120, and a paper in the former volume of these Essays, p. 94.

long been in the hands of a series of usurpers), called
Gurthrigernus by Gildas, and by later writers Vortigern, invited the Saxons from Germany to his assistance, and thus brought over Hengist and Horsa,
who from allies soon became enemies, and persecuted
the natives even more savagely than the Picts and
Scots, until they were defeated in battle by Aurelius
Ambrosius, one of the Romans of rank who had been
left in the island. From that time, the supposititious
Gildas tells us, till the battle of Mount Badon (said
to be Bath), followed a long series of battles, in which
sometimes the Saxons and at others the Britons
had the better.* He subsequently declaims against
the wickedness and profligacy of five British chieftains, his contemporaries, whom he represents as
reigning at the same time in different parts of the
island, Constantinus (in Damnonia), Aurelius Conanus,
Vortiporius, Cuneglasus, and Maglocunus.† There
was probably some ground for these names, as they
resemble in form those found on the late Roman inscriptions in this island.

   It is not necessary for the present purpose to show
that this history must have been in a great measure
legendary; it is adopted by our earliest historian
Bede, and, with some trifling additions made by him
from other sources (not British), is all that the Anglo-
Saxons in subsequent times seem to have known of
the events of that period which intervened between
the loss of Britain as a province to the Roman empire, and the establishment of their own supremacy.
In the earlier Norman period, Ordericus Vitalis, who
collected his historical materials with so much indus-

* See the *Historia Gildæ*, § 14—26.
† See the *Epistola Gildæ*, § 28—33.

try, and from his connection with the borders of
Wales might be supposed to have known something
of Welsh traditions, only repeats the words of Bede.
It is tolerably clear, in fact, that this was all that
was known of British history during the first quarter
of the twelfth century.

Towards the end of the reign of Henry I, or a
little before the year 1135, appeared William of
Malmsbury's " History of the English Kings." This
writer is the first who adds anything to the previous
outline of the earlier history of the island. He gives
us the story of Vortigern and Rowena; and, besides
some other slight additions to the narrative of the
wars between the Britons and Saxons, as given by
former chroniclers, he relates Hengist's fatal " par-
liament," and makes direct allusion to the prowess of
king Arthur, adding, " *Hic est Arthurus de quo Brit-
tonum nugæ hodieque delirant, dignus plane quem non
fallaces somniarent fabulæ, sed veraces prædicarent
historiæ, quippe qui labantem patriam diu sustinuerit,
infractasque civium mentes ad bellum acuerit.*"* A
very slight comparison is sufficient to convince us
that William of Malmsbury, an active inquirer after
historical documents during the greater part of his
life, derived this new information from the *Historia
Britonum*, which has since passed under the name of
Nennius.

There are two circumstances of importance in this
passage of the English historian ; in the first place,
it is the earliest known allusion to the pseudo-Nennius, and in the second place it shows that as early as
the reign of Henry I. the name of Arthur was cele-

* Will. Malmsb. de Gestis Reg. Angl. lib. i. p. 9, ed. Savile.

brated in fables or romances (*nugæ, fabulæ*) among
the Bretons of Armorica, for to them alone could the
Latin name *Britones* be then applied.   In Nennius
only did William of Malmsbury find mention of the
deeds of a British king named Arthur, and he immediately makes the reflection, this must be the Arthur
who is the subject of Breton romance.   In a subsequent part of his history, the same writer alludes to
different legends current in his time relating to the
death of Arthur's nephew Walwanus (the Sir Ga-
wayne of later romance), but none of them agree with
the story as told by Geoffrey of Monmouth.*

It is evident that the book which bears the name of
Nennius had then first made its appearance in England.   Henry of Huntingdon, whose English history
was composed between the date of William of Malmsbury's history and the year 1147, makes more extensive use of the book just alluded to than William has
done, and cites it once directly under the name of
Gildas, but he speaks of it with great caution and
apparent suspicion . . . *apud quendam authorem re-
peri . . . . dicitur . . . . scripserunt quidam, &c.*   I
would remark, that it was next to impossible at this
time to detect a literary forgery, because there was
no rule of historical criticism by which to test it internally, and as to its external appearance, when any
one found a manuscript in a monastic library, or in
private hands, he was obliged to take it for what it
pretended to be, as the modern appearance of a manuscript only showed that it was a recent copy, and
it would have been in vain to attempt to trace back
the prototypes. It may also be observed, that in most

---

* Will. Malmsb. de Gestis Reg. Angl. lib. iii. p. 115.

of the earlier manuscripts of this work it is either given anonymously, or ascribed to Gildas.

That the *Historia Britonum* of Nennius is an absolute forgery no one who has given it a careful perusal can doubt for a moment; but where it was forged, when, and for what special purpose, it would be difficult even to conjecture. It is a strange jumble of indigested materials. It commences with some chronological details relating almost entirely to Bible history, and copied apparently from a common and not very accurate authority. Then we have a few sentences descriptive of the island of Britain, followed by the fabulous history of its first inhabitants, who are stated to have been Trojans led to Italy, after the ruin of their country, by Æneas, the wife of whose grandson Silvius being pregnant, it was foretold by the soothsayers that she would bear a son who should kill his mother and his father, and become an object of aversion to his countrymen. This child was named Bruto; his mother died in childbirth, and he subsequently killed his father Silvius by accident while shooting with an arrow, and thus fulfilled the prophecy. Bruto and his companions were obliged to leave Italy, and, after various adventures, reached Britain, where they founded a new kingdom. Equally fabulous accounts of the origin of the Picts, Scots, and Irish follow. These stories were founded on the common ethnological speculations of the day, filled up by means of imaginary derivations of names, and a perversion of the fables of antiquity. The legend of the birth of Brutus is found elsewhere told of other persons, and under a variety of different forms; it was during the middle ages a popular legend as well among the Christians of the west as

among the Mahommedans of the east, who had the
same tendency to a belief in fatalism; but its prototype is recognized in the classic story of Œdipus.

The pretended Nennius now leaps over the British
history to the period of the Roman invasion, his account of which is founded on the common narratives,
but disguised, so as to give it the air of having been
written by a native of the island, who tells the story
to the disadvantage of the invaders.   The history of
the Roman emperors is taken chiefly from Prosper of
Aquitaine.   That of the Saxon invasion, and of the
subsequent religious mission of St. Germanus, is
abridged from Bede.   But alterations are made in
the narratives of these writers, with the aim of giving
to the compilation the appearance of an independent
authority.   The compiler adds to them, first, a story
of Vortigern's marriage with his own daughter; next,
the legend of Merlin, which seems to have been derived from the East, for it is found in Oriental writers;
and, lastly, the battles between Vortimer and the
Saxons, and the murder of the British chieftains at
the meeting with Hengist.   After these various
matters, the legend of St. Patrick is inserted, and
then the writer suddenly returns to the wars between
the Britons and the Saxons, to mention the name of
Arthur and enumerate the twelve battles in which
he was victorious, the last being that memorable con-
flict of Mount Badon, already alluded to.   The book
concludes with the pedigrees of the different Anglo-
Saxon kings, copied very carelessly from some of the
lists which were then common, and are not now uncommon, and betraying the same design in the compiler of appearing a different person from what he
really was that we trace in other parts of the book.

Most of the earlier manuscripts of the pseudo-Nennius belong to the latter half of the twelfth century; two only are of an earlier date, but I believe that their antiquity has been much over-rated, and that they are probably not older than the beginning of the twelfth century. But the most remarkable circumstance connected with these two early manuscripts is, that they appear to have been written abroad, and in fact never to have been in England, until one of them was bought a little more than a century ago for the library of the earl of Oxford. This manuscript had formerly been in the library of the monastery of Montauban in Quercy, not far from Toulouse. The other early manuscript is now preserved in the Vatican, and had formerly belonged to the monastery of St. Germain at Paris. Everything, in fact, seems to show that this book was new in England when it fell into the hands of William of Malmsbury and Henry of Huntingdon; and, the circumstances just mentioned being taken into consideration, we may fairly be allowed to presume that it was brought from France.

It appears to have been in the autumn of the year 1147* that Geoffrey of Monmouth completed his

* The book is dedicated to Robert, earl of Gloucester, who died in October, 1147. In the preface to the seventh book, Geoffrey speaks of his patron Alexander, bishop of Lincoln, as recently dead—the bishop died in August, 1147. He said that when he had proceeded so far in his history, the prophecies of Merlin beginning to be much talked of, the bishop called him off from the history to give an authentic translation of those prophecies, which, now he had finished his history, he inserted in it as a seventh book.

A difficulty regarding the date is caused by a statement of Henry of Huntingdon in a MS. at Lambeth, which would seem to prove that Geoffrey's History had been at least partially published a few years earlier. I have not had an opportunity

Historia Britonum, a far more remarkable book than
that of Nennius, and here the author appears before
us in his own character and makes a statement relating to his undertaking. He says that he had often
wondered why Gildas and Bede had handed down to
posterity no account of the kings who reigned in
Britain before the Christian era, or of Arthur and
the various British kings of the subsequent period,
whose glorious deeds were nevertheless traditionally celebrated—*a multis populis*—by many peoples.*
While occupied with these thoughts, his friend Walter
Calenius, archdeacon of Oxford, showed him a very
old book in the Breton language which contained the
deeds of all the kings from Brutus first king of the
Britons to Cadwalader the son of Cadwalon. At his
friend's request, and struck with the interest of this
volume, he undertook to translate it into Latin, and
he pretends that his own history is a translation of
the Breton book. At the conclusion he speaks jeeringly of William of Malmsbury and Henry of Huntingdon, " whom I command not to write on the
kings of the Britons, since they have not that book
in the Breton language, which Walter archdeacon of
Oxford brought over from Britany."†

It seems clear from this, and from what has been
said above, that before Geoffrey of Monmouth wrote,

of examining the MS. and it is of no importance for the question agitated in the present paper.

* In mirum contuli, quod intra mentionem quam de eis
Gildas et Beda luculento tractatu fecerunt, nihil de regibus qui
ante incarnationem Christi Britanniam inhabitaverunt, nihil
etiam de Arturo, cæterisque compluribus qui post incarnationem successerunt, reperissem ; cum et gesta eorum digna æter-
nitatis laude constarent, et a multis populis quasi inscripta
jucunde et memoriter prædicentur. Galf. Mon. Epist. dedicat.

† Galf. Mon. Hist. Brit. lib. xii. c. 20.

nothing further was known in England relating to
these pretended British kings than the brief unsatisfactory account which had been furnished by the
pseudo-Nennius, and Geoffrey distinctly refers his
materials to that same country, Britany, where Arthur
had been the subject of fables several years before,
as we are assured by William of Malmsbury. The
manner in which the new history was received can
leave no doubt on our minds of the novelty which
characterized it, and it was too romantic not to be
widely popular as it became known. It seems to
have produced everywhere an extraordinary sensa-
tion, and copies were rapidly multiplied and spread
abroad. An Anglo-Norman trouvère named Gaimar,
whose patroness the lady of Ralf Fitz Gilbert obtained through a northern baron named Walter Espec
the loan of the book from the earl of Gloucester, translated it into Anglo-Norman verse not long after its
publication. This translation appears to be now lost,
though Gaimar's history of the Anglo-Saxon kings,
which formed a continuation, is preserved in several
manuscripts. Nearly at the same time, a monk of
Beverley named Alfred, endeavouring to dispel from
his mind the grief caused by troubles in which his
monastery was involved, by collecting historical materials, began, as he tells us, to hear people talk of
British kings of whom he was entirely ignorant; and,
ashamed of being obliged to confess so often that he
was unacquainted with them, he became anxious to
obtain a sight of the new history, and with much difficulty succeeded in borrowing it for a short time, during
which he made an abridgment of it,* which has been
preserved and was printed by Thomas Hearne. Very

* See Alfred's Prologue to his History.

soon after this, another trouvère, the well-known Wace,
began a new version of Geoffrey's History in Anglo-
Norman verse, which he completed in 1155, and to
which, from Brutus the pretended colonizer of Britain,
was given the title of the *Roman de Brut*. Wace was
a native of Jersey, and, having spent his youth in
Normandy and Britany, was well acquainted with
the legends of both countries. He frequently am-
plifies his original, and sometimes adds incidents
which we may suppose he borrowed from the original
traditions of Britany.

While some were thus expressing their astonishment, without being incredulous, at such an extraordinary narrative of the earlier history of this island,
there were others who looked upon it in a very
different light. These, however, were not numerous,
though they are important by their character. William of Newbury wrote as an old man at the end of
the century, and speaks the impressions of his youth.
" A man in our times," he says, " called Geoffrey,
and who received 'the *agnomen* of Arturus because he
cloaked with the honest name of history, by giving
them the clothing of the Latin tongue, the fables
concerning Arthur taken from the old tales of the
Bretons and *increased from his own imagination*.
Moreover, what he calls the history of the Britons,
how petulantly and impudently he lies in almost
every part of it, no one, unless he be ignorant of the
old histories, when he meets with that book, is left in
any doubt. I omit how much of the acts of the
Britons before Julius Cæsar that man invented, or
wrote from the inventions of others, which he set
forth as authentic," &c.* Giraldus Cambrensis, a

* Wil. Neub. de Rebus Anglicis, prœm.

Welshman well acquainted with the legends of his country, who was born before the *Historia Britonum* was published, and bears testimony that it was not supported by Welsh traditions, tells us of one of his countrymen who had the faculty of seeing evil spirits, and who gave an unerring judgment on the truth or falsity of books placed before him or in his hands, by the freedom with which the evil spirits approached them: "Once," says Giraldus, "when he was much tormented by the evil spirits, he placed the Gospel of St. John in his bosom, and they immediately vanished from his sight, flying away like birds; afterwards he put the Gospel away, and for the sake of experiment took the History of the Britons by Galfridus Arthurus in its place, when they returned and covered not only his body, but the book in his bosom, far more thickly and in a more troublesome manner than usual."* A story like this indicates a general impression in Wales against the veracity of Geoffrey of Monmouth. Giraldus elsewhere speaks of the "fabulous history" of Geoffrey.†

William of Newbury seems to have been perfectly right in his judgment that much of Geoffrey's book was his own invention, for it is far from probable that the *Historia Britonum*, in its entire, can have been translated from any book in the Breton tongue. I cannot dissuade myself that the history of the wanderings of Brutus is a fiction of Geoffrey's founded upon Nennius, and filled with a strange medley of classical names, taken mostly from Virgil. In the opening chapter of this story he has adopted

* Girald. Cambr. Itin. Cambriæ, lib. i. c. 5.
† Girald. Cambr. Walliæ Descrip. cap. vii.

words and phrases from Nennius, whom he must therefore have had before his eyes; and, which is still more singular, in his description of the route of Brutus in his way to the Western ocean, he takes from Nennius nearly verbatim a passage which in the original applies, not to Brutus, but to the eastern colony who, according to that account, peopled Ireland.* We are here dealing with Latin words, and the similarity could not have arisen accidentally in a translation from the Breton tongue. In the course of his wanderings Brutus is made to arrive in Aquitaine, where he builds the city of Tours (*civitas Turonorum*), and names it after his nephew, a Trojan named Turonus, who was slain in battle there. Here, for once, Geoffrey adduces a pretended authority, and, of all other authorities that he might have chosen, none would serve his turn but Homer! *quam, ut Homerus testatur, ipse postmodum construxit.*† This surely is an authority which was not likely to have been obtained from a Breton book. Geoffrey's first

---

* The passage in Nennius (§ 15) is,—

" At ille per quadraginta et duos annos ambulavit per Affricam [he was coming from Egypt] ; et venerunt ad Aras Philistinorum per lacum Salinarum, et venerunt inter Rusicadam et montes Azariæ, et venerunt per flumen Malvam, et transierunt per maritima [Mauritaniam, *in other MSS.*] ad Columnas Herculis, et navigaverunt Tyrrenum mare," &c.

Geoffrey, Hist. Brit. lib. i. § 11, 12, says of Brutus and his companions,—

" Et sulcantes æquora, cursu triginta dierum venerunt ad Africam: nescii adhuc quorsum proras verterent. Deinde venerunt ad Aras Philenorum, et ad locum (*leg.* lacum) Salinarum; et navigaverunt intra Rusicadem et montes Azaræ. . . . . Porro flumen Malvæ transeuntes, applicuerunt in Mauritaniam; deinde . . . . refertis navibus petierunt Columnas Herculis. . . . . Utcumque tamen elapsi, venerunt ad Tyrrhenum æquor."

† Galfr. Mon. Hist. Brit. lib. i. § 14.

book ends with the foundation of Brutus's capital,
named by him New Troy, but since better known by
the name of London.   With an affectation of chronological knowledge, which is carried through the
work, and seems to have been designed as a trap for
the credulity of the reader, Geoffrey informs us that,
when London was built, Heli ruled in Judea, and the
Ark of the Testament was taken by the Philistines;
the sons of Hector reigned in Troy, after having
driven out the descendants of Antenor; and Silvius,
the son of Æneas, reigned in Italy.   It is not worth
the trouble to show the absurdity of such statements.

The second and third books contain the history of
the descendants of Brutus until the period of Cæsar's
invasion, which seems to be a mere invention by
Geoffrey himself.   The names of these personages
are chosen such as to give plausible derivations of the
names of towns, rivers, &c.   Thus the three sons of
Brutus, Locrin, Albanact, and Kamber, divide the
island among them, and the three divisions are called
after their names Loegria, Albania, and Cambria.
In their time Humber, king of the Huns, invades the
island, but being defeated, he is drowned in the river
which thence took his name.   Locrin falls in love
with his captive Estrild, Humber's daughter, and con-
ceals her from his wife in a subterranean chamber
which he built for her within London, sixteen feet
under the ground.*   She bears him a daughter
Sabren, who with her mother is drowned by Locrin's
wife (after the king's death) in the river called after

* This is about the depth at which the floors of houses of
Roman London would be found.   Is it not probable that the
origin of Geoffrey's tale about the subterranean chamber was
the discovery of the foundations of a Roman house in digging
some pit in the city?

her the Severn (*Sabrina*). Another king, Ebraucus,
built York, called after him *Ebrauc*. Geoffrey was
here deceived by a corrupt form of the ancient
Eboracum. This Ebrauc had in succession twenty
wives, who bore him twenty sons and thirty daughters:
he sent his daughters to Italy, where they were
married to the noblest of the Trojans who had settled
there; his sons he sent to conquer Germany. After
three generations king Bladud founded Bath, and
taught his subjects necromancy. He also invented
wings to fly, but they betrayed him, and he fell upon
the temple of Apollo in London, and broke his neck.
This is the classic story of Dædalus. His son Lear
built Leirchester, or Leicester. Leicester took its
name from an old name of the river on which it stands
—under the Romans it was called Ratæ. After several
generations came Dunwallo Molmutius, concerning
whom our author quotes from Gildas what is not found
either in Gildas or Nennius. He was the author of
the Molmutine laws, which, Geoffrey says, were still
in force among the English in his time. Next we
have the extraordinary history of Brennius and Be-
linus, who are said to have conquered Rome. The
latter, on his return, built Billingsgate, and gave his
name to it. Then, after a numerous succession of
kings, we arrive at Lud, who was contemporary with
Cæsar, and who gave his name to Ludgate, which he
erected.

Three more books include the history of the
Romans in Britain, and that of the Saxon invasion to
the time of Arthur. It is a mere romance, built
upon the historical facts which were universally
known, and reads much better in Anglo-Norman
poetry than in grave Latin prose. A story is in-

vented to show how the Roman conquest was effected
only by means of domestic treason—it is a kind of
first edition of Hengist and Vortigern.   The emperor
Claudius landed at Porchester, and he, like Cæsar,
was defeated by the Britons; his general, Hamo,
was slain on the beach at the place since called after
him Hampton (Southampton).   The British king
Arviragus married Genuissa, the daughter of the
emperor Claudius, and in honour of the marriage
Claudius built Gloucester.   According to others it
was a son of Claudius, named Gloius, who gave name
to this city.   After the death of Allectus, his col-
league Livius Gallus was besieged in London, and
the city being taken by assault, Gallus was slain near
the stream which passed through the city, and was
afterwards called from him *Gallbrook* or *Wallbrook*.
When Maximian led all the soldiery from Britain
into Gaul, he established a large part of them under
Conan in Armorica, called afterwards from them
Britany: in order to supply them with wives, the
eleven thousand virgins were sent from their native
land.   This appears to be a perversion by Geoffrey
of the ecclesiastical legend.   Vortigern was an usurper,
and when Hengist and a few Saxons were thrown by
chance on the British coast, they were brought to
him as a race of people who had never been seen or
heard of before, and, after cross-examining them, he
took them into his service to support him in his
usurpation.   Hengist obtained his first grant of land
by a stratagem: he asked for as much only as he
could surround with one leathern thong, which was
readily granted, and the artful Saxon took a large
bull's hide, and cut it into one very fine and very long
thong, with which he marked out as much land as

I.   L

was necessary to build a strong castle, which the
Saxons, in memory of the transaction, called Than-
caster. This story was of course taken from Virgil;
it was the classic legend of the building of Carth-
age:—

> Devenere locos, ubi nunc ingentia cernes
> Mœnia surgentemque novæ Carthaginis arcem ;
> Mercatique solum, facti de nomine Byrsam,
> Taurino quantum possent circumdare tergo.
>
> Æn. I. 365.

The history of the Saxon wars is built upon Gildas
and Nennius. The story of the meeting at which the
British nobles were treacherously slain, and the subsequent building of Stonehenge to commemorate the
tragedy, may have been a local legend. The history
of Merlin is, as I have before observed, of eastern
origin: it is found in the collection of apologues
which, in its European dress, passed under the title
of the Seven Sages, and occurs among the early
Indian and Persian story-books.* The seventh book
of Geoffrey's history consists of Merlin's Prophecies,
which were very popular in the twelfth century, and
are quoted in a late part of the historical work of
Ordericus Vitalis.

Geoffrey's eighth book contains the history of
Aurelius Ambrosius and Uther Pendragon, and
appears to be made up partly in the same way as
those we have been considering. In it, however, we
have the amours of Uther (taken from the classic
story of Jupiter and Alcmena) and the birth of king
Arthur, whose history occupies the ninth and tenth

---

* See my edition of the Seven Sages, p. 78, and the Introduction, pp. lvi. lvii.

books. This part of the work, if any, may have been taken partially from a Breton book, of which Geoffrey speaks again at the commencement of the eleventh book, and there acknowledges that part of his information was taken from the recital of archdeacon Walter, and not from the written document.*

The eleventh and twelfth books contain the history of the British kings from the death of Arthur to that of Cadwallader, which Geoffrey places in 689. Most of the British kings whose adventures are here narrated were probably made for the occasion, and their history, with the exception of what is interwoven into it from the Anglo-Saxon historians, is about as authentic as the earlier part of the work. It is only necessary to state that the first four kings of Britain who follow king Arthur, are four of the chiefs whom Gildas enumerates as living contemporaneously in different parts of the island, Constantinus, Aurelius Conan, Vortiporius, and Malgo (or, as Gildas calls him, Maglocunus), and that Geoffrey of Monmouth actually misunderstands the figurative language of the old writer, and charges Malgo with a detestable vice of which Gildas does not accuse him.†

* Sed ut in Britannico præfato sermone invenit, et a Gualtero Oxinefordensi in multis historiis peritissimo viro audivit, vili licet stylo, breviter tamen propalabit.   Galf. Monum. Hist. Brit. lib. xi. § 1.

† Gildas, in his invective against the Britons, § 33, says to Maglocunus,—" Quid tu, enim, insularis draco, multorum tyrannorum depulsor tam regno quam etiam vita, supradictorum novissime in nostro stylo, prime in malo, major multis potentia simulque malitia, largior in dando, profusior in peccato, robuste armis, sed animæ fortior excidiis, Maglocune, in tam vetusto scelerum atramento, veluti madidus vino de sodomitana vite expresso, stolide volutaris?"

Geoffrey of Monmouth says of his Malgo (lib. xi. § 7),—"Cui

We may in this instance also see the manner in
which Geoffrey's imagination built long stories upon
small foundations, for on the mere expression of
Gildas that Maglocunus was *multorum tyrannorum
depulsor*, (the word *tyrannus* was applied to any independent chief or noble,) he makes his British king
Malgo, at the time when the Britons were rapidly
bowing beneath the yoke of the Saxon invaders, not
only gain the supremacy at home, but conquer and
reduce under his dominion Ireland, Iceland, Goth-
land, the Orcades, Norway, and Denmark!

This very slight review of the contents of Geoffrey
of Monmouth's British History will, I think, be sufficient to show that as a whole it could not be translated from any book in the Breton language.   The
purely classic names which are introduced in the
earlier part of the history, selected from Virgil,—
the strange mixture of names in other parts, which
could not have been found together, for one or two
of his British and Pictish names, such as Rodric (lib.
iv. c. 17), Cheulphus (lib. iii. c. 1), are of a German
origin,—the ingenuity with which names are invented,
so as to seem to have been the origin of names of
places and things which we know have quite other
derivations, and to work in bits from Latin writers, so
as to seem to make an agreement between the British
history and that of other nations,—all these betray
the manner in which Geoffrey's History was put together.   We know that it was a fashion in his time
to derive not only names of places, but even names

successit Malgo omnium fere Britanniæ pulcherrimus, multorum
tyrannorum depulsor, robustus armis, largior cæteris, et ultra
modum probitate præclarus, nisi sodomitana peste volutatus
sese Deo invisum exhibuisset."

of sciences, &c. from those of men who were supposed to have built or discovered them,* and little
attention was paid to the real meaning of the words.
Many of the stories in Geoffrey of Monmouth are
invented in this way; and they must have been invented by a man in England who was acquainted
with localities, and who had a design to practice upon
people's credulity in such derivations.   Thus Ludgate, and Billingsgate, and especially Wallbrook,
(which we know was so called because it passed under
the London wall,) and many others, which are all
Saxon, are not likely to have found their derivations
in an old Breton book.   The story of Lear and his
daughters was taken from the mediæval romances:
it was Geoffrey of Monmouth who connected it
with Leicester (Leir-caster), and made it a part
of British history.   The name of the town was,
as I have said, derived from the old name of the
river on which it stands.   It is too absurd to suppose
that any old Breton book should have told us that an
early British queen named Marcia (a Roman name
long before the period of the Roman invasion) compiled the laws called after her *lex Martiana*, and that
king Alfred translated them into Anglo-Saxon, and
called them after the original name, Mercna-lage;†

---

* For instance, the mediæval name for Arithmetic was Algorismus. Instead of seeking its real source, the writers on the
subject tell us gravely that the name was derived from a king
named Algor, who first treated of it. Non invenientes sed
doctrinam traditam de numerorum progressione ab Algore rege
quondam Castelliæ suo in Algorismo, &c. Johannis Norfolk
in artem progres. summula, MS. Harl. 3742. Hæc præsens
ars dicitur Algorismus ab Algore rege ejus inventore. MS.
Bibl. Reg. 12 E. I.

† Galf. Mon. Hist. Brit. lib. iii. § 13.

or, that a still more ancient British king, Dunwallo Molmutius, enacted the code of laws called after him the Molmutine laws, which Gildas translated from British into Latin, and king Alfred translated from Latin into English, under which form they became the laws of England, which continued in force in Geoffrey's time.* What could Breton minstrels know about Anglo-Saxon laws or king Alfred's translations? It is not improbable that some of the stories which Geoffrey has worked up into his book, such as that of Stonehenge erected by supernatural means, may have been English local legends.

The earliest translation of Geoffrey's History, now extant, is Wace's Roman de Brut, in Anglo-Norman verse, completed in the year 1155. I have already stated that Wace was intimately acquainted with Breton traditions. He informs us in his other great work, the Roman de Rou, that he had visited the forest of Brecheliant to seek the wonders which the Bretons said were to be seen there, and which in fact are celebrated in the romances of the cycle of king Arthur, but his search was vain, and he somewhat naïvely acknowledges his folly.

> Là alai-jo merveilles querre,
> Vis la forest e vis la terre ;
> Merveilles quis, maiz ne's trovai ;
> Fol m'en revins, fol i alai,
> Fol i alai, fol m'en revins,
> Folie quis, por fol me tins.
> > Roman de Rou, l. 11534.

Wace's version of the whole of the *Historia Britonum* antecedent to king Arthur, is a close copy of the ori-

* Galf. Mon. Hist. Brit. lib. ii. § 17, and lib. iii. § 5.

ginal, with the mere poetical amplifications in descriptions and reflections that any other rhymer would have made; he evidently knew nothing of the history he was translating independent of the book he was translating from.   The concluding portion of Wace's Brut, subsequent to the death of Arthur, is also closely translated from Geoffrey of Monmouth.   It is in the history of this mythic Romance hero, whose name was cherished by the Bretons of Armorica, that Wace's imagination appears less fettered, and that he seems to be more at home in his subject.   And although Wace adds nothing of much importance to Geoffrey's history of Arthur, we learn from him the valuable fact that the romances of the Round Table (which is not mentioned by Geoffrey of Monmouth) were popular among the Bretons in the middle of the twelfth century, and there is an apparent implication that these romances differed very much from Geoffrey's account of the Breton hero—in fact, it was the difference between romance taken as romance, and the same romance metamorphosed and moulded into a history.

> Fist Artus la Roonde Table,
> *Dont Breton dient mainte fable :*
> Iloc seoient li vassal
> Tot chievalment et tot ingal ;
> A la table ingalment seoient,
> Et ingalment servi estoient.
>
> Roman de Brut, l. 9998.

It is now quite clear that in the first half of the twelfth century the romances of Arthur were popular in Britany ; and it seems equally certain that English and Norman writers only knew of them as popular in Britany.   When we consider Geoffrey of

Monmouth's history in itself,—when we examine its
artificial structure, and see the manner in which the
materials are continually betraying themselves,—
when we bear in memory how common a practice it
was among romantic and poetical writers in the
middle ages to call their works translations, when
we know that they were not translations, in fact that
this was a sort of conventional formula when authors
wished to claim a mysterious or an especially authentic
origin for their productions,—I think we shall have
no difficulty in coming to the conclusion that Geoffrey
deceived his readers as to the character of his book.
Perhaps the wish expressed by William of Malmsbury with regard to the fabulous Arthur, *dignus
plane quem non fallaces somniarent fabulæ, sed veraces
prædicarent historiæ*—may have given him the hint:
the book which had then become known under the
name of Gildas or Nennius offered him a brief outline, which his imagination easily filled up; and if he
did use any Breton book, it was one of those *fabulæ*
or romances relating to Arthur which were prevalent
in Armorica, and he seems to have altered it and
worked it up so that it should be neatly dovetailed
into the body of his history.

Geoffrey's book formed a new era in the history of
the romances to which I am alluding. They had
hitherto been mere popular tales of the country, the
amusement of a dreary evening, or chanted by the
minstrel in his patron's festive hall. They had now
gained a place in literature which was shortly to
give them a celebrity in almost every corner of the
known world, for they were told in Greek among the
poets of the East, and they were not unknown to the
Arabs of the South. That involuntary process of

localizing legends in countries to which they were
really strangers, which was so prevalent in the
middle ages, was active in several different countries,
and soon connected the name of king Arthur with
many spots and objects in various parts of this island.
Later on in the twelfth century an old coffin was dug
up at Glastonbury, and the monks immediately declared that it was king Arthur's body, and they with
equal facility found the body of his frail queen Gwe-
nevra. It was said that a Welsh minstrel had declared
that king Arthur was buried there, and that the place
had been further revealed in a dream to king Henry.*
It was chiefly through the encouragement given to
literature by this monarch and his court that the
Breton romances were at length reduced to writing
in a form more accordant with their real character, in
the French or Anglo-Norman prose of Robert de
Borron and Walter Mapes, who also pretend to translate, but, singularly enough, they talk of Latin originals.   The Romances of the Saint Graal, of Merlin, of Lancelot du Lac, and of the Quête du Saint
Graal, appear to contain the mass of the stories of the
cycle of the Round Table current among the Bretons
in the twelfth century; stories, however, which belong to the same cycle, and are not found in these
large romances, are alluded to by contemporary
writers.   A comparison of them with the history of
Geoffrey of Monmouth shows that that writer must
have used the Breton romances only as the foundation
of his narrative of the deeds of king Arthur, which
he completed probably from his own inventive genius.

* See the account of this discovery in the work of Giraldus
Cambrensis de Instructione Principum (published by the Anglia
Christiana Society), p. 191.

We might pursue the literary history of this cycle of romances, and show how it was gradually enlarged and extended in the different hands through which it passed during another century. The old feeling that it originated in Britany still prevailed. But Geoffrey of Monmouth's History remained as an insulated romance : it received no addition or explanation from the increased knowledge of the romances to which its great hero, Arthur, belonged. No documents or authentic traditions confirmed it; and it seems only to have received some amplification from the English monk Layamon, who worked up into his English version a few more of those local legends (such as that of the destruction of Cirencester by the agency of sparrows) of which Geoffrey himself had already made use.

XI.

ON SAINTS' LIVES AND MIRACLES.*

 REMARKABLE contrast is presented
by the circumstance, that while in France
—a Roman Catholic country—writers
are investigating, in a purely philosophical spirit, the legends and miracles of those morally
dark ages, from the influence of which we have
fortunately been long emancipated, there are found
men in Protestant England—men bound by their
duty to defend the church which they are deliberately
undermining—eagerly engaged in republishing these
legends to the world, and recommending them even
with more than popish bigotry.

It is singular that any modern religious party, instead of resting its claims on some show of reason,
should reject contemptuously the plainest dictates of
common sense, and exact a blind acceptance of the
most ridiculous and most disgusting portions of the
belief of the middle ages.   With these men, absur-

* This paper appeared originally in the " Edinburgh Review,"
vol. lxxxv. in April, 1847, as a review of 1. " Lives of the English Saints;" Parts I. to XII. 12mo. London, 1844-5 ; and, 2.
" Essai sur les Légendes Pieuses du Moyen-Age."   Par L. F.
Alfred Maury, 8vo. Paris, 1843.

dity is the extreme of wisdom; and the very errors
which liberal-minded Romanists now reject are, by
our would-be " Catholics," held forth as the gauge
of orthodoxy.   Justification is not sought in scriptural or apostolical authority; and the pure and
simple faith which Jesus taught to his disciples is
represented to be but a rude outline, an *ébauche,*
which it required the " wisdom " of the dark ages to
develope.   The testimony of history is rejected, for
it has too much to say : while the mere *belief* of the
" Catholic " is the only sure evidence of truth, in this
new school of religious professors.   Such, at least, is
the doctrine expressly inculcated in the tracts before
us; which are generally attributed to a late proselyte
to Romanism, who, at the time of their publication,
was a member of the Church of England, and was
receiving wages at its hands.

With regard to the principle upon which these
Lives have been composed, and on which it is intended
that they should be now studied, there is neither dis-
guise nor reservation.   We are warned, from the
beginning and throughout, that in matters of this
high order our belief is relieved from subjection to
the ordinary rules of evidence.   In a completely un-
historical account of the primitive British church,
(given in Part III, and containing the first portion
of the life of St. Augustine,) after stating the want
of historical evidence of the pretended visits of the
apostles Paul and Peter to Great Britain, the writer
observes, " yet it has undoubtedly been long received
as a *pious opinion* by the Church at large;" after
which, he immediately informs us, that " this sort of
argument, although it ought to be kept quite distinct
from documentary and historical proof, and will form

no substitute for such proof with *those who stipulate for something like legal accuracy* in inquiries of this nature, will not be without its effect upon *devout minds.*" In telling a miracle of a saint of the seventh century, which is not mentioned before the fourteenth century, our historian adds:—" This story is given on the authority of Capgrave, not of Bede; not that there seems any reason for *doubting its truth.*" After the relation of several absurd miracles, without meaning and without object, we meet repeatedly with remarks like the following:—" And from not understanding them (the saints,) we go on to criticise them, not always or at once remembering, that ' the natural man discerneth not the things of the spirit,' and that, in the case of certain given persons, it is on the whole far more likely that *such as we should be in the dark*, than *such as they in the wrong.*" " If the reader so far forgets that he is occupied upon a portion of ecclesiastical history as to *stumble at the marvellous portions* of the present biographical sketch, it is hoped he will at least suspend his judgment till a few pages further on, or accept the statement, subject to any qualifications which may secure them from the chance of irreverent usage, and him from the risk of that *especial blasphemy* which consists in slighting the manifestations of God's Holy Spirit; a sin, one should have thought, denounced by our blessed Lord in language sufficiently awful to make the possibility of it an unspeakably more formidable alternative than *any amount of credulity.*" " When, to the readers of one age, the miracles of another long past away *appear so grotesque as to provoke amusement*, their seeming eccentricity is *no ground for rejecting them.* If men are to be taught, the teaching will be shaped for them, adapted to their way of looking at things, corresponding to their habits of thought, and, as it were, echoing the actual life and manner of the times. Supposing a miracle wrought for the conversion of a barbarous people, will it not almost certainly *have a barbarous aspect*, and be what a philosophical age would deem a *gross* display of supernatural power or goodness?" Somewhere near York, St. Augustine restored a blind man to his sight in the name of Jesus Christ. At this time of day, there is something unusually *naïve* in the exclamation :—" Why should not that name work miracles at any time ?· *Why not among ourselves now-a-days ?* Truly, because we lack the conditions of its power—Catholic faith and Catholic sanctity !" This is precisely the way in which the late Mr. Irving accounted for the withdrawal of miraculous powers from modern prayers. In another place we are gravely told that the reason why we cannot believe the miracles of the saints is, that we are labouring under an intellectual darkness caused by three centuries of Heresy !

Ravings like these may appear at first sight undeserving of notice. Can they have any weight with any body ? But when we look further into the body of the tracts themselves, (and they have been widely distributed,) we find their fallacious doctrines put forth so Jesuitically, the poison so cunningly hidden beneath the sugar, that it is right to exhibit the working of the system in its true colours. The object of this writer may be discovered without difficulty. He knows that the voice of the past, if impartially listened to, is against him—therefore he would cast a discredit upon all but *ecclesiastical* history. The cross-examination of his witnesses by a skilful advocate must be fatal—therefore he would impress upon us not only the *danger*, but the " *especial blasphemy*," of criticising. The scheme, too, has been to a small degree successful; because the experiment has fallen upon an age, when people are off their guard. At the time of the Reformation, the whole case was before the eyes of every body; the conviction of its rottenness was general among as many as ventured to inquire, because the evidence was overwhelming. On the contrary, our own age, satisfied with the judgment of our forefathers, has been gradually forgetting the evidence by which that judgment was obtained, until at last a little special pleading is enough to throw doubts upon its justice among the credulous and simple-minded. The only remedy is to produce the evidence again; and fortunately we shall find that in the present case it is increased rather than diminished by lapse of time. The Romanist knows this well, and therefore he sets his face against historical criticism and the publication of historical documents. This is the spirit exhibited in these new " Lives of the English Saints;" on which account it will not, we think, be uninteresting, to examine a little into the materials of which those extraordinary fabrications called *Lives of Saints* were constructed, and into the mode in which they were put together.

The Lives of Saints may be arranged in several classes. Some were mere forgeries, inventions to serve the purposes of those who first compiled them; others, equally lives of persons who never existed, had their foundation in nothing but popular fables, and even in mistaken allegories; in other instances, they are the mere legends which during ages had gathered round the memory of some personage known

only by name, and committed to writing long after
the period at which he lived; while, in many cases,
we have the life of an individual written by his contemporary, sometimes a friend, almost always a prejudiced chronicler, intentionally or unwittingly in-
serting much which it would have been very difficult
indeed to have ever authenticated or ascertained.
The saints of this latter class (the only one which has
much historical importance) are of two races.   They
gained a place in the calendar, either by the part they
took in supporting the usurpations of the church upon
the civil power, during the long struggle in which
the former was not over-delicate in the choice of its
weapons, or by their activity as missionaries in con-
verting the heretics or the heathen to the Church of
Rome.   In general, the more authentic the lives, the
fewer the miracles; and, in like manner, the earlier
lives of the same saint contain much fewer miracles
than the later ones.   The mass of the mediæval
miracles appears to have originated in the mixture of
ideas produced by the conversion of the pagan tribes
by men who, though Christians, were as superstitious
and credulous as themselves.

When the missionaries first entered upon their
labours among the people of western and northern
Europe, they found a creed which acknowledged two
classes of supernatural beings,—the gods (*dii majores*)
of the respective tribes, such as Odin, Thor, &c.—
and a multitude of lesser spirits, who were believed to
haunt wood and valley and mountain, and to inhabit
air and water, continually intermixing visibly or in-
visibly with mankind, and exerting over individuals
an influence for good and for evil.   The worship of
the gods was the province of the higher classes, and

was the business of the priests; the minor spiritual
beings, elves or nymphs, held intercourse with individuals at their pleasure, or sometimes by compulsion.
And these individuals (the originals of the sorcerers
and witches of later times) obtained by this means
miraculous powers : for instance, the power of curing
diseases, of working good or evil, like the spirits themselves, and of foretelling future events. They were
consulted by those who laboured under such diseases,
who had sustained losses by accident or robbery, or
who sought to gratify revenge or conciliate love.
As the monkish missionaries made their way, they
banished the heathen priests—whose gods and their
worship were gradually forgotten—while their mythic
histories were preserved in the form of romances and
popular stories. But the elves and minor spirits, in
whose existence the monk believed equally with the
peasant, still held their sway; and sorcerers and
witches continued to follow their occupations.

We trace, indeed, everywhere the attempts of the
ecclesiastics, down to a late period, to turn the popular superstitions to their own purposes. Elves and
nymphs were, in their creed, innumerable hosts of
demons, against whom they had to contend. The
martyrs of the primitive ages of the church had suffered for refusing to worship idols of wood and stone;
the monkish saints advanced a step further, and em-
barked in a more substantial warfare with spiritual
beings. These imaginary demons were naturally
opposed to the intruders; and we find them seizing
every opportunity of tormenting the missionaries and
their converts. In the seventh century, St. Sulpicius, while a mere child, went to pray by night at
a ruined church near his father's house; two black

demons, who haunted the ruin, would have scared
him from his devotions, but he drove them away with
the sign of the cross. With the same weapon his
contemporary, St. Frodobert, at that time also a boy,
drove away a devil which used to stop him on his
way to school. So late as the beginning of the thirteenth century, the Belgian St. Juetta, when she
went to her devotions at night, was persecuted by
demons who appeared to her in every variety of form,
ludicrous as well as fearful. We might fill a volume
with such stories. The tricks which these demons
played upon their spiritual adversaries are often of
the most frivolous kind; precisely such as are laid
to the charge of the playful elves of the popular mythology. When St. Frodobert was at his nightly
devotions in the church, a devil overthrew his candle-
stick and put out the light. A demon stole the bread
of St. Amatus, abbot of Remiremont. St. Benedict,
the father of monachism in the west, lived for some
time at the summit of a rock, and his food was sent
up by a rope to which a bell was attached; one day
the evil one threw a stone at the bell, and it was
broken, whereby the saint could no longer make
known his necessities. In a majority of cases, the
demon exhibited much greater malignity; as in another adventure of St. Amatus, when the fiend threw
down the upper part of a lofty rock, that it might
crush him in his cell; but the saint caused it miraculously to stop in the midst of its descent. Like the
spiritual beings of the popular mythology, we often
find the demons in possession of ruined cities or fortresses; we have already had an example in which
they haunted a ruined church; St. Salaberga en-
countered a whole host in the ruins at Laon, who

appeared in the shapes of fierce wild beasts.   But, in
the Teutonic mythology, the special haunts of spirits
of almost every description were the wild morasses
and the unfrequented woods.   It was in such places
that the mythic heroes of the pagan creed went to
encounter them, or that the charmer consulted them;
accordingly, when their imitators, the monks, had
gained strength in the country, and were no more
subject to the attacks of the demons at home, they
began to act upon the offensive, and followed the
enemy into his own dwelling-place.   Under these
feelings, St. Guthlac took up his residence amid the
marshes of Croyland, and St. Cuthbert established
himself in the island of Farne; where the legendary
histories of these saints describe their long-continued
struggle with their spiritual adversaries.   People im-
plicitly believed that such places could only be rendered
habitable by the holiness of the saints.   We sometimes find these saints contending with water-demons,
the nickers of the ancient creed, the memory of whose
transformation is still preserved in the popular name
of " Old Nick."   In a district in France, there was
in the seventh century a certain whirlpool (*gurges*)
in the river, which the pagans had " consecrated to
their demons," and these demons dwelt in it, and, if
any entered the river in its vicinity, they dragged
him to the bottom and he was drowned.   The people
of the neighbourhood prayed St. Sulpicius to drive
away these demons, which he did, but as it appears
ineffectually; for a man falling in soon afterwards
was strangled by the fiend, and brought out lifeless.
The saint, to save his own credit, restored the drowned
man to life.   The nymphs of the older mythology
also acted their parts; according to the popular fables,

they became frequently enamoured of men, and had
intercourse with them, an intercourse which is the
foundation of many romantic stories.   The monks
and hermits were no less frequently the objects of
their amorous propensities, and had need of all their
piety and miraculous powers to withstand their seduc-
tions.   Water-nymphs appeared to St. Gall (Act. Ss.
Bened. sec. ii. p. 237); a nymph (or, according to
the legend, a devil in woman's form) came by night
to St. John, abbot of Moultier, in the diocese of
Langres, and tried her seductive arts upon him in
vain; a similar attempt was made upon St. Benedict,
and it was repeated with a multitude of other saints.

Such, evidently, was the origin of a considerable
portion of the multifarious demoniacal agency, which
fills the mediæval saints' legends.   The monks borrowed another class of miracles from the observances
of paganism, in their desire to vindicate to themselves powers, the same as those with which popular
superstition had invested priests and sorcerers.   The
heathen priest, as well as his Christian rival, cured
diseases: and that by charms, which were in many
cases identical, if we except the mere insertion of
Christian terms.   For instance, the pagans applied to
their priests and sorcerers for the detection of robbers, and for the recovery of goods lost or stolen; in
due course this attribute was transferred to the monkish saints, whose legends are so full of instances of the
miraculous detection of theft and robbery, that it is
unnecessary to particularize them.   We know what
reverence our heathen ancestors paid to fountains—
the favourite objects of their pilgrimages and religious ceremonies.   These also enter extensively into
the saints' legends; and were everywhere translated

into objects of Christian worship under the Romanized Christianity of the middle ages. If we believe
the legends, the saints made so many of the fountains
now in existence, that the pagans can hardly have
found a spring to worship at. The stories of fountains produced miraculously by the saints are repeated, by the compiler of our new *Lives of Saints*,
without a smile,—on the contrary, he seeks to awe
us into the impression, that it would be a "special
blasphemy" to disbelieve them. (See the *Life of
St. Augustine*, p. 87.) The monks even fell into the
reverence with which the people cherished the barrows, or graves, of their ancestors, and they sometimes dug up their bones to make relics of them.
Thus, while the unconverted Saxon revered the
barrow, because he believed that it was from time to
time revisited by the spirit of its tenant, the English
monk, with a grosser superstition, worshipped the
bones, the last mouldering witnesses of his mortality.
On the site of the present town of Ludlow, in Shropshire, stood, in early times, a large barrow, probably
Roman. It was an object of popular superstition,
and in Christian times a church was built beside it.
In 1199, as we learn from a document printed in
Leland's *Collectanea*, (iii. 407,) it being found necessary to remove the mound, three sepulchral interments were discovered. The clergy of the adjoining
church carefully gathered up the bones, and placed
them in a coffer; telling people that they were the
blessed relics of three saints of Irish extraction—
St. Fercher, St. Corona, and another, whose name is
preserved only imperfectly in the document!

One of the most common exploits of the heroes
of the Teutonic mythology was the destruction of

dragons, which were supposed to have the care of
treasures concealed in old ruins and in the barrows
of the dead.   The monks would have their saints
rival these mythic heroes. When St. Julian preached
the gospel to the Franks, a dreadful dragon brooded
in a ruined temple at " Artinas," which the saint immediately put to flight.   Nearly at the same period,
in another part of France, (*in deserto Thornodorensi,*)
a dragon, the terror of the neighbourhood, dwelt in
an ancient pit or well; it was killed by St. John of
Remiremont. When, in the sixth century, St. Tozzo,
St. Magnus, and St. Gall had wandered through
France to the borders of Switzerland, they came to
the Roman Campodunum, (Kampten,) which was
then a deserted mass of ruins.   A presbyter of the
neighbourhood told the strangers that the people of
the country sometimes visited the ruins by day; but
that at night the access was dangerous on account of
the fearful dragons and serpents which had their dens
there, and which frequently slew such incautious
hunters as might be led thither by their eagerness in
the chase.   In the midst of their conversation, " a
great serpent called a boa" (*egressus est foris de op-
pido vermis magnus qui dicitur boa*) suddenly issued
from the ruined town and approached the saints;
Tozzo and one of his companions sought refuge in a
tree; but St. Gall miraculously slew the assailant,
and afterwards cleared the old town of its noxious
occupants. In the sequel of their journey, the saints
came to a narrow pass in the mountains of Switzerland, called Rosshaupten, which was strictly guarded
by a ferocious dragon; they pitched their tent, and
spent the night in prayers for the overthrow of the
monster, and in the morning they found it stretched

lifeless on the ground. St. Maximin, abbot of Micy, in the diocese of Orleans, slew a dragon which vomited flames, and ravaged the country far and wide, sparing neither age nor sex. By his own desire, the saint was buried on the spot where he vanquished this dragon, and many miracles were afterwards performed at his grave. Towards the end of the seventh century, his bones were dug up and carried to the church of Micy, where they were preserved as relics endowed with miraculous powers. It is probable that these also were nothing more than bones found in an ancient barrow, the hero of which was believed to have slain a dragon. St. Samson, bishop of Dol, slew several dragons in Britany; St. Gildas destroyed a dragon in Italy; and St. Lifard killed another at Méhun, in the diocese of Orleans. M. Alfred Maury (in the work indicated at the head of the present article) enumerates nearly forty saints who slew dragons, chiefly in France. There is no room for mistaking the animals slain; they were the identical dragons of the Teutonic mythology — imaginary beings, in the existence of which we will, fearless of the consequence of our " irreverence to the saints," venture to disbelieve.

The outline or groundwork of the lives of many other of the saints is clearly taken from some of the stories of the earlier mythology of the people, or of the mediæval romances which sprung out of it. The saint is often a creature of the imagination; while sometimes the story is attached to a name which had been handed down almost without a history. Thus, from the early writers, we know little more of St. Furseus, than that he was the hero of a vision of purgatory. But a monk, at a later period, has com-

piled a wild and extravagant life, in which we are told
that his father had contracted a secret marriage with
a king's daughter without the monarch's consent;
and that, when the damsel was discovered to be with
child, her father, in his wrath, ordered her to be
burnt for her incontinence. As she was dragged to
the place of execution, the child, which was Furseus,
cried out from its mother's womb, and declared that
it was unworthy of a king to condemn his daughter
without a trial. The king treated the admonition
with contempt, and the lady was thrown into the
fire; but she shed so large a flood of tears that the
flames were instantly extinguished. The king, finding that he could not burn his daughter, banished
her from his kingdom; and she gave birth to Furseus
in a foreign land. This is an incident which occurs,
with some variations, and without the miracle, in
several mediæval romances, from one of which it was
doubtless taken. The mother of St. Samson of Dol
was barren, to the grief of her lord; they went to a
wise man or priest, by whose blessing the lady's in-
firmity was removed; and his prophecy that she
should soon give birth to a son was confirmed by the
visit of an angel, to announce to the mother her
pregnancy. A similar story is told of the birth of
St. Molagga, and it is repeated in the legends of
other saints. A somewhat similar incident occurs
also in some of the mediæval romances, such as that
of Robert le Diable ; but, in the *Saints' Lives*, it is
probably imitated directly from the New Testament.

Invention, we are aware, is a rare talent. Nevertheless, we are surprised at finding how often the
same incident is repeated in the lives of different
saints. St. Mochua was attended by a multitude of

people in a wild district, where he had nothing to offer them for food.   In this dilemma, the saint called to him stags from the forest, and, having killed them, they were soon eaten up; but he had given strict orders that the bones and skin should be carefully preserved and kept together.   Next morning, after he had said a blessing or a charm over them, the stags were restored to life and vigour, and hurried off to their old haunts in the woods.   St. Euchadius was, on one occasion, obliged to kill a favourite cow to regale his guests; after the meal, he placed the bones in the skin, and restored the animal to life.   St. Finnian performed the same exploit with a calf.   These are all variations of one original story, and that story, singularly enough, is found in the ancient mythology of the North.   We quote it from the readiest source at hand—Pigott's *Manual of Scandinavian Mythology*, p. 117.   Thor, on one of his expeditions against the giants, went in his car, drawn by two he-goats, to seek a lodging in the hut of a peasant.   " The peasant's family consisted of himself and his old wife, and of a son and daughter, Tialf and Roska.   The old woman lamented to Thor, that she had nothing to offer him for supper but some roots.   Thor answered that he would provide food, and bade her prepare the table. He then took Miölner, his hammer, and slew his two he-goats; and having stripped them of their skins, put them into the boiler.   The skins were spread out carefully before the hearth, and Thor desired the peasant to be sure to put all the bones into them. When the meat was cooked, they all sat down to supper . . . . . During the supper, however, Tialf, the boy, had contrived to get a thigh-bone of one of the goats, which he brake for the sake of the marrow.

I.   M

Thor stayed over the night in the cottage. The next morning, before dawn, he rose, and taking Miölner in his hand, he swung it in the air over the goat-skins and bones. The goats immediately sprang up in life and spirits; but one of them was lame in the hind-leg. Thor's anger on this was kindled. He said that the peasant or his people must have been careless with the bones, seeing that a thigh-bone had been broken." Mr. Pigott observes in a note, that "the heathen Finlapps still take care not to break the bones of the animals which they sacrifice, saying that the gods may put flesh and skin on them again." It would not be easy to conceive a more convincing illustration of the source of the mediæval legends of saints. *

If more of the stories of the earlier mythology of the Teutonic race had been preserved, we should without doubt be enabled to identify in this manner many particulars in the outlines of the saints' legends, of the origin of which we are now ignorant. With such a beginning, it was easy to fill the canvass; and we shall find that, in the composition of the life of a saint, almost every class of materials was made to con-tribute. In illustration of this part of the subject, we would point out to particular attention the number of interesting facts collected together by M. Maury, in his *Essay on the Pious Legends of the Middle Ages.* He has divided the mediæval miracles into three classes—1. Miracles imitated from the Gospels, and from the Old Testament; 2. Legends formed by

---

* Several of the saints, like St. Colman, left the imprint of their feet or hands on rocks, which were afterwards worshipped. These marks had no doubt been objects of pagan reverence, as we still find them in the East.

confounding the figurative meaning with the literal, in consequence of the tendency of uncultivated minds to refer everything to material life; and, 3. Miracles or legends invented to explain figured symbols or emblematical images, the real meaning of which had been forgotten. Instances of the latter class meet us at almost every turn. We know that, even in modern times, people are frequently inventing fables to account for pictured representations which have been handed down from the past without any authentic explanation. The number of imitations — evident copies—of the Scriptural miracles, found in the legends of the saints, is perfectly extraordinary. M. Maury cites imitations of the Annunciation in the lives of fourteen different saints; twenty-nine imitations of the miraculous multiplication of food, and of the changing of water into wine; and so on with every miracle in the Old and New Testaments. Instances of the two other classes of miracles are equally numerous; even the Gospel parables, or eastern apologues, are thus transformed. After this fashion, in the coarse comprehension of these monkish biographers, the odour of sanctity, or its reverse, become material scents; the bones of the saints, when dug up from the grave, smell like roses, while those of sinners and pagans stink insufferably. The new writer of *Saints' Lives* gravely informs us, that "it is said of the holy Sturme, a disciple and companion of Winfrid, that in passing a horde of unconverted Germans, as they were bathing and gamboling in a stream, he was so overpowered by the intolerable stench [of sin] which arose from them, that he nearly fainted away." Thus, also, the fervour of holiness becomes a material warmth. It is related in

the life of St. Fechin, how his piety was so fervent,
that when he bathed himself in cold water, the water
was rendered nearly boiling hot.　A similar unspiri-
tual conception led the monks of Mont St. Michel
to show amongst their relics the spear and shield
with which St. Michael was armed when he encoun-
tered the dragon of the Revelations; and we have
read that some relic-monger of old, mistaking the
symbolical representation of the Holy Spirit for a
real pigeon, exhibited to the pious gaze of his hearers
a feather of the Holy Ghost!

Then the immense profusion of miracles!　This is
a characteristic of the mediæval lives of saints, which
immediately attracts the attention of the reader.　In
scriptural history, the Creator interrupts rarely the
laws which he has given to nature, and that only on
occasions of extraordinary importance; on the other
hand, the monkish saints seem to be so overburdened
with the miraculous power, that they daily perform
miracles, the only object of which appears to be the
relieving themselves of the desire of exercising it.
Their frequency must have changed altogether the
aspect of society.　Prisons are so often miraculously
opened by their intervention, that the ordinary course
of justice must have been constantly at fault; while
between those whom they relieved from wounds and
sickness, and the dead whom they recalled to life by
dozens and scores, the land must have been peopled
for successive generations with a population literally
stolen from the grave.　When the Franciscans compared the miracles of their founder with those of the
Saviour, they boasted that, for Christ's single transformation, St. Francis had exhibited twenty; that
Jesus had changed water into wine but once, whereas

St. Francis had performed the same miracle thrice; and that in place of the small number of miraculous cures enumerated in the Gospel, St. Francis and his disciples had restored more than a thousand blind to their sight, and more than a thousand lame to the use of their limbs, and raised more than a thousand dead to life.

The writer of the *Lives of the English Saints* argues insidiously, that as the object of the miracles was *teaching*, we have no right to judge, by our present standard, of the homely and ridiculous character which they often possess. The criterion which he proposes is—were they fitted to the manners and comprehension of the age? In anything but miracles, an argument like this might have its weight. But, instead of considering the false logic implied in it, let us show that it is founded on an untrue statement. A majority of the saints' miracles are performed for the most frivolous causes—often with selfish motives and for personal revenge, and very commonly in private. A few examples, taken at random, will give the best idea of their usual character.

The object of many of these miracles was the mere personal convenience or advantage of the saint. When St. Mochua wanted a fire in his cell, he called down a flame from heaven to light it. The candles of the saints were often lit in a similar manner. When St. Senan found that he had only one small candle, and that no more were to be obtained, he caused it miraculously to burn during a whole week without consuming. When St. Faro of Meaux (*Meldis*), was at supper, his cup-bearer let fall the vessel from which he drank, and it was broken to pieces. The saint, by a miracle, made it whole, and continued his

meal. St. Goar, of Treves, seeking a beam to hang
up his cape, saw a sunbeam that came through the
window, on which he suspended it, and it remained
hanging there till he took it down.   The biographer
observes, that " it is not to be wondered at if a ray of
the sun assumed the hardness of wood in obedience
to the holy man, since, to one who lives in devout
intimacy with the Creator, the creature is subjected
by the Creator's will."   The same miracle was performed by (among others) St. Aicadrus, abbot of
Jumièges, who similarly hung up his gloves on a sunbeam.   St. Leufroi, when in summer the flies in-
fested his cell, and settled on his food, drove them
away by a miracle.   By another miracle, St. Columbanus kept the grubs from his cabbages, when other
gardens were overrun by them.   St. Cuthbert, in a
similar manner, kept the field he had sown with corn
from the intrusion of birds.   St. Fechin, on his return
from a distant excursion, finding that he had a long
way to travel before he regained his monastic home,
and perceiving the approach of night, caused the sun
to stand still, in order that he might not be overtaken
by darkness.   Thus the miracle which God had once
vouchsafed in the hour of battle for the salvation of
his chosen people, was here repeated at the caprice
of an individual to avoid a very slight inconvenience.
The want of a meal was a sufficient cause for a miracle.
When St. Fintan expected company, having no flour to
make bread, and there being no water to turn the mill,
he ordered the mill to work of itself, and it obeyed.
When St. Cadoc was travelling in Cornwall, and
overtaken by thirst in a district where there was no
water, he struck his staff into the ground, and a beautiful stream at once administered to his wants.   When

St. Mael was in want of fishes, he caught them on dry ground, and when another Irishman, St. Berach, wanted fruit, he caused the willows to bear apples. When St. Aidan, bishop of Ferns, was hungry, he took a handful of leaves and turned them into bread; and when St. Fechin wanted meat, he took acorns and turned them into pork. St. Tillo, on visiting his monks, finding they had no wine to give him, filled their barrel by a miracle. St. Romaric also miraculously filled a vessel with wine, and another with ale. Turning water into wine was the most common of miracles.

In the course of their travels, the saints had still more frequent occasions for the exertion of their miraculous powers; which, to judge from the narratives of their biographers, must have rendered their labours extremely easy. In the first place, they were not liable to be wet. When St. Albin, a French saint of the sixth century, (even in his youth,) went forth with his companions, he alone was untouched by the heaviest rain. When St. Roger, abbot of Elant, fell into a river, he was brought out perfectly dry. The saints, indeed, seem to have possessed the same power over the elements as the witches and sorcerers, from whom probably the idea was derived. St. Columbanus forbade the rain to wet his corn in harvest time, and when the reapers of St. Geneviève were occupied in the field, she ordered the rain away, that they might not be inconvenienced by it. When St. Gildas and his companions resolved to take their lodging in an island that was inconveniently small, it miraculously expanded at their desire. When St. Trivier, with two or three companions, was on his journey to Italy, and they lost their way in the woods, at his prayer two wolves came forward to offer themselves as guides. It may be observed, too, that he must have been only a second-rate saint; for Bolland, who prints his life from a manuscript, acknowledges that he could not find his name in any of the calendars. When St. Fechin was travelling, he came to where a large tree had fallen across his path; instead of taking the trouble to walk round or scramble over it, he merely ordered it to make way: and immediately it raised itself upright in its place. St. Dominic, under similar circumstances, beheld a large beech-tree falling upon him; he stretched out his arms towards it, and it drew itself back and fell in the contrary direction. St. Corbinian travelled on horseback from France to Bavaria; in his way through a forest, a savage bear rushed out, and killed and devoured his horse: another saint would have restored the horse to life, but a word from Corbinian rendered the bear as tame as a lamb; the saint saddled and bridled it, and so proceeded on his journey. On St. Mochua getting tired of walking, he called to the nearest wood for a wild stag, which became as tame as St. Corbinian's bear.

No amount of water was any obstacle to their progress. When St. Mochua with his disciples came to a deep and rapid river, he threw his cloak on the water; and they all passed over upon it as in a boat. A lady saint, St. Fanchea, passed over the sea on her cloak in a similar manner. In the popular mythology, we frequently meet with nymphs and witches passing the water on carpets, sieves, or other articles of magical power. Another lady, St. Cannera the virgin, when she had to pass the sea, walked upon the water. This was a very common practice. One

day as St. Scothinus was walking in this manner across
the Irish channel, he met St. Barras the bishop passing him in a ship.   The bishop appears to have been
jealous, and asked him what he was walking upon ;
to which St. Scothinus replied that it was a beautiful
green meadow.   When St. Barras denied this, he
stooped down and gathered a handful of fresh flowers.
St. Barras, to refute him in his own way of arguing,
also stooped down, and, dipping his hand in the
water, drew it out full of fishes.   This is duly set
forth in the authentic life of the saint printed by
Colgan.   St. Aidan, or Maedhog, bishop of Fern, at
the beginning of the seventh century, was one day
walking over the sea from Ireland to Wales ; upon
which, an angel came and checked him for his pre-
sumption in performing a miracle like this without
God's permission.   He returned, however, by the
same road ; and on his arrival in Ireland, finding that
he had inadvertently left a bell behind him, he had
only to wish for it, and the sea brought it over to the
Irish shore.   This saint subsequently made a practice
of taking his horse to exercise at sea.   Either the
same, or another saint with a similar name, drove a
waggon and a team of horses over an Irish bog ; and
as often as he and his friends went out to sea on
horseback, the water became hard under their horses'
hoofs.   The saints who rode thus were chiefly Irish ;
and every one acquainted with the fairy mythology
of the sister island, will remember its stories of troops
of horsemen riding over lakes and seas.   Other saints
advanced a step in the miraculous: St. Patrick passed
over the sea, and St. Cuanna over a lake, mounted
on a large flag-stone instead of a boat.   When St.
Cadoc came with twenty-four of his disciples to a

M 2

wide and rapid river, he struck it with his staff; the
waters separated and left a dry path to the other side.
In like manner, St. Serenicus caused the waters of a
river in the diocese of Sens, in France, to divide, that
he might pass over dry. These, of course, are imitations of the passage of the Red Sea by the people of
Israel.

There is another problem, which has attracted the
attention of several ingenious persons—the possibility
of being in two places at once. The saints long ago
approached very near to its solution. The compiler
of the original life of St. Cadoc, having confounded
a British saint with an Italian, and finding that the
same person was thus on the same day in Italy and in
Britain, tells us that, as he was occupied about his
affairs in the latter country, he was suddenly seized
up in a cloud or whirlwind, and that in the winking
of an eye (*quasi in palpebræ motu*) he was set down at
Beneventum. It is scarcely necessary to observe,
that this was precisely the method of travelling
practised by the witches, fairies, and other beings of
the popular creed. Several saints might be mentioned as repeating this experiment of passing to a
distant place "in the winking of an eye." St. Scothinus, already cited for his exploits on the sea, usually
went to Rome in a day, transacted his business there
the same evening, and returned to Ireland the next
morning.

We may trace this rage for miracles into every
department of the monastic life. When St. Fechin
designed to build a magnificent church in a valley that
was too narrow, he ordered one of the hills to move
further off, and was obeyed. When St. Laumer was

building a monastery at the place called after him, Laumer-le-Moutier, a large oak stood in a position where it was difficult for the woodmen to cut it; he said a prayer, (a Pagan would have called it a charm,) and the oak at once moved to a more convenient place. St. Maedhog was desirous of building, and had no architect; he took the hand of a rough, untaught labourer, named Gobban, and blessed it; and Gobban in an instant became a most skilful architect, and built for the saint a noble church.* One of the most common miracles connected with building, was that of lengthening a beam which the carpenter had made too short. This was performed by St. Amatus and St. Gall for their cells or oratories; and by St. Pardulf, St. Æmilian, and St. Augustine of Canterbury, for their monasteries and churches. It was repeated by several English saints. The earlier monasteries were sometimes built in elevated positions. When the monks complained of the labour of fetching water from the plain, their founders, as in the cases of St. Benedict and St. Basoli, brought the fountains to the top of the hill. St. Fechin built a mill on a hill-top; the carpenter employed upon it accidentally exclaimed, in the midst of his work, that he wished he might live till he saw there water to work it. The saint reproved him for his want of faith, and walked to a lake about a mile distant, into

---

* " Quodam tempore cum B. Maedhog basilicam sibi ædificare voluisset, non potuit artificem tum invenire. Confidens in Deo, benedixit manus cujusdam ineruditi nomine Gobbani, et statim subtilissimus artifex est factus. Postea in summa arte illam basilicam ædificavit."—*Acta Sanctorum Bolland. Mens. Jan.*, vol. ii. p. 1118.

which he threw his stick; the stick followed him on his return, and the water after it: a plentiful stream soon set the mill to work.

It would be an endless task, and by no means an agreeable one, to mention all the different miracles said to have been performed with no other object than to increase the comforts of the monks, individually or collectively, as soon as they were established in their monasteries. St. Fechin's monastery had once the misfortune to have a monk so ugly that he was ashamed to show himself among his brethren; the saint spat on the ground, and anointed his ill-favoured features—they instantly underwent so great a change, that he was ever afterwards remarkable for his beauty. St. Berach also made an ugly man handsome, and a short man long. St. Gerald and St. Abban, both Irish saints, changed girls into boys. All these are incidents of the old fairy legends. The same may be said of another marvel; that of purses or vessels endowed with the quality of furnishing a constant supply of money or liquor. These stories figure among the myths of Scandinavians and Germans. St. Odilo of Cluny, visiting a dependent cell, found that there was only a small vessel full of wine to serve a large number of monks; nothing daunted, he ordered them to pass it round, and, after every one had drunk his fill, the vessel was found to be just as full as when they began. A similar miracle was ascribed to St. Patrick. There can be but little doubt, that the principal precedent upon which the worthy man proceeded in this instance, would be that of Elijah and the widow's cruise.

As we have already intimated, many of these miracles were performed with no other apparent object than the gratification of a very petty feeling of revenge. St. Roger, abbot of Elant, was treated with disrespect at a priory he visited; he went away praying fervently that the uncourteous monks might be punished. The priory immediately took fire and was burnt to the ground. A man who refused to carry St. Fechin in his boat, was drowned. St. Cadoc made some trifling demand of a peasant, which the latter refused jeeringly; the saint turned up his eyes to heaven—and at his prayer fire came down and destroyed the clown who had thus offended him. Men who laughed at St. Præjectus of Clairmont, were struck dead. A monk, who had offended St. Molagga, died immediately. This revengeful feeling of the saints was cherished even towards animals. In the life of St. Bertulf, we are told that a monk named Leopardus had the care of his vineyard, where, one day, he found a fox devouring a bunch of grapes. Leopardus rebuked the fox, and forbade its touching the grapes in future. But the fox, unable to resist the temptation, returned to the vineyard, seized a bunch of grapes in its mouth, and instantly dropped down dead. St. Attracta changed dogs, which disobeyed her, into stones. The same fate was experienced by two wolves, which attacked the sheep of St. Cadoc. As St. Marius, abbot of Revons in France, in the sixth century, was proceeding to visit his dependent cells, a dog ran after him and tore his robe. A simple ejaculation from the saint was sufficient to call two wolves from a neighbouring wood: and they immediately devoured the offending animal. St. Ebrulf had a monastery in the wilderness of Ouche; a raven built its nest near him, and frequently stole the provisions of the monks; on which one of them, who wished to try his hand at a miracle in imitation of his master, prayed that it might be punished, and it was immediately afterwards found dead.   A raven flew away with one of the gloves belonging to Columbanus; but it came back and restored it at the call of the saint.   In the same manner a fox, which had stolen a cock belonging to St. Condedus the hermit, was made to bring back its prey with the greatest contrition.   Some crows carried away part of the thatch of St. Cuthbert's hut to build their nests ; at his rebuke, they not only made an apology, but they brought him a piece of hog's lard (which they must have stolen from somebody) to make him amends for the injury he had sustained.   This miracle is told by Bede, whose authority our modern miracle-mongers look upon it as little less than blasphemy to doubt.

The class of miracles which our new writers of saints' lives are willing to consider as coming under the title of " grotesque," but which they think there is nevertheless " no ground for rejecting," is also extremely numerous.   We confess that we do not always very easily perceive their object or utility, even for " teaching."   For instance, St. James of Tarentaise, a disciple of St. Honoratus, hoping to conciliate the favour of the Burgundian prince, Gundicarius, by a present of ice in the summer, carried it on the back of an ass : by miraculous interference, the sun, though intensely hot, had no effect upon it. But the saint and his attendants, having forgotten to put themselves under protection of the miracle, were soon overcome by the heat, and they retired to a shady spot to seek repose.   Here a raven suddenly pounced upon the head of the ass, tore out one of its eyes, and flew away. The saint, on learning what had happened, made a hasty invocation: upon this, the raven instantly returned, croaking forth its penitence, and carrying the eye in its beak. The eye was replaced in its socket, and, wonderful to relate! the sight of the ass was so perfectly restored, that the animal arose more vigorous than ever, and continued its journey. The Irish St. Ita, finding a man with his head cut off, restored it to his shoulders, and sent him about his business. St. Cronan caused a wild beast, which had killed and eaten a man, to reject the meal from its stomach, and he then brought back the man to life. St. Maclou found a boy weeping for the death of one of his swine; he stretched out his hand, and it immediately rose up alive. St. Melorus having lost his hand, caused another to be made of silver, which became fixed to his arm and as pliable as a hand of flesh and muscles. St. Benedict employed a man to clear the thorns and brushwood from the side of a lake, and lent him an axe for the purpose. While he was actively employed in his work, the head of the axe flew from the handle into the lake. St. Benedict, informed of this accident, took the handle, blessed it, and cast it into the lake; it sank, and then returned to the surface of the water, with the head firmly attached to it. St. Leufroi performed the same miracle in a river; both, of course, copies of the miracle of the prophet Elisha, in the Old Testament.

Such, it appears, is the trash in which "devout minds" are required to believe; and for the sake of believing which, we are called upon to relinquish our right of investigating and judging. We have taken our examples very indiscriminately, from less than a tithe of the materials of this description which have been committed to print, and among which may be found many more absurd miracles than those here alluded to. Several, indeed, of the very worst class are retailed with becoming gravity in the *Lives of the English Saints*, which are lying before us. What, for instance, shall we think of the following? We are told of St. Augustine's missionary wanderings, that " there is no record, or even tradition, of his reception in the north of England having been otherwise than favourable, and even hearty. Very different from this are the accounts of his travels in Dorsetshire. While there, we hear of his having come to one village where he was received with every species of insult. The wretched people, not content with heaping abusive words upon the holy visitors, assailed them with missiles, in which work, the place being probably a seaport, the sellers of fish are related to have been peculiarly active. Hands, too, were laid upon the archbishop and his company. Finding all efforts useless, the godly band shook off the dust from their feet and withdrew. The inhabitants are said to have suffered the penalty of their impieties even to distant generations. All the children born from that time bore and transmitted the traces of their parents' sin in the shape of a loathsome deformity."—(*Life of St. Augustine*, p. 327.) The insult put upon the saints was that of attaching the tails of fish behind their robes. To explain the nature of the deformity, it will be enough to state that, according to the narrator of this miracle, the inhabitants of the village in question were ever afterwards born with tails! It was probably in reference to this judgment, pronounced on some of their countrymen by their great apostle, that the English crusaders who accompanied Richard I. are reported to have been mocked with the title of *caudati*, or the people having tails.

Vast as was the number of miracles said to have been performed by the saints while alive, they bear no comparison with those performed in after ages by their bones.   This is one of the many startling problems, which are to be found among Pascal's " Thoughts."   " The lives of saints," says their modern biographer, in " many cases do not end with their deaths; their influence over the visible church is often more signally exerted through their relics than it was in their sojourn upon earth.   Somewhat of that power which they now have in their glorified state is permitted to be transfused into their mortal remains, and through them to act upon the church. Many of the saints have lived and died almost in obscurity, whose relics have worked wonders for centuries; God, who saw them in secret while on earth, thus manifesting them openly after He has taken them from us."   In fact, some of the saints, who lived not in obscurity, but of whose lives we have more authentic memorials than of the others, worked no miracles until ages after their death; and when their marvellous qualities had become a matter of pecuniary importance.

It takes but a step to pass from the age of saints to that of relics.   The worship of relics, and a faith in the miracles performed by them, are surely a degrading superstition under any system.   In all ages, and under all creeds, a reverence for the memory of the individual has often been transmitted to his mortal remains, and to the spot in which they are deposited.

It is the same universal sentiment, which makes us
desire to fix some lasting memorial over the graves of
departed friends; and in credulous ages, it easily degenerated into a belief that the relics of the dead
possessed something more of the living individual
than their mere physical structure might indicate.
Under this impression, the bones of the saints (the
most durable parts of their frames) were looked upon
as representing the saints upon earth and purified
from fleshly taints.   From this supposition it was an
easy step to believe that they possessed the power of
working miracles — greater than they had worked
while in the flesh.   For it seems to have been the
vulgar notion, that the miracle was not so much done
by God at the saint's intercession, as by some mysterious influence with which the latter was endowed.
The bodies of individuals whose sanctity was thus
acknowledged became the objects of pilgrimage, and
were believed to perform miraculous cures on those
who solicited their aid.   As few would seek a benefit
of this kind without making some offering in return,
(this offering being not unfrequently the measure of
the efficiency of the relics,) they soon became a
source of great riches to the church or monastery
which possessed them.   When this was once discovered, the relics themselves increased rapidly in
number; until there was scarcely a parish church but,
if it could not boast of a whole saint, could at least
show a fragment of one.   This gave rise to an extensive and disgraceful system of jugglery and de-
ception, which was carried to the most extraordinary
lengths.   It was only necessary to open some long-
forgotten grave, or to meet by accident with a heap
of unknown bones; a monk of the house was brought

forward to declare that he had received a divine in-
timation, either in a vision or in a dream, that they
were the remains of a saint; the bones were carried
with great ceremony into the church; and, if such a
saint had never been heard of before, the fertile
brains of the same or of some other monk, soon produced a life filled with marvellous details.   Such, in
all probability, was the origin of three-fourths of the
saints in the calendar.   Whence the materials were
chiefly derived, has been already shown.   We have
seen, in at least one instance, bones taken out of a
Pagan barrow and turned to this purpose.   The
period during which the greatest number of relics
were thus miraculously discovered, was that of the
rebuilding of monasteries which followed the devas-
tating invasions of the Danes and Normans.

It was a very suspicious circumstance attendant on
these relics, that in general they gave no miraculous
evidence of their existence, except while they were
in the hands of those who were making a profit of
them.   St. Marcellus, the pope, was buried in the
monastery of Hautmont, in the diocese of Cambrai.
It had been almost destroyed by the Huns, and lay
ruined and neglected till the eleventh century.   At
that period, abbot Ursio ruled over it; and it was
reduced to such extreme poverty that, tormented by
enemies, and perhaps by creditors, the abbot searched
every part of the house in the hope of discovering
some lost object of value which might be turned into
money.   Abbot Ursio and his monks found, accordingly, in a lumber-room, a coffer of silver; but they
were totally ignorant of its contents, and are said to
have felt some unaccountable hesitation in opening it.
After consulting together, they laid their doubts

before the bishop of Cambrai, and, by his advice,
proceeded to examine it with becoming reverence.
When they opened it, a sweet odour issued from the
interior, where they found a parcel of bones, which
a document—placed there, it was said, in the time of
Dagobert—stated to be the relics of St. Marcellus.
There was now nothing but rejoicing among the
poverty-stricken monks. A new and elegant shrine
was constructed; the bones, which had been so long
dormant, began to work miracles anew; and a crowd
of devout worshippers soon relieved the monastery
from its pecuniary embarrassments. The tomb of St.
Frodobert had in like manner been forgotten, and
the church in which he lay had long been a ruin. As
long as they had been unknown, his bones had
worked no miracles; but some pious and rich individual took it into his head to rebuild the church in a
stately manner. Upon this, the saint gave information of his resting-place; and, as soon as due honours
and *offerings* were paid to his tomb, he vouchsafed to
perform an endless list of miraculous cures.

We are the more surprised at the caprice with
which the relics sometimes kept themselves long
hidden, when we compare this with the jealousy with
which, at other times, they punished the slightest
disrespect or neglect. When enemies ravaged the
territory of Arbonne, a soldier who attempted to
open the coffin of St. Gall was seized with madness.
A man who struck the tomb of St. Erminold irreve-
rently, fell down dead. A hundred similar instances
might be quoted. This jealousy was cherished even
against those who robbed the shrine of its dues. A
good dame of Ratisbon, unable by the severity of
her disease to go herself, sent another woman, who

dwelt with her in the same house, to offer for her a
piece of money and light candles at the tomb of St.
Erminold. She came with a crowd of devotees, and
offered her money and lighted her candles; but, in
the confusion created by the crowd of offerings, in-
cited by covetousness, she drew back the money with
her hand. She was putting it in her purse, when
her fingers became suddenly stiff and contracted, and
adhered so firmly to the coin, that she was compelled
in her agony to confess her crime. On receiving
absolution, her hand was restored to its natural condition. Considering the innumerable miracles of this
kind which are related in the Romish legends, it seems
remarkable that, when the Reformers (who certainly
provoked such manifestations as much as any Pagan
invaders) drew forth these time-worn relics at a later
period, and scattered them to the winds, no miracle
was ever wrought for their protection. The age of
saints' relics, as well as that of saints' miracles, was
then past; and a second time—

> " Peor and Baalim
> Forsook their temples dim."

In older times, if we believe their story, this jealous
spirit of self-defence was often found necessary to
guard against pious, as well as impious, depredators;
for the possession of relics was sometimes the cause
of dire war, even between the inmates of different
religious establishments. When St. Fanchea died
in Ireland, the inhabitants of two petty kingdoms
assembled in separate parties to fight for her body,
almost as soon as the breath had left it. Instead of
loathing the quarrelsome spirit which had brought
them together, the saint declared by a miracle to

which party she wished to belong. The body of St. Furseus, in like manner, was nearly the subject of a battle.

Sometimes, when a larger or more influential party were in want of the relics of a saint of celebrity, they looked round for a weaker who possessed them, and plotted a pious theft. If they succeeded, it was a miracle by which the saint showed his preference for the new place of abode; if they failed, the miracle was in favour of the old possessors. The bones of St. Neot were preserved at the church in which he had been buried, St. Neot's in Cornwall, until the year 974. A powerful Saxon earl at that time founded a priory at Eynesbury, now St. Neot's in Huntingdonshire, and wanted a patron saint. He obtained for his praiseworthy attempt the sanction of three powerful individuals, Brithnod abbot of Ely, Athelwold bishop of Winchester, and king Edgar. The official guardian of the shrine in Cornwall was corrupted: he secretly fled with the treasure entrusted to his care, reached Huntingdonshire in safety, and was received into the earl's house, as the monastic buildings were not yet completed. The people of the Cornish St. Neot's, when they discovered the theft, armed themselves hastily, and pursued the fugitive to Eynesbury, where they besieged the house, and demanded their relics. But the king sent an armed force to drive the Cornishmen out of the village, with orders to put them to the sword without mercy, in case of resistance. It was proclaimed that the saint, having been disgusted with the sins of the Cornishmen, had miraculously made known his wish to seek a new and more splendid shrine in the county of Huntingdon.

In the tenth century, the relics of St. Bertulf were deposited at Boulogne. They were one night stolen in order to be carried over to England to king Athelstan. But the robber had proceeded no further than the Flemish port of Audinghem, when he was overtaken by the clergy of Boulogne, and obliged to surrender his prey. A miracle had withheld him from passing the sea. In the latter part of the eleventh century, the clergy of Laon made an attempt to steal the body of St. Theodoric (or Thierri), abbot of Rheims, which had been laid in a richly ornamented coffin by abbot Raimbald. There was at this time a dispute between the clergy of Laon and the abbot of Rheims. The relics of St. Theodoric were carried to Laon to decide the cause, and were honourably received in the church. As appears to have been the custom in such cases, the guards of the sacred deposit were chosen from the clergy of Laon, and not from those of Rheims. This circumstance furnished the looked-for opportunity for the theft. In the dead of the night, when the treacherous keepers were intentionally off their guard, two persons entered the church, silently lifted the cover of the shrine, and introduced their hands. To their astonishment they found the coffer empty. Supposing that they had been anticipated, they left the church as noiselessly as they came : and the clergy of Rheims carried home their relics in safety. The thieves, however, subsequently made a full confession : and it was placed among one of the most remarkable miracles of the saint, how his relics had become invisible and intangible, when an attempt was made to steal them. This system of relic-stealing had become so common, that in some houses extraordinary precautions were taken

to prevent it.   We are told that it was an ordinance
strictly enforced in the church of St.   Cadoc at Beneventum, that no native of the British Isles should be
allowed to pass the threshold, in consequence of an
old prophecy that a monk of Lancarvan would one
day steal and carry away St. Cadoc's relics.   Other
arts than that of robbery were employed at times to
gain possession of relics.   St. Romanus, the abbot,
was buried at Fontrouge, near Auxerre.   It appears
that the clergy of this place did not make the most
of his relics, and, under pretence that the saint was
dissatisfied with so obscure a resting-place, they were
removed to a church in Auxerre.   There they soon
became famous for miraculous cures, and the bishop,
not without much trouble, effected their translation
to his cathedral.   But even here they were not
allowed to rest quietly ; for, at a subsequent period,
the archbishop of Sens employed similar intrigues to
obtain them for his metropolitan church.

It was not only found necessary to guard against
these attempts to steal the bodies of the saints : there
were many depredators on a smaller scale, who
attempted to gain possession of a bone or a fragment.
In such cases the bones, when taken away, either
lost their power of working miracles, or they became
hurtful, and even fatal, in the hands of their new
possessors.   The bodies of St. Deicolus and St. Columbanus were deposited in shrines in the church of
Lure.   The countess Hildegardis was anxious to
carry some portion of the relics with her into Alsace:
she went to the church, and tried in vain to lift the
cover of the coffin of St. Deicolus.   As she persisted
in her attempt, a sudden earthquake, accompanied
with thick darkness, shook the monastery from its

foundation, and struck the inmates with terror. The countess now desisted; and, turning to the shrine of St. Columbanus, opened it with comparative ease, and abstracted a tooth. From this moment, until the time she returned and publicly restored the tooth, we are told that the countess was never free from excruciating toothache! When the relics of St. Genevieve were carried about in fear of the Norman invaders, an abbot, Herebert, more pious than wise, (*zelum quidem pietatis habens, sed non secundum scientiam,*) stole one of the teeth; but he was punished with a succession of fearful dreams and visions, until he restored it. Something of a similar kind happened to the relics of the Belgian hermit, St. Gerlac. A stranger came from a distance to offer at his shrine, and under pretence of devoutly kissing his head, drew out a tooth unperceived, and went his way, exulting in the possession of so holy a relic. His joy, however, was not of long duration; for, within a year, he brought back the relic in penitent humility, and showed the guardians of the shrine that, in the interim, he had himself lost every tooth in his head.

When, however, the clergy *sold* their relics, which they often did by bit and bit, their virtues remained unimpaired; and this became, in course of time, a very lucrative source of revenue. Long before the Reformation, the bones (or pretended bones) of the principal saints of the Romish ritual had been scattered over every part of Europe; and, by some mysterious power of development or multiplication, there were often found as many heads, arms, hands, &c., of the same saint, as, put together, would have made a dozen individuals.

Such is, in brief, the history of saints' lives and

saints' miracles. It must be confessed, not a very
flattering one for human reason; although an instructive one for those who would study the errors of the
past in the light of a warning for the future. The
Reformers were not far from the truth when they
charged with idolatry the church of the middle ages;
that church which, after it had once lost its original
purity, seems to have gone on adopting some of the
most exceptionable characteristics of almost every
pagan creed with which it came in contact. At first,
probably, these corruptions were taken up unwittingly : and various allusions in old canons and
homilies would seem to show, that there were at all
times enlightened members of the Roman communion
who set their faces against them. There are instances
of fathers of the mediæval church lifting up their
voices against these pretended miracles, as mere instruments of worldly vanity. Few, indeed, of the
wiser Catholics, even of the middle ages, who must
have known well the secrets of their order, can have
ever looked upon them as anything better than as
parts of the painful chapter of serviceable frauds.

   If anything on such a subject ought to astonish us,
the *revival* of these legends in our own age and
country is surely an astonishing phænomenon. But
it is useless to talk of reason and of evidence to en-
thusiasts, young or old, who have made up their
minds to believe, without evidence and against reason.
We will end with a modern story, which our readers
may apply. Everybody has read of the miraculous
cures performed, not long ago, by prince Hohenlohe.
In 1821, the magistrates of Bamberg forbade him to
exercise his miraculous powers without first acquaint-
ing the police, nor unless in the presence of a com-

mission deputed by the authorities, nor unless one or more physicians were in attendance. The prince appealed to the pope. The pope ordered him to conform to the restrictions. The miracles have not been heard of since.

—— " Ghosts prudently withdraw at peep of day."

XII.

ON ANTIQUARIAN EXCAVATIONS AND
RESEARCHES IN THE
MIDDLE AGES.

MONG the ornaments of the splendid votive altar exhibited to the Society of Antiquaries some years ago by M. le colonel Theubet were three antique engraved gems, one of which, I believe, represented a head of Socrates, another a scarabæus, and the third a figure offering sacrifice at an altar. We have many proofs of the care with which ancient gems and cameos were sought and preserved in the middle ages, and it is probable that some of the most beautiful specimens known in modern times have been derived from the monastic treasuries. The superstition of a barbarous age regarded these relics as things endowed with magic qualities, which possessed healing and protective virtues that rendered them precious to the possessor. It appears that they were sometimes even regarded as natural productions, not formed by the hand of man. As early as the twelfth century (at least) we meet with regular inventories of such gems, with an enumeration of their virtues according to the figures they bore; and I now publish an inventory of this

kind in Latin, which is the one of most common occurrence in manuscripts.   It appears to me that it
possesses considerable interest, and that it may be
appropriately introduced by a few anecdotes from old
writers illustrative of the excavations and researches
amid the ruins of antiquity made by monks and others
in the middle ages.

Under the Anglo-Saxons, down to a late period,
our island appears to have been covered with the
majestic ruins of Roman towns and cities; although
people had been gradually clearing away many of
them in order to use the materials for new buildings.
As early as the middle of the seventh century, when
the monks of Ely wanted a stone coffin for the body
of the abbess Etheldrida, they sought for it among
the ruins of the Roman city the site of which is
now occupied by the town of Cambridge.   They
" came to a small deserted city which, in the language
of the Angles, is called Grantchester, and presently,
near the city walls, they found a white marble coffin,
most beautifully wrought, and neatly covered with a
lid of the same kind of stone."*   At a much later
period we shall find the abbots of St. Alban's collecting the materials furnished by the ruins of Verulamium (or, as the Saxons called it, Wærlam-ceaster)
to build their church.   Many Anglo-Norman and even
later works still existing are built in part of Roman
materials.

We find also that at an early period people, not
content with taking what was above ground, made
excavations under the soil in search of the relics of
ancient days.   It seems probable that the different
tribes who occupied the ground frequently opened

* Bede, Hist. Eccl lib. iv. c. 19.

the barrows of the tribes who had preceded them in
search of treasures.   The earliest mediæval poems,
such as the romance of Beowulf, speak of the
treasures of a primeval age, consisting of cups and
other vessels, personal ornaments, and weapons,
rescued by their heroes from beneath the tumulary
mounds of the giants (according to the belief of the
unconverted Germans), or of the heathen (according
to the Christianised notions).   We hear of the opening of barrows as late as the thirteenth and fourteenth
centuries,* and the discovery of funereal deposits and
of treasures.   The Anglo-Saxons appear to have
collected immense quantities of articles of Roman
manufacture by excavating, particularly vases and
other vessels of different materials ; and the earlier
rituals frequently contain forms for blessing these
implements of pagan manufacture in order to make
them fit for Christian use.   One of these benedictions
(*Benedictio super vasa reperta in locis antiquis*) prays
the Almighty to "deign so to cleanse these vases
fabricated by the art of the 'Gentiles" (*hæc vascula
arte fabricata Gentilium*), that they may be used by
the believers in peace and tranquillity ; and another
runs in these words, "God, who by the coming of
thy Son our Lord hast cleansed all things for thy
believers, attend propitious to our invocations, and
cleanse by the amplitude of thy grace these vessels,
which, by the indulgence of thy piety, after a length
of time being taken from the gulph of the earth, thou
hast restored to the use of men."†   In many in-

* See curious instances in my History of Ludlow, pp. 14
and 28.

† See the Anglo-Saxon Ritual of the Church of Durham
(published by the Surtees Society), p. 97.

stances, particularly in the earlier times of the Anglo-
Saxons, these Roman utensils appear to have been
buried again in Anglo-Saxon barrows, which accounts
for the discovery of mixed deposits of earlier and
more recent articles in one place. Mr. C. Roach
Smith exhibited to the Society a brazen bowl of
Roman workmanship, which had been mended with
pieces of metal bearing proof of Saxon art.*

The traces of these excavations appear not unfrequently in popular legends. It seems probable, from
legends preserved by the old chroniclers, that the
Italians of the tenth, eleventh, and twelfth centuries
penetrated into some of the Etruscan tombs. Gerbert
the mathematician, after he had become pope as Syl-
vester II., was a great excavator.† A story told of
this celebrated man by William of Malmsbury, and
which afterwards entered into the compilation of tales
known by the name of the Gesta Romanorum, seems
to refer to the discovery of some spacious subterranean
tomb of the early inhabitants of Italy ;‡ and the
same historian tells us that in the eleventh century
the Romans discovered the " body of Pallas the son
of Evander."§ More than a century after this a
tomb was opened in the neighbourhood of Glastonbury, which, it was pretended, contained the body of
king Arthur.‖

---

* Engraved and described in vol. xxx. of the Archæologia,
p. 133.

† Denique thesauros olim a gentilibus defossos, arte necro-
mantiæ molibus eruderatis inventos, cupiditatibus suis implicuit.
W. Malmsb. De Gest. Reg. Angl. lib. ii. p. 65.

‡ Ibid.   § Ibid. p. 86.

‖ Giraldus Cambrensis, De Inst. Princip. gives an account
of this discovery. See before, p. 225 of the present volume.

The earliest systematical excavations in England, of which we have a definite account, were made among the ruins of Verulamium in the earlier part of the eleventh century by two successive abbots of St. Alban's, Ealdred and Eadmer. We learn from Matthew Paris that abbot Ealdred overthew and filled up all the "subterranean crypts" of the ancient city, as well as the vaulted passages, with their windings, some of which ran under the bed of the river. He did so because they had become hiding-places for thieves and depraved women. The subterranean ruins of Roman Paris are described as the haunts of a similar class of society in the twelfth and thirteenth centuries. Ealdred also destroyed and filled up as much as he could the fosses of the ancient city, and certain caves, which afforded a place of refuge to the robbers who prowled in the neighbouring woods. The abbot laid up carefully all the unbroken tiles or bricks, and the stones which were fit for building, as materials for the new church which it was his intention to erect. With this object he made great excavations in order to discover stone buildings. As the workmen were digging near the bank of the river they found oak planks, with nails in them, and covered with pitch, apparently part of a ship, as well as old rusty anchors and oars, which proved, as Matthew Paris thought, that the sea had once encircled the town. Moreover, they found shells such as are commonly cast upon the sands of the sea shore. The places where these were found received the appropriate names of Oyster-hill, Shelford, Anchorpool, Fishpool, &c. There was also a deep den, surrounded by a hill, with a subterranean cave, which had been inhabited by a dragon, and was called Wurmenhert; this likewise abbot Ealdred filled up and defaced, leaving, however, traces of its former condition. When Ealdred had collected together much materials, both of stones, tiles, and wood, he died prematurely in the middle of his labours. His successor, Eadmer, continued the excavations. As the workmen were digging up the walls and foundations of the old buildings they uncovered the foundations of a vast palace, and they found a hollow in the wall like a cupboard, in which were a number of books and rolls, which were written in ancient characters and language that could only be read by one learned monk named Unwona. He declared that they were written in the ancient British language, that they contained " the invocations and rites of the idolatrous citizens of Wærlamceaster," with the exception of one, which contained the authentic life of St. Alban; the abbot preserved the latter, and had it translated into Latin, and as soon as the translation was completed the original crumbled into dust. This story was probably in part a pious fraud, designed to give authority to the legend of the saint. That remains of books were found is rendered probable, by the fact of some being termed rolls, which we know was the form of books among the Romans, and not among the Saxons. The other part of the story is also probably a fable, that it appeared from these books that the two principal deities of the citizens of Verulamium were Phœbus and Mercury, " called by the English, Woden," it being chiefly inhabited by merchants, of whom Mercury was the patron. These idolatrous books the abbot committed to the flames. " And as the abbot before mentioned diligently turned up the earth where the ruins of Verulamium appeared, and found squared stones with

N 2

bricks and columns, which he reserved for the erection of the church he proposed to build for St. Alban, the workmen found in the foundations of the old building pots and amphoras, elegantly formed of pottery and turned on the lathe, as well as glass vessels containing the ashes of the dead, for the ancients used to burn the bodies of their dead, whence the word *funus*, quasi *fumus*. There were also found the ruins of temples, altars overturned, and idols, and various kinds of coins which were then used." The idols were, without doubt, Roman statues and bronzes; the abbot, with characteristic Vandalism, ordered them all to be broken to pieces. *

<hr>

* *Ealdredus octavus.*—Ealdredus abbas. Iste antiquas scripturas (*lege* cryptas) subterraneas veteris civitatis, quæ Werlamcestre dicebatur, perscrutatas, evertit omnia et implevit; tracones vero et vias cum meatibus subterraneis, et solide per artificium arcuatis, quorum quidam subtus aquam Warlamiæ, quæ quondam maxima civitati fuit circumflua, transierunt, diruit, implevit, aut obturavit. Erant enim latibula latronum, vespilionum, et meretricum. Fossata vero civitatis et quasdam speluncas, ad quas quasi ad refugia redeuntes malefici et fugitivi a densis silvis vicinis fugerunt, in quantum potuit explanavit. Tegulas vero integras et lapides quos invenit aptos ad ædificia seponens, ad fabricam ecclesiæ reservavit. Proposuit enim, si facultates suppeterent, diruta veteri ecclesia, novam construere. Propter quod terram in profunditate evertit, ut lapideas structuras inveniret. Quod cum fecissent fossores, juxta ripam asseres quernos cum clavis infixis, pice navali delinitos (quales solent esse in carinis), invenerunt. Necnon et quædam navalia armamenta, utpote anchoras rubigine semirosas, et remos habienos, in certum et manifestum signum aquæ marinæ, quæ quondam Warlamcestrense vexit navigium, repererunt. Quæ unda, quomodo in parvum rivulum nunc contrahatur, et quo miraculo, Historia de sancto Albano explanat evidenter. Conchilia vero et conchas, quales litus maris solet educere vel projicere cum arenis æquoreis (quas insolito vestigio cives Verolamiæ properantes ad martyrium novi martyris quondam calcarunt) non sine admiratione invenerunt. Unde nomina

From these and other excavations on the same spot were probably derived some of the valuable gems enumerated in the inventories of the relics of the abbey of St. Alban's, preserved in the two Cottonian

locis ubi talia repererunt incolæ hæc videntes vel imposuerunt vel retulerunt se a veteribus relata meminisse, utpote, Oistre-hulle, Selleford, Ancrepol, Fispol, nomen vivarii regii ex reliquiis aquæ diminutæ. Specus quoque profundissimum, monte continuo circumseptum, cum spelunca subterranea, quam quondam draco ingens fecerat et inhabitavit, in loco qui Wurmenhert dicitur, in quantum potuit explanavit; vestigia tamen æterna habitationis serpentinæ derelinquens. · Iste autem Ealdredus, cum jam multam tam in lapidibus et tegulis quam materia lignea ad fabricam ecclesiæ coarvasset quantitatem, matura nimis morte præventus, imperfecto negotio, viam universæ carnis est ingressus.

Eadmarus nonus.—Eadmarus abbas. Iste pius ac mansuetus, et sacris literis sufficienter eruditus, sæculari et claustrali floruit probitate. Iste quæ prædecessor ejus viriliter imprimis est prosecutus, non in tantum placuit Deo ac martyri ut domum ipsius martyris ædificaret et consummaret, similis factus Salomoni. Adquisita tamen, tam in thesauris quam in materiæ adunata ad ecclesiam construendam, non dispersit vel consumpsit. Istius abbatis dum fossores muros et abscondita terræ rimarentur, in medio civitatis antiquæ cujusdam magni palatii fundamenta diruerunt, et cum tantorum vestigia ædificiorum admirarentur, invenerunt in cujusdam muri concavo deposito, quasi almariolo, cum quibusdam minoribus libris et rotulis, cujusdam codicis ignotum volumen, quod parum fuit ex tam longæva mora demolitum. Cujus nec litera nec idioma alicui tunc invento cognitum præ antiquitate fuerat; venustæ tamen formæ et manifestæ literæ fuerat, quarum epigrammata et tituli aureis literis fulserunt redimiti. Asseres querni, ligamina serica, pristinam in magna parte fortitudinem et decorem retinuerunt. De cujus libri notitia, cum multum longe lateque fuerat diligenter inquisitum, tandem unum senem jam decrepitum invenerunt sacerdotem, literis bene eruditum, nomine Unwonam, qui imbutus diversorum idiomatum linguis ac literis legit distincte et aperte scripta libri prænominati. Similiter quæ in aliis codicibus, in eodem almariolo et in eodem habitaculo repertis, legit indubitanter, et exposuit expresse. Erat enim litera, qualis scribi solet tempore quo cives Warlamecestram

manuscripts, Nero D. i., and Claudius E. iv.   One
at least of these gems was an ancient cameo.   The
sketch below is an exact copy of the drawing of it

inhabitabant, et idioma antiquorum Britonum, quo tunc temporis utebantur.   Aliqua tamen in Latino, sed his non opus
erat ; in primo autem libro, scilicet majori, cujus prius fecimus
mentionem, scriptam invenit Historiam de sancto Albano Anglorum protomartyre, quam ecclesia diebus hodiernis recitat le-
gendo. Cui perhibet egregius doctor Beda testimonium, in nullis
discrepando. In aliis vero libris passim inventis, reperit lector
prædictus invocationes et ritus idolatrarum civium Warlam-

made by Matthew Paris, by whose hand the first of
the manuscripts just mentioned was written.   His
description of this relic is given in the note;* it

cestrensium. In quibus comperit, quod specialiter Phœbum deum
solis invocarunt et coluerunt ; quod perpendi potest, per Historiam Sancti Albani, si eam sedulus lector intelligat ; secundario
vero Mercurium, Woden Anglice appellatum, quo quartus dies
septimanæ intitulatur, deum videlicet mercatorum, quia cives
et compatriotæ, propter navigium civitatis et commodum loci
situm, per unam dietam tantum a Londoniis distantem, fere
omnes negotiatores et institores fuerunt. Abjectis igitur et
combustis libris in quibus commenta diaboli continebantur,
solus ille liber in quo historia sancti Albani continebatur in
thesauro charissime reponebatur. Et sicut prædictus presbyter
illum antiquo Anglico vel Britannico idiomate conscriptum, in
quo peritus extitit, legerat, abbas iste Eadmarus per pruden-
tiores fratrum in conventu fecit fideliter ac diligenter exponi
et plenius in publico prædicando edoceri. Cum autem con-
scripta historia in Latino pluribus ut jam dictum est innotuis-
set, exemplar primitivum ac originale (quod mirum est dictu,)
irrestaurabiliter in pulverem subito redactum cecidit annul-
latum.

Et cum abbas memoratas profundiora terræ, ubi civitatis
Verolamii apparuerunt vestigia, diligenter perscrutaretur, et
antiquos tabulatus lapideos cum tegulis et columnis inveniret,
quæ ecclesiæ fabricandæ fuerunt necessaria sibi reservaret quam
proposuit sancto martyri Albano fabricare, invenerunt fossores
in fundamentis veterum ædificiorum, et concavitatibus subterraneis, urceos et amphoras opere fictili et tornatili decenter
compositas, vasa quoque vitrea, pulverem mortuorum continen-
tia. Solebant enim antiquitus cadavera mortuorum comburere,
unde *funus* quasi *fumus* dicebatur. Inventa sunt insuper fana
semiruta, altaria subversa, et idola, et numismatum diversa
genera quibus utebantur, et quæ idola coluerunt antiqui cives
Verolamii idolatræ. Quæ omnia ex præcepto abbatis sunt
comminuta.—*Matth. Paris, de Vit. Abbat. ed. Watts*, pp. 40, 41.

* Hunc lapidem preciosum, qui videlicet constat ex sardo-
nice, calcedonio, et onice, præter hoc quod intrinsecus latet,
verum ipse totus vulgariter *kaadman* appellatur, dedit Deo et
ecclesiæ sancti Albani devotus ipsius ecclesiæ filius et frater de
capitulo, bonæ memoriæ Æthelredus pater beati Ædwardi, rex

must have been a very handsome gem. Matthew
Paris tells us, that it was of great efficacy for women
in child-birth. It was named *kaadman* (perhaps
another mode of spelling *cadmeus* or *cameus*). Two
stories were current relating to the manner in which
it had come into the possession of the monastery :
according to one, it had been given by king Ethel-
red ; according to the other, it was a present of one
of the abbots. To reconcile these two statements it
was said that a noble lady, having sent for it in the
pains of labour, and experienced its efficacy, kept it

Anglorum. Qui cum una dierum veniens ad Sanctum Alba-
num capitulum ingrederetur, detulit secum dictum lapidem, et
benigne ac gratanter contulit ecclesiæ, ipsum commendando et
virtutem ejus pronuntiando, postulavitque ut ipse abbas et con-
ventus inferrent ilico sententiam excommunicationis in omnes
qui illud donum suum aliquo tempore forent ablaturi. Iste
lapis, quia speciosus est et magnus, cum provideretur ei locus
idoneus ut collocaretur in feretro interiori tempore Galfridi
abbatis fabricato consilio eorum qui præerant opere aurifabrili,
reservatus est et depositus in thesauro, ut utile suæ virtutis
officium temporibus exerceret opportunis. Mulieribus enim
parituris efficax confert patrocinium, invocatoque fideliter beati
Albani Anglorum prothomartiris nomine non permittit partu-
rientes alicui discrimini subjacere. Dicitur autem quod si
violenter aut fraudulenter amoveatur ab ecclesia memorata,
virtutem suam penitus est lapis amissurus. Noverintque tam
obstetrices quam paritura quod lapis ponendus est supra pectus
inter mamillas parituræ, paulatim et successive versus occiduam
corporis partem submittendus ; infantulus enim nasciturus lapidem subterfugit appropinquantem. Insculpitur autem eidem
lapidi ymago quædam pannosa, tenens in dextra hastam, quam
serpens rependo ascendit, et in sinistra puerum vestitum tenentem ad humerum quoddam ancile, et aliam manum versus ipsum
ymaginem extendentem, prout in antecedenti pagina figuratur.
Plures quoque colores habet, campum videlicet fuscum, limbum
quoque ad instar iris, habentem [ex aer]eo et subrufo colore
compositum, [ymagi]num vero pars aerei coloris est, [pars
quoque]subrufi ; forma quoque oblongus [est, qu]antitate vero

fraudulently from the abbey, pretending that it had been sent home. After her death her daughter also retained it during her life, so that the monks had almost forgotten that they ever possessed such a relic, when, on her bed of death, the latter lady repented, and restored it privately to the then abbot, who took upon himself the glory of having given it to the abbey. It appears from the lives of the abbots of St. Alban's that many other engraved cameos were in the possession of the abbey.* The name *cameo* was itself of mediæval formation. We find mention of them in many monastic inventories and other documents. In the

semipeda[lis; s]ex autem tenaculis in suo castone [forti]ter roboratur. In quo scilicet castone nomen possessoris, videlicet beati Albani, eɃ nomen datoris, piissimi videlicet regis Anglorum Æthelredi, insculpuntur nigellata.

Contigit autem quondam ut cuidam potenti matronæ partui proximæ lapis iste accommodaretur, et cum prospere peperisset, et se iterum sperasset sæpius parituram et gemmam sibi profuturam, retinuit et abscondit ipsum lapidem fraudulenter, asserens palam mentiendo quando reposcebatur se domum ipsum remisisse. Et post vitam illius matronæ, filia ejus simili ducta intentione ipsum multis annis retinuit. Elapso autem multo tempore moritura confessa est veritatem, et quod diu fraudulenter retinuerat, pœnitendo et veniam postulando resignavit. Abbas autem cujus tempore hæc facta fuit resignatio, quia non in propatulo facta fuerat, jactitavit se hunc lapidem huic ecclesiæ contulisse. Casus autem consimilis in pluribus aliis solet evenire, ut quod silicet redimitur vel restituitur aut sponte resignatur, adquisitioni et industriæ abbatis qui pro tempore fuerit ascribatur. Ponderat autem lapis memoratus cum suo castone argenteo quinque solidos et ii. den.—MS. Cotton. Nero, D. ɪ. fol. 145, vᵒ. Collated with MS. Cotton. Claudius E. ɪv. fol. 352. See M. Paris, de Vit. Abbat. p. 59.

* Nobilibus lapidibus insculptis quas camaeos vulgariter appellamus. Vit. Abbat. S. Alb. p. 42. Allati quidam ampli lapides, quos sardios onicleos appellamus, et vulgariter cadineos [*l.* cadmeos] nuncupamus.—*Ibid.* p. 59.

inventory of the church of Anicy, made in 1444, we
find a gold pontifical ring with a cameo, on which
were four figures. * In 1321, Geoffrey, bishop of
Laon, gave to his church a ring with a cameo.† Among
the precious stones adorning the mitre of .the abbot
of St. Victor at Marseilles in 1358 was a cameo with
the figure of a man's face looking to the left.‡ Other
instances will be found in the Lexicon of Ducange.§
An immense number of cameos (*kamahutis, camautis,
&c.*) and engraved gems appear among the ornaments
and plate in the treasury of St. Paul's Cathedral in
London, in the year 1295.‖ These engraved gems
were frequently inserted in the counter-seals of secu-
lar and ecclesiastical personages of rank, and contrast
singularly with the rude engravings of the seals themselves.   A number of impressions of such counter-
seals still existing are engraved in the plates of the
first volume of the Vetusta Monumenta of our society.

The cameo of the abbey of St. Alban's, drawn by
Matthew Paris, forms a curious illustration of the
following mediæval inventory of engraved gems and
their virtues.   It is difficult to fix the date at which
this inventory was first composed: but there can be
little doubt that it contains a description of ancient

* Item unus anulus auri pontificialis cum uno camayeu cum
quatuor   imaginibus.—Inventarium ecclesiæ Aniciensis, an.
1444, ap. Ducange, v. *Camæus.*

† See Ducange, v. *Camahutus.*

‡ In mitra inter quatuor grossos lapides est camasil habens
faciem hominis respicientis ad sinistram.—Inventarium Abbatis
S. Victoris Massil. an. 1358, ap. Ducange, v. *Camasil.*

§ Conf. Ducange, sub vv. *Camæus, Camahelus, Camaholus,
Camahutus, Camasil, Camaynus, Camayx.*

‖ See the curious inventory of this date printed in Dugdale's
History of St. Paul's Cathedral, ed. Ellis, pp. 310, 314.

engraved gems which once existed, and many of
which are probably still preserved. A considerable
portion of them belong to the numerous class of these
beautiful relics which are distinguished by the name
of abraxas; indeed the inventory itself has somewhat of an oriental character. There is something
of what the French term *bizarre* in the contrast between the descriptions of the ancient engravings and
the mediæval enumeration of virtues attached. Thus,
the first on the list is a gem representing Pegasus, or
Bellerophon; this stone was good for warriors, and
gave them boldness and swiftness in flight. Another
bore a figure of Andromeda; it had the power of
conciliating love between man and woman. A gem
bearing the figure of Hercules slaying a lion or " other
monster" was a " singular defence to combatants."
The figure of Mercury on a gem rendered the possessor wise and persuasive. The figure of Jupiter,
with the body of a man and the head of a ram, made
the man who bore it beloved by everybody, and he
was sure to obtain everything he asked. If you find
a stone bearing the figure of a hare, it will be a
defence against the devil. If you find a dog and a
lion on the same stone, it will be a preservative against
dropsy or pestilence. The figure of Orion was believed to give victory in war. If you find a stone on
which is Perseus, holding in his right-hand a sword
and in his left the Gorgon's head, it is a preservative
against lightning and tempest, and against the as-
saults of devils. A stone on which is engraved a
long-bearded man sitting on a plough, with a bending
in his neck, and four men lying down, and holding
in his hands a fox and a vulture, this, suspended
about the neck, enables you to find treasures. If you

find a dove with a branch of olive in its mouth, engraved in pyrites, and mount it in a silver ring and
carry it with you, everybody will invite you to be
his guest, and people will feast· you much and frequently.   The figure of a syren, sculptured in a
jacinth, rendered the bearer invisible.   A fair head,
well combed, with a handsome face, engraved on a
gem, gave to the bearer joy, reverence, and honour.
Such were the qualities attached to ancient gems in
the superstitious belief of the middle ages.

It will be observed, that in the inventory these
gems are not spoken of as things then made, but as
articles *to be found* (*si inveneris lapidem, &c.*); its object is to instruct the finder in the particular value
and use of the article he may chance to discover.
During the middle ages (and even up to a very recent
time) antiquities were always objects of superstition.
Great earthworks, or extraordinary structures, were
the work of demons.   Tumuli were guarded by
dragons, or were the abode of fairies.   Ancient vessels needed consecrating before a christian would dare
to use them.   Engraved gems were looked upon as
magical amulets, and the finders endeavoured to preserve and take advantage of, rather than to dispel, the
charm.   When they became an object of commerce
it was the interest of the dealer to enhance their value
by the display of their virtues.   It must have been
after such articles had become tolerably common that
some one composed the singular code or inventory
I here communicate.   The statement that they were
made by Solomon for the children of Israel would
seem to point out a Jew as the inventor.   A para-
graph at the end of one copy of the inventory informs
us that they were made under Xerxes, king of the

Persians, by the advice of all the astrologers of Egypt, Chaldea, and Persia.*

SOME time ago the Society of Antiquaries did me the honour of listening to, and printing in its Transactions, a few remarks on the antiquarian excavations made by the monks during the middle ages; on the destruction of many ancient monuments by this process; and on the purposes to which the articles thus brought to light were turned. Perhaps I may be permitted to recall the attention of the members of the Society to this subject, which will be hardly considered an uninteresting one, in order to show how much may be learnt on the subject of local monuments of antiquity in this country from a careful perusal of the legendary literature of the church. So general was the custom of turning old popular legends into religious legends, and so universally were such popular legends attached to ancient sites and monuments, that we need not be surprised at the great importance which these monuments often assume in the histories of the lives and miracles of saints, and at the numerous and curious descriptions of these monuments which we find in the peculiar class of literature to which I allude.

I am convinced that a large portion of the reliques of saints shown in the middle ages were taken from

* I have added a French version, not always agreeing with the Latin original, from a very early printed book, entitled, *Le Lapidaire en françois, composé par messire Jehan de Mandeuille, chevalier.* It is described by Brunet, Manuel, tom. ii. p. 417, and these extracts are given in M. Le Roux de Lincy's Livre des Legendes, from whence they are here reprinted.

the barrows or graves of the early population of the countries in which they were shown. It was well understood that those mounds were of a sepulchral character, and there were probably few of them which had not a legend attached. When the earlier Christian missionaries, and the later monks of Western Europe, wished to consecrate a site, their imagination easily converted the tenant of the lonely mound into a primitive saint—the tumulus was ransacked and the bones were found—and a monastery, or even a cathedral, was erected over the site which had been consecrated by the mystic rites of an earlier age. In some cases, without disturbing the bones of the dead, the legendary character of the spot had induced some still earlier hermit to make it his abode, before it was thus chosen for the site of a religious edifice. It appears from the early life of St. Guthlac that the monastery of Croyland was built on the site of what was probably a Roman barrow, and one which had already been broken up in search of treasure, which was often the case with monuments of this description. The biographer of the saint tells us that " there was on the island (Croyland) a great mound raised upon the earth, which of yore men had dug and broken up in hopes of treasure. On the other side of the mound a place was dug, as it were a great water-cistern. Over this cistern the blessed man Guthlac built himself a hut."

I think I may venture to say, that with very little trouble, I might adduce from the monastic legends from fifty to a hundred distinct examples in which barrows were opened for the sake of finding the bones of saints. The notices to which I would call attention at present relate merely to the still interesting remains of the ancient city of Verulamium (near St. Alban's), and occurred to me in the course of a hasty perusal of the Chronicle of Roger of Wendover, a monk of that house.

It is highly probable, not only from the circumstances of the case, but from some modern discoveries, that the abbey church of St. Alban, erected on the spot where the bones of that saint were pretended to have been discovered, was built on the site of a Roman cemetery attached to the ancient city. The legendary account of the discovery of the remains of his spiritual teacher, St. Amphibalus, and his companions, is more definite and curious in its details.

This discovery took place in the year 1178. I must be permitted to give a little of the mere legendary part of the story. "There was," says the historian just mentioned, "a certain man who lived at his native town St. Alban's, and enjoyed a character free from reproach among his fellow-townsmen. . . . As he lay in bed one night, about the hour of cock-crowing a man of tall and majestic mien, clad in white, and holding in his hand a beautiful wand, entered the room. The whole house was illuminated with his appearance, so that the chamber was as light as at noon-day. Approaching the bed, he asked, in a gentle voice, 'Robert, are you asleep?' Robert, trembling with fear and wonder, replied, 'Who art thou, lord?' 'I am,' he said, 'the martyr St. Alban, and am come to tell you the Lord's will concerning my master, the clerk who taught me the faith of Christ; for, though his fame is so great among mankind, the place of his sepulture is still unknown, though it is the belief of the faithful that it will be revealed to future ages. Rise, therefore, with speed, and I will show you the spot where his precious remains are buried.' Robert then, rising from his bed, as it seemed, followed him, and they went together along the public street (*in strata publica*) towards the north, until they came to a plain which had lain for ages uncultivated near the high road (*regiam viam*, the Watling Street)." Matthew Paris adds to Wendover's narrative, that " on their way they conversed with one another, as is the custom between friends travelling together, at one time on the walls of the destroyed (*dirutæ*) city, at another on the decrease of the river (the draining of that part of its course which had anciently formed the lake of Verulam), and of the common street (or road) adjacent to the city."* Wendover, proceeding to describe the plain just alluded to, says, " Its surface was level, furnishing a good pasturage for cattle, and a resting-place for weary travellers at a village called Redbourn, about three miles from St. Alban's. In this place were two mounds, called the *Hills of the Banners*, because there used to be assemblies of the faithful people held around them, when, according to an ancient custom, they yearly made a solemn procession to the church of St. Alban's."

This custom of holding assemblies or wakes about ancient barrows was common among our Anglo-Saxon forefathers, and several examples might be cited. The narrative goes on to say that St. Alban

* A friend well acquainted with the ground suggests that, though their imaginary route may have passed at St. Michael's over the river into Verulamium, and then along the principal street northwards, or along a footpath by the side of the north-eastern wall, yet most probably, the course described, instead of crossing the river, continued on its north-eastern side along the road which, till the lake was drained, was the main road from St. Alban's through Redbourne.

took the man to one of these mounds, which he told
him was the sepulchre of St. Amphibalus, and touching it with his finger, it appeared to open, and he saw
a cist, which he was told contained the bones of the
saint. Next day the man told his story abroad, and
it was carried to the abbot, who set a watch upon
the mound until it was opened, for so many people
crowded to the spot that, during the time of the digging, it presented the appearance of a fair. At length
the happy moment arrived—the monkish barrow-
diggers discovered the bones, and, to use Wendover's
words, " The holy martyr Amphibalus lay between
two of his companions, whilst the third was found
lying crossways in a place by itself. They also found
near the place six others of the martyrs, making
with St. Amphibalus himself, ten in all. Among
other reliques of this champion of Christ were found
two large knives, one in his skull and the other near
his breast, confirming the account which was handed
down from ancient times in the book of his martyr-
dom. For, according to that book, whilst the others
perished by the sword, Amphibalus himself was first
embowelled, then pierced with lances and knives, and
finally stoned to death; for which cause, also, none
of his bones were found entire, though in all the
corpses of his companions not a bone was broken."
The chronicler goes on to tell how the bones were
carefully gathered up, and carried in solemn triumph
to the abbey church.

The story of the vision was no doubt an invention
of the monks to gain authority among the vulgar for
their discovery ; but the opening of the barrow is too
vividly described to have been a fiction. The village
of Redbourn is about four miles to the north-west of

St. Alban's, and modern observations might perhaps throw some further light on the narrative of the ancient monk. It appears to have been a Saxon burial-place; for any one who has been in the habit of opening Saxon barrows will at once recognize the position of the spear-head (which might be taken for a large knife), which is invariably found by, or sometimes under, the skull, and the knife (supposed to be the seax) which is found near or very little below the breast. We do not find Romans buried with their weapons.

The allusions to the ruins of the ancient city, and to the walls, which were then probably nearly if not quite perfect, are curious. I have no doubt that at Verulamium, as at other sites of Roman cities in England, much of the walls of the houses, as well as of the public buildings, remained standing, at least as late as the twelfth century, and perhaps still later. At Verulamium great destruction had already been committed by the monks in collecting building materials for their church, but no doubt the havoc which has been committed in the subsequent period has been still more extensive. Any one who has seen the modern houses and walls—almost whole villages— along the line of the Roman wall in the North, built out of its materials, will understand easily how the buildings of the Romans have disappeared throughout the island. I will point out an implied allusion which seems to me to show that large remains of its public buildings were still visible on the site of Verulamium in the thirteenth century.

Roger of Wendover has inserted in his Chronicle several rather long purgatory legends. Among these, there is one which is found in no other writer, except

Matthew Paris, who republished Wendover with additions, and which for that reason I am strongly inclined to believe was composed by a monk of St. Alban's, and preserved only in the abbey there. This vision is said to have happened to a countryman in a place named Tunstead, in the bishopric of London (which has been supposed to be Twinstead in Essex), in the year 1206, so that the account must have been written subsequent to that period. It is a singular legend, and the visitor to purgatory wanders among walls and buildings until you are almost forced into the conviction that it was imagined by some one while he was strolling among the scattered ruins of an ancient city, or at least that he had a vivid impression of such a scene in his mind.

After having witnessed a great number of strange sights, the visitor to the shades was shown what are termed in the title of the chapter " The theatrical sports of the demons." " After this," the legend tells us, " saint Domninus said to the devil (one of the demons who had fallen into conversation with them), ' We wish to go with you to see your sports.' The devil answered, ' If you wish to go with me, do not bring this labourer with you, for he would on his return amongst his fellow mortals disclose our acts and secret kinds of punishment to the living, and would reclaim many from serving us.' The saint said to him, ' Make haste and go forward, I and St. Julian will follow you.' The demon therefore went on in advance, and the saints followed him, bringing the man with them by stealth. They then proceeded to a northern region, as if they were going up a mountain; and behold, after descending the mountain, there was a very large and dark-looking house, sur-

I.   O

rounded by old walls, and in it there were a great many lanes (in the Latin text *plateæ*—perhaps it should be *placeæ*, wich in the Mediæval Latin means simply *places*), as it were, filled all around with innumerable heated iron seats.   These seats were constructed with iron hoops glowing white with heat, and with nails driven in them in every part, above and below, right and left, and in them there sat persons of different conditions and sexes; these were pierced by the glowing nails all over their bodies, and were bound on all sides with fiery hoops.   There was such a number of those seats, and such a multitude of people sitting in them, that no tongue would be able to reckon them.   *All around* these places were *black* iron *walls*, and by these walls were other seats, in which the devils sat *in a circle*, as if at a pleasant spectacle, grinning at each other over the tortures of the wretched beings, and recapitulating to them their former crimes.   Near the entrance of this detestable scene, on the descent of the elevated ground, as we have said, there was a *wall five feet high*, from which could plainly be seen whatever was done in that place of punishment.   Near this wall, then, the beforementioned saints stood outside, looking on at what the wretched beings inside were enduring, and the man, remaining concealed between them, plainly saw all that was going on inside."   The legend then goes on to describe these punishments; and it appears that the suffering souls were brought in their turn from the seats to act on the stage the different crimes they had committed on earth, and that such performance ended in inexpressible torments.

I think that there can be no doubt that the writer of the above description had in his view the plan of a

Roman theatre. There were no theatres in the middle ages, and I am acquainted with no Roman author, known to the monks, whose writings could have conveyed to them any distinct idea of one. Where then did a monk of St. Alban's, supposing one of those monks to have been the author of the legend, derive his notions of such a building? Recent discoveries on the site of Verulamium, I think, furnish the answer.

The members of our society will recollect that, a few years ago, the remains of a theatre were discovered, and partially excavated, within the walls of the city of Verulamium. It was a Roman theatre of very great extent, and perhaps the only one in Britain. A description of it, with a plan, was published in the following year by R. Grove Lowe, esq. By comparing the description in the legend with the plan of this theatre, few and slight as the definite allusions in the former are, I cannot help thinking that it will appear evident that the writer of it had that building in his mind. The *plateæ*, lanes, or the *placeæ*, places —whichever be the correct reading—were no doubt the seats around the orchestra, which were probably at that time perfectly visible. The theatre at Verulamium, like the Roman theatres discovered on the Continent, had two parallel outer walls in a semi-circle,—or, in this case, somewhat more than a semi-circle, which, from what we know of Roman theatres, inclosed a corridor, with elevated seats above. The corridor was probably standing in Wendover's time, and the seats above it were those by *the outer wall*, which in the legend were occupied by the demons who sat as spectators of the infernal "sports." The wall, *five feet high*, behind which the two saints and the countryman concealed themselves, was probably one of the walls near the stage and proscenium, and would naturally give them a full view of the area of the theatre.* The monk of St. Alban's, probably, did not understand that part of the site covered with the ruins of the stage, and he supposed that the spectacles were exhibited in the central space devoted to the orchestra. It is very probable that, at the beginning of the thirteenth century, the walls of the theatre, where most dilapidated, still stood as much as five feet above the ground.

I will merely add that the theatre at Verulamium is in many respects one of the most remarkable discoveries of this kind that have been made in our days, and it must be a subject of regret that the excavations were discontinued. The site might be rented for a year, and at no very great expense the whole remains of the theatre uncovered. I cannot help thinking that such an undertaking was worthy the attention of government.

In concluding these brief notes, I would again beg to press upon the attention of antiquaries the necessity of examining, in illustration of English local antiquities, not only the documents alluded to above— the religious legends, but a variety of others which have been too long neglected. Among these not the least curious are the descriptions of boundaries in the old Anglo-Saxon charters. These documents describe

---

* Or the three spectators may be supposed to have stood behind part of the inner wall of the corridor, near the front entrance— towards which the land sloped from the adjoining hill. At such spot there was discovered, I am informed, on the recent excavations, the only remaining fragment of wall which rose above the bonding course of tiles laid on the original level of the theatre.

the limits by reference to visible objects, which were
often ancient monuments, and the way in which these
are referred to and the names given to them are sometimes in the highest degree interesting.   The collection published by Mr. Kemble is a treasury of information of this kind.   I will only refer to one charter
of as early a date as the year 955, a grant of land in
Berkshire, in which the description of limits makes
us acquainted, among other objects, with the names
then given to two of the barrows which are so numerous in the district to which it relates, Hilda's low
and Hwittuc's low, and with that ancient monument
now so celebrated by the popular name of Wayland
Smith.   This early notice of the latter is valuable, as
showing to us that the legend in connection with this
locality existed as early as the middle of the tenth
century ; and it shows us further, that the term which
has been corrupted into the name of an individual
was in reality that of the monument, for the Saxon
name given to it in the document, Welandes smiððan,
means simply *Weland's smithy.*

DE SCULPTURIS LAPIDUM.

MS. Harl. No. 80, fol. 105, r°. of the 13th cent. compared with
MS. Arundel, No. 342, fol. 69, r°.

I.

1. Si inveneris lapidem in quo sit equus alatus qui dicitur
Pegasus, optimus est militantibus, et in campestri bello; bel-
lantibus enim præbet audaciam et velocitatem, et dicitur libe-
rare equos ferentes super se tales lapides ab acutis infirmitatibus
et ab infusione. Hic lapis præest arieti, et vocatur Bellerofons,
i. bellorum fons.

2. Si inveneris Andromedam, qui habet crines sparsos atque
manus remissas, ille lapis in quo hoc signum est habet potestatem reconciliandi amorem inter virum et mulierem, et inter
nebulones et adulteras.

3. Si inveneris lapidem in quo sit Cassiopea virgo sculpta,
habens manus suas ad modum crucis extensas, et triangulum in
capite, in cathedra sedens, hic lapis est solamen post laborem et
requies post infirmitatem. Hic lapis fessa et debilia corpora
reparat, et sana sanitati conservat.

4. Serpentarius est qui habet serpentem procinctum, cujus
caput dextera manu tenet, et in sinistra caudam. Hic lapis
gestatus vel bibitus liberat hominem a veneno sumpto sive
ante prandium sive post prandium.

5. Si inveneris lapidem in quo sit Hercules, genu flexo, habens
in dextera manu clavam interficientem leonem seu aliquid aliud
monstrum, si quis hunc lapidem in pedestri bello portaverit,
victor existet. Hic etiam pugilibus est singulare præsidium.

6. Si inveneris lapidem in quo sit ursus seu serpens dividens
utrasque versas, hic lapis hominem reddit astutum, fortem, in
proposito manentem, Deo et hominibus placentem.

7. Si inveneris lapidem in quo sit Saturnus depictus, habens
in dextera manu falcem, hic lapis reddit se ferentem potentem,
cujus potestas crescit semper usque dum eum habuerit.

8. Est et alius lapis in quo habetur qui vocatur Jupiter,
habens hominis formam et caput arietis; si quis illum habuerit,
diligetur ab omni creatura, et si quid ab aliquo petierit impe-
trabit.

9. Est et alius lapis in quo habetur Mercurius, habens alas in dextra, et in sinistra manu virgam serpente involutam ; qui hunc habuerit tantum abundabit sapientia atque gratia ut nemo sibi resistere possit. Gratus erit Deo et omni populo, et perpetua gaudebit sanitate.

10. Si quis in aliquo lapide invenerit serpentem sculptum, habentem super se urnam, in cauda corvum, qui hunc lapidem habuerit omnibus bonis abundabit, et erit astutus et providus contra futura. Creditur enim hic lapis posse resistere nocivo calori ; hoc enim habet a cancro sub quo suum caput et caudam dirigit usque ad centaurum.

11. Si quis invenit lapidem in quo sit centaurus, habens in sinistra manu leporem suspensum cum cultello, et in dextera baculum in quo est bestiola infixa cum lebete suspensa, hic lapis reddit se ferentem perpetua sanitate præditum ; et inde dicitur quod centauri fuerunt armigeri Archillis, et hunc lapidem manu ferebant.

12. Si inveneris lapidem in quo sit sacrarium, i. in modum casulæ ferentis sacra, hic lapis reddit se ferentem ornatum perpetua virginitate, et facit eum gratum Deo et hominibus, licet sequatur caudam scorpionis.

13. Cetus invenitur in fine piscium et in principio arietis, habens magnum tuber in dorso, et in ventre aliud, et serpentinum caput cristatum inferius et superius ; qui hunc lapidem habuerit, in quo cetus sit descriptus, erit felix in terra et in mari, prudens, amabilis, et si qua ei ablata fuerint recuperabit.

14. Si inveneris lapidem in quo sit navis habens velum in altum et protensum, in omni negotio eris superior.

15. Si inveneris in lapide leporem sculptum, quamdiu illum habueris ab aliqua dæmoniaca lædi non poteris.

16. Si inveneris canem qui est cum leone in aliquo lapide sculptum, cum leo sit igneæ et siccæ naturæ, futuram hydropisim non timebis, nec pestilentiam vel communem morbum.

17. Si inveneris lapidem in quo sit Orion descriptus, habens in manu sua ensem, qui est in fine tauri existens, in bello victor eris.

18. Si inveneris lapidem in quo sit aquila, quæ præest capricorno, ille lapis conservat tibi veteres honores et acquiret novos.

19. Si inveneris lapidem in quo sit cignus, qui præest aquario, ille lapis proculdubio liberat a paralysi et a febre quartana.

20. Si inveneris lapidem in quo sit Perseus, habens in dextera

manu ensem et in sinistra caput Gorgonis, ille lapis Deo dis-
ponente reddit se ferentem a fulmine et tempestate et incursu
dæmonum securum.

21. In quocunque lapide inveneris arietem, leonem, et sagittarium insculptum, illi lapides ignei sunt et orientales, et se
ferentes faciunt Deo et hominibus gratos, et liberant eos a
febribus cotidianis et hydropisi, et reddunt eos facundos et
ingeniosos.

22. In quibuscunque lapidibus inveneris taurum, virginem,
et capricornum, hii lapides frigidi sunt et meridionales, et per-
petuo reddunt se ferentes liberos a synocha febre.

23. Si inveneris lapidem in quo sit libra, gemini, et aquarius,
tales lapides calidi sunt et aerei et occidentales, hii vero proculdubio liberant se ferentes a quartanis febribus et paralysi, et
faciunt Deum placatum.

24. Si inveneris scorpionem, cancrum, seu piscem apidi im-
pressos, illi sunt frigidi et aquatici et septentrionales, defen-
dunt se ferentes ab ethica [al. eptica] febre et tertiaria et causon,
et hii omnes sunt consecrati perpetua conjuratione.

25. Si in lapide inveneris cervum, vel venatorem, vel canem,
vel leporem impressum, ille habet potestatem curandi dæmo-
niacos, lunaticos, maniacos, et in nocte militantes, atque frene-
ticos.

26. Si inveneris lapidem in quo sit homo habens in manu sua
palmam sculptam, ille reddit ferenti se potestates et principes
benevolentes et placidos.

27. Si inveneris in berillo locustam marinam sculptam et sub
pedibus ejus corniculam, sub genibus poni debet herbæ savinæ
modicum in auro inclusum.

II.

1. [In berillo sculpitur locusta marina, et sub pedibus ejus
cornicula, et sub pedibus poni debet herbæ savinæ modicum
auro inclusum.]

2. Calcedonius debet perforari et scetis ascelli et collo et
brachiis suspendi.

3. In corallo debet inscribi natura noctilucæ, hoc est accate
[al. eichete; leg. Hecate]; signatur autem in eo Gorgonis
figura.

4. Crisolitus debet perforari et in sinistro brachio suspendi.

5. Adamas debet includi in auro, vel argento, aut ferreo
anulo, et debet in sinistro brachio ligari.

6. In smaragdo debet sculpi scarabæus, et sub eo positus
psittacus cristatus. [In saphiro debet sculpi integra, et in alio
sculpitur scarabæus.]
7. In jaspide opportet sculpere Martem armatum, aut virginem solam cum veste circumfusa tenentem laurum, et ita con-
secratur perpetua consecratione.

* * * * * *

III.

Incipit liber secretus filiorum Israel.

1. Si inveneris sigillum in lapide sculptum, s. virum sedentem
super aratrum, longibarbum, curvaturam habentem in collo,
iiij^{or}. homines jacentes, et tenentem in manibus vulpem et vul-
turem, hoc sigillum ad collum suspensum valet ad omnes plan-
tationes et ad inventiones thesaurorum. . . .
2. Si inveneris sigillum in jaspide rubeo sculptum, hominem
ad collum clipeum habentem, in caput galeam gestantem, erec-
tum tenentem gladium, serpentem pedibus conculcantem, hoc ad
collum suspensum gestans nullum licet fortissimum timeas
inimicum. . . .
3. Si inveneris in jacincto albo equum sculptum super se co-
codrillum depictum ferentem, hujusmodi sigillum in omnibus
placitis et causis valere cognoscas. . . .
4. Si inveneris in corneolo sigillum sculptum, s. hominem
sedentem, et mulierem ante illum stantem, cujus capilli ad renes
dependunt, virque sursum respiciat, hoc sigillum in anulo aureo
pondere sigilli duodecies exæquato ponas. . . .
5. Si inveneris in ametisto sigillum taliter factum vel sculptum, s. equum spumantem et fervidum, et desuper virum sedentem et sceptrum manu tenentem, hoc sigillum hiis valet qui
potestatem exercent. . . .
6. Si inveneris in crisolito sigillum sculptum, s. hominem
habilem et altum, accensam in manu candelam tenentem, hoc
se gestantem divitem facit, et debet poni in auro purissimo, in
quo ejus virtus utilior ei esse cognoscitur.
7. Si inveneris cristallum in quo sit tale sigillum sculptum,
s. mulierem in una manu avem tenentem et in altera piscem
bajulantem, hoc sigillum in capiendis avibus piscibusque vim
confert. Hoc ergo ad manum tecum in argenteo anulo portes.
8. Si inveneris in aliquo preciosorum lapidum sigillum tali
modo sculptum, cornutum videlicet alias equum gestantem

inferius, qui capram trahat dimidiam, si inveneris hujusmodi sigillum in anulo plumbeo habitum, in alendis et domandis omnibus animalibus sive bestiis gestatori suo maximam confert gratiam.

9. Si in aliquo preciosorum lapidum sigillum taliter sculptum inveneris, s. militem super equum tibicinantem, et arborem ante illum stantem sculptam, hoc venatoribus multam venandi gratiam præstat, si ad tale exercendi opus secum gestaverint.

10. Si inveneris in turchesio tale signum, s. virum flexis genibus sculptum, sursum respicientem et pannum tenentem, pone in auro optimo, tecum caste defer et diligenter, nimiam gratiam in emendis omnibus seu vendendis accumulabit tibi.

11. Si in pirite sigillum hoc modo sculptum inveneris, turturem s. et ramum olivæ ore tenentem, in argenteo anulo ponas et tecum deferas. A cunctis enim invitaberis, et multa convivia tibi parabunt, et in illis conviviis ubi præsens fueris nullus qui ad os manu dextera cibum deferat saturabitur, sed omnes te conspicient et mirabuntur.

12. Si in aliquo preciosorum sigillum taliter sculptum inveneris, s. scorpionem et sagittarium inter se pugnantes, in anulo ferreo pone, et si vim ejus velis cognoscere, figuram ejus in ceram exprime, et quoscunque ex eadem cera tetigeris inter se discordantes altrinsecus et male volentes perpetualiter facies.

13. Si in aliquo preciosorum lapidum inveneris hoc modo sculptum, arietem videlicet et semibovem, in argenteo anulo pone, et quoscunque tetigeris discordantes pacificabis.

14. Si inveneris sigillum in jacincto marino hoc modo sculptum, semifeminam videlicet et semipiscem, tenentem in una manu lanceam et in altera ramum, hoc sigillum in auro obrizo pone, et vim ejus talem cognosce, anulum in quo sigillum fuerit cera cooperi, quod in pugno stricte tenens et invisibilis quocunque volueris ire poteris.

15. Si in aliquo preciosorum lapidum sigillum taliter sculptum inveneris, virum videlicet arantem et desuper dominicam manum signum + facientem, et aliquot stellas juxta sculptas, et tecum deferas, et messes et fructus regionis in qua fueris nulla tempestate periclitabuntur.

16. Si inveneris sigillum in jaspide viridi sculptum, caput s. et collum ab humero et supra, hoc in anulo argenteo vel æneo pone, et quocunque cum illo perrexeris vel navigaveris, sive in mari vel in fluminibus, nullo modo periclitaberis.

17. Si in aliquo preciosorum lapidum sigillum inveneris taliter sculptum, s. basiliscum et imaginem personæ, cujus una feminæ

et altera serpentis, hoc sigillum si tecum feras omnia venenalia animalia sive reptilia tractare poteris.

18. Si inveneris in corneolo basiliscum et draconem pugnantem et caput bovis desuper, hoc sigillum suspende ad collum, et si cum aliqua ferali bestia sive marina sive silvestri vel alia qualicunque pugnaveris, victa subcumbet.

19. Si inveneris sigillum in gagate sculptum, s. virum nudum et inflatum, et alium bene indutum et coronatum, et teneat in una manu gristum et in alia ramum herbæ, et pone in quovis anulo, et omnis febricitans hoc secum deferens per triduum sanabitur.

20. Si inveneris sigillum in quovis lapide sculptum, s. virum stantem, cujus caput capiti bovis sit simile, et pedes aquilæ pedes ejus, hoc sigillum exprime in cera, et ipsam ceram tecum porta, et non invenies aliquem vel aliquam quæ tibi male loquatur.

21. Si inveneris sigillum in diacoco sculptum, virum magnum et rectum, et tenet in una manu diabolum et in alia serpentem, et super virum solem et lunam, et sub pedibus leonem, hoc sigillum pone in anulo plumbeo, et sub lapide pone radicem artemesiæ et radicem fæniculi Græci, et fer tecum super ripam aquæ, et invoca quemlibet de malignis spiritibus, et habebis responsum de qualibuscunque interrogaveris.

22. Si inveneris sigillum in jaspide viridi obscuro sculptum, virum stantem s. fasciculos herbarum ad collum deferentem, grossos renes et amplis scapulis habenti præsidium erit. Si vero medicus fueris, in discernendis ægritudinibus et cognoscendis medicinis et herbis et in dandis potionibus gratiam maximam dabit. Si autem lapis guttatus fuerit quasi guttis sanguineis, pone in argenteo anulo, et si emoptoicus secum detulerit in digito mox curabitur. Hoc sigillum fertur habuisse Galienus. *Explicit.*

Additions from MS. Arundel, No. 342.

De luna et sole.—In quocunque lapide inveneris lunam sive solem sculptum sive aliquo modo impressum, ille lapis perpetua consecratione consecratus est; semper illum feras tecum, et bonam ducas vitam.

De aliis non credat.—Si quis alias sculpturas invenerit, eas non credat. Hii enim lapides perpetua consecratione consecrati sunt in templo Appolli[ni]s secundum cursum signorum et horas planetarum, sub Xerase rege Persarum, consilio omnium

astrologorum tam Ægyptiorum quam Caldeorum, atque omnium
Persarum. In nomine Dei pii et misericordis, soli Deo honor
et gloria.—Amen.

THE SAME SUBJECT, FROM THE FRENCH
" LAPIDAIRE."

*S'ensuit le livre Techel des philosophes et des Indois, et dit estre
des enfans d'Israel, mention faisant de plusieurs pierres pre-
cieuses et de leurs vertus et propriétés.*

Cy apres s'ensuyvent plusieurs pierres entaillées et erlentées,
lesquelles sont appelées *pierres de Israel*, selon les saiges philosophes, les aucunes sont artificielles, c'est-à-dire qu'elles ont été
ouvrées.

Premierement, en quelque maniere de pierre que tu trouveras entaillé à l'ymaige du mouton, ou du lyon, ou du sagittaire, elles sont consacrées du signe du ciel. Elles sont très
vertueuses, car elles rendent l'omme amyable et gracieulx à tous ;
elles resistent aux fievres cothidianes, quartaines, et autres de
froide nature. Elles guerissent les ydropiques et les palatiques,
et aguisent l'engin et rendent beau parler, et font estre seur en
tous lieux, et acroist honneur à celluy qui la porte, especiale-
ment l'ymage du lyon.

En quelque pierre que vous trouverés entaillée ou eslevé
l'ymage du tourel, ou d'une vierge, ou du capricorne, elles sont
consacrées et meredionnales, et de froide nature. Elles guerissent de la continue et autres chauldes maladies, et fait seur
celluy qui la porte, et le fait entrer en devotion envers Dieu.

En quelque pierre où tu trouveras entaillé jumeaux et balances
et l'aquaire, elles sont consacrées et occidentales. Elles guerissent de melancolie et du palasim, et rend le porteur gracieulx
et amyable.

En quelque pierre que tu trouveras entaillée ou eslevée l'es-
crevisse et l'escorpion, elles sont consacrées et septemtrionales.
Elles gardent d'estre etique et de fievre tierce et d'autres ; et
encline l'omme à estre bordeur et menteur.

Toutes les pierres dessus dites sont consacrées à la consecra-
tion du ciel et de leur entailleure, de quelconque figure qu'elle
soit, et aussi sont consacrées les pierres qui ont figure de planette,
ou de soleil, ou de lune.

La pierre de la planette qui est appellée *Saturne* a ymage d'ung vieillart, et a en sa dextre main une faulx ; celle pierre esmeut l'omme à honneur et le fait puissant.

La pierre de la planette qui est appellée *Jupiter* a ymage d'omme qui tient la teste du mouton ; elle rend l'homme amyable et conferme grace de tous hommes et de toutes bestes.

La pierre de la planette qui est appellée *Mars* est d'ung homme armé, ou d'une vierge vestue de larges vestemens, tenant ung rain d'olivier. Elle fait victoire, et delivre des causes adverses et contraires.

La pierre de la planette *Venus* a ymage tenant une palme en sa main ; elle donne victoire aux princes, et rend gracieulx celui qui la porte.

La pierre de la planette *Mercure* est une ymage qui a esles es piés ; et en la senestre main une verge et ung serpent, et est enveloppé entour elle; fait habonder sapience et donne joie, santé, et grace.

La pierre qui a ymage d'ung veneur, ou de lune, ou d'ung chien, ou d'ung serf, ou d'ung lievre, elle guerit les lunatiques et frenetiques, et ceulx qui ont le dyable au corps.

La pierre qui a le dos d'un serpent, d'une buire, et dessus la queue du serpent ung corbeau, fait l'omme riche et saige. Elle appaise trop grant chaleur.

La pierre qui a ymage d'omme seant en ung trepié jusques aux espaules et jusques aux genoulx, elle garde l'omme de luxure, et donne gracieux estatz.

La pierre qui a forme de nez et une vielle, fait avoir souvenance de son fait, et donne sapience.

La pierre qui a ung lyon et ung chien en sa bouche, et que le lyon soit de nature de feu, cette pierre garde d'ytropisie, et guerit la morsure des chiens envenymés.

La pierre où il y a ung homme tenant une faulx et une espéee, elle fait victoire en batailles.

La pierre qui a ung aigle garde et donne honneur.

La pierre qui a ung cheval à elles, que on appelle *Pegasus*, ceste pierre est bonne aux chevalliers, car elle fait le cheval legier et hardy contre autres chevaulx.

La pierre qui a ymage de femme qui a les cheveulx espars et les tient en ses mains, celle pierre a pouvoir de reconceillier amour entre mary et femme.

La pierre qui a ymage d'une vierge qui ait ses mains en maniere de croix, et soit à trois coustés ung chief, et soit assise en une chaire, celle pierre rend soulas et repos après labeur et maladie, et reconforte le membre grevé en quelque maniere que ce soit.

La pierre où il y a ung homme qui tient ung serpent en sa destre main, celle pierre delivre de venin, et preserve et garde d'emprisonnement.

Se en une pierre est ung homme qui flechisse son genoil, et en sa dextre main tienne vourle dont il tue ung lion et tiengne le poil en sa main, ou qu'il tiengne une courte faulse beste contre nature faicte, elle donne amour et victoire en toutes batailles ; mais il la convient nettement tenir sur luy sans soullure.

Se en une pierre a deux vurles, et qui'il y ait avec un serpent, celle pierre rend seurté et hardiesse et gracieuseté.

Se en une pierre est ung homme à tout ung escu à son col, ou en sa main, et tiengne en l'autre main une lance, et dessoubz ses piés soit ung serpent, celle pierre donne vertu.

Se en une pierre est ung homme qui ait longues oreilles, elle vault contre males bestes et contre ceulx qui sont hors du sens et qui n'ont point d'entendement.

Se en une pierre a ung lion, elle vault contre ydropisie et plusieurs autres maladies.

Se en une pierre a ung aigle et capricorne, elle vault à toutes besongnes.

Se en une pierre a ung dromadaire qui ait ses cheveulx espars sur les espaules, elle fait concorde entre mary et femme.

Une pierre où il y a ung homme en ung mont de pierres, assis ou debout, tenant en sa main une pierre, c'est la figure de Nostre-Seigneur qui, selon le philosophe, fut veu en une montaigne de pierre de dyamant.   Ceste pierre vault contre toutes tempestes et contre dyables, et tous ennemys, et rend l'omme devot et obeyssant à Dieu.

Un sagittaire en semblence de vassal, donne grace et amours à celluy qui la porte, et le rend très agreable à Dieu et aux hommes.

Ung beau chief bien pigné, qui ait une belle face, donne liesse, reverance, et honneur.

Uu lait chief hericé, qui ait la face yrée, donne à celluy qui la porte deffenses à ses contraires et seurté en faisant toutes choses, et donne victoire contre ses ennemys.

Ung chief qui ait long cheveulx et entremeslex, en semblence et face de viellart fort barbu, donne sapience et stabilité en œuvres, et fait dilection de droitz et de loix.   Elle suppedite les ennemys, et enchasse les dyables, et resiste au serpent et au venin, et vault contre impetration de songes.

Se tu trouves ung homme qui tiengne en sa destre main ung livre et en la senestre une verge, celle pierre mise en or a vertu de apaiser les discordans, et donne victoire en causes, et vault contre les mauvaises bestes, et fait l'omme estable. Ceulx qui se meslent de nigromancie usent souvent de celle pierre.

Se tu trouves en une pierre ung homme couronné, tenant en sa destre main une serre et en la senestre une palme, et dessoubz ses piés estamel, celle pierre mise en or a grand dignité, car ce que on requiert au saulveur du monde, souventes fois luy est sa requeste ottroiée, quant elle est juste et raysonnable.

Se en une pierre on trouve ung homme qui en sa destre main tiengne une lampe, et à la senestre une teste de femme, elle vault à accorder homme et femme. Qui aura celle pierre sur luy, il ne se esveillera pas de legier.

Se tu trouves en une pierre ung torel et un mouton, celle pierre vault à faire beau parler et contre ydropisie.

Ung homme en une pierre qui ait esles es piés et tiengne ung baston en sa main, elle donne grace et amour.

Ung homme en une pierre qui tiengne une verge en sa main, vault à avoir domination et seignourie.

Ung homme en une pierre qui ait un cor à son col, il oste raige et fantosme.

Ung homme en une pierre qui soit moitié bœuf, elle conserve les honneurs et enferme les sens à bien.

Une pierre où il y ait une nef à tout le mast et une voille, vault à entretenir ses besongnes.

Ce en une crisolite a une femme qui ait en une de ses mains ung soleil et de l'autre ung poisson, elle vault à ceulx qui vont en gibier d'oyseaux ou de poissons.

Ce en une pierre a une torterelle avec ung rain d'olivier, celle pierre fait estre aymé de tous.

Ce en une pierre est ung serpent et ung sagittaire qui se combate, celle pierre a pouvoir d'accorder les discordans.

Ce en une pierre est moitié figure de femme et figure de poisson, comme la serayne, et tient en sa main ung mirouer et en l'autre ung rain d'olivier, celle pierre mise en or, enclose en sa main, a vertu de faire la personne invisible.

Ce en vert jaspe a figure de croix, elle a vertu que celui qui la porte ne peut noier.

Ce ung basilict a une seraine, elle donne seurté d'aller contre les serpens.

Ce tu trouves ung homme seant sur ung liepart, et tiengne

en sa main une cedule escripte, elle vault contre les bestes et garde de peril et d'eaue.

Ce en une pierre est ung homme qui tiengne en sa main la figure d'ung dyable qui ait cornes et esles, et en l'autre main ung serpent, et dessoubz ses piez ung lion, et sus ses figures soit la figure du soleil et de la lune, celle pierre doit estre mise en plong et a vertu de contraindre les dyables à respondre à tout ce que on leur demande.

Ce en une pierre a ymage d'omme qui porte en son col ung faisseau d'arbres, et soit assise en argent, elle a vertu de savoir discerner entre les maladies; elle restraint le sang, et donne grace et honneur; et dit-on que Galion portoit celle pierre en ung anel.

Ce on trouve en une noire pierre un homme pourtant ung sestre en une main, et en l'autre ung oisel qui ait ses esles tendues, et au dessus une figure cothodrille, ceste pierre est bonne contre les enchanteurs et les illusions des dyables et contre tous ennemys.

Ung homme tenant en sa destre main ung livre et en sa senestre une verge, celle pierre, mise en or ou en argent, fait obtenir les jugemens et les sentences, et aide en toute necessité et convertit les ennemys; et c'elle est portée en bataille, elle fait victoire honneste. Les nigromanciens usent fort de ceste pierre.

Ung homme fort et robuste, lequel ait face terrible, et soit comme courroucé et yreulx, restraingnant en soy le front, tenant en sa main destre une lance et en sa main senestre ung cheval, et qu'il y ait dessoubz ses piés ung homme qui soit gissant, adonc doit estre mise en euvre. Elle donne victoire en batailles; et se aucun assiet ung cristail, et il le pourte autour d'ung chastel, tantot ceulx qui seront dedans se combatront et se rendront.

Se en une pierre est figure de temple ou de moustier, elle garde de luxure, et rend l'omme agreable à Dieu et aux hommes et femmes.

END OF VOL. I.

CHISWICK PRESS:—PRINTED BY WHITTINGHAM AND WILKINS, TOOKS COURT CHANCERY LANE.

For EU product safety concerns, contact us at Calle de José Abascal, 56–1°,
28003 Madrid, Spain or eugpsr@cambridge.org.

 www.ingramcontent.com/pod-product-compliance
Ingram Content Group UK Ltd.
Pitfield, Milton Keynes, MK11 3LW, UK
UKHW010349140625
459647UK00010B/948